NILE VALLEY CIVILIZATIONS

PROCEEDINGS OF THE
NILE VALLEY CONFERENCE,
ATLANTA, SEPTEMBER 26-30, 1984

EDITOR
IVAN VAN SERTIMA

Morehouse College Edition

Third printing, 1989.

Library of Congress Catalog Number: 80-643869
ISBN: 0-88738-622-9 (paper)
Printed in the United States of America

Cover design by Jacqueline Patten-Van Sertima
Cover photo: Statue of Thutmoses III, 18th Dynasty

NILE VALLEY CIVILIZATIONS

Incorporating JOURNAL OF AFRICAN CIVILIZATIONS,
November 1984 (vol. 6, no. 2)

Contents

Since Ancient Egyptian words are composed of consonants and the vowels are sometimes optional, the reader may observe several different spellings of various words that have been translated (for example, *Kemetic* and *Kamitic* both appear in this volume).

Dedication

This special issue of the *Journal of African Civilizations* is dedicated to Dr. Hugh M. Gloster, President of Morehouse College, who paved the way for our scholars to march back into classical Egypt and recover the ancient African cradleland of world civilization.

Dr. Hugh M. Gloster,
President of Morehouse College

Morehouse College
Office of the President
Gloster Hall-Suite 322
830 Westview Drive, Southwest
Atlanta, Georgia 30314
(404) 681-2800, Ext. 440

June 1, 1989

Dear Readers:

The Nile Valley Conference held September 26 through September 30, 1984 at Morehouse College represented the lighting of a fuse that has caused an explosion of information regarding the ancient sources of world civilization. Five years ago this conference put us on the threshold of a door to a wider mansion of African history. Today, it is clear in every conceivable human endeavor that the African contribution was the original and decisive one in aeronautics, agriculture, architecture, astronomy, calendars, education, engineering, ethics, language, law, literature, mathematics, medicine, mining, mystery, myth, navigation, philosophy, physics, religion, technology, and writing. These facts have been confirmed in this century by leading historians, palaeontologists and paleoanthropologists, such as Richard E. Leakey, Donald C. Johanson, Cheikh Anta Diop, and William Leon Hansberry.

As president of Morehouse College, I am pleased that one of our alumni, Dr. James Adam Wilborn, and the Union Baptist Church of Atlanta, Georgia have made it possible for our Dean of Chapel, Dr. Lawrence Edward Carter Sr., to reissue *Nile Valley Civilizations*. These lectures first delivered at Morehouse College in the Martin Luther King Jr. International Chapel will help reaffirm the mission and task of Black colleges to educate and uplift people of African descent, and ultimately all human persons, all over the world. They will help restore the credibility of what Dr. Martin Bernal called "the ancient model," i.e., the ancient Nile Valley world view.

Morehouse College is grateful to Dr. Ivan Van Sertima and all of the presenters for giving the Nile Valley Conference through this volume world wide attention.

Sincerely,

Leroy Keith Jr.
President

Introduction

THE NILE VALLEY CONFERENCE: NEW LIGHT ON KEMETIC STUDIES

Charles S. Finch

It has been said that the only thing that is new is that which has been forgotten. From September 26th to 30th, 1984, at the Martin Luther King, Jr. International Chapel on the campus of Morehouse College in Atlanta, Georgia, the light of a new dawn cast its glow over some of the forgotten realities of history. This light, in the form of the Nile Valley conference, signalled an end to the murky obscurantism that has surrounded everything to do with the worldwide history of African peoples. This cloud hiding African history from view has caused a corresponding beclouding of the collective African mind. It is as if African peoples have been mentally adrift in a Sargasso Sea of ignorance and confusion, without moorings, without direction, without a helm to steer by. In the aftermath of the Nile Valley Conference, we can now perceive that the "Dark Ages" of African history may finally be drawing to a close.

The Nile Valley Conference was eighteen months in the making, starting out as a germ of an idea and then taking seed in the newly-formed Bennu Study Group under the co-convenership of Dr. Charles S. Finch and Mr. Larry Williams. Conversations began almost immediately with Dr. Ivan Van Sertima who vigorously endorsed the idea and committed the *Journal of African Civilizations* to co-sponsorship. Atlanta commended itself as an optimal choice of locale for a number of reasons: (1) it is the transportation, financial, and media "capital" of the South where nearly 60% of African-Americans still reside, (2) the seven Atlanta University Center institutions contain the largest concentration of Black students and scholars in private institutions anywhere in the world, and (3) Atlanta has historically been the setting of many of the most important political, cultural, and historic developments of African-American people.

In January, 1984, the Human Values in Medicine Program of the Morehouse School of Medicine, under its Director Dr. Mwalimu Imara, became the third co-sponsor of the conference, giving it formal institutional backing for the first time. Shortly thereafter, the Martin Luther King Jr. International Chapel of Morehouse College, under Dean Lawrence E. Carter, also took up the challenge and became the fourth and final co-sponsor of the Nile Valley Conference. The King Chapel was designated as the conference site.

Nile Valley or Kamitic Studies is such a vast discipline that it was not possible in a four-day conference to cover all the relevant areas of study. It was felt from the first that the conference should bring into focus the research of the last 10-15 years on the Nile Valley which has changed forever ideas about who created the Nile Valley civilizations, what they achieved, and the impact they left on Africa and the world. Fundamental to this was an "Afro-centric" as opposed to an "Euro-centric" worldview, for only such a worldview could hope to shed any meaningful light on the study of these ancient African civilizations. It is evident that conventional Egyptology has reached its limit in what it can teach us of Kamitic civilization. Aside from crippling itself by perpetuating the "big lie" about the non-African origins of ancient Kemit (Egypt), it has also exhausted creative energy to which it may have once laid claim. Increasingly, modern Egyptologists—refusing to acknowledge the African origin of ancient Egypt—are talking in circles, accumulating ever-growing mounds of archaeological facts but contributing little new to our understanding of these ancient civilizations. Without the Afro-centric perspective, modern Egyptology is a dead science, fit only for musty curators maundering over marginal artifacts. The Afro-centrism that must be inherent in Nile Valley studies is not, unlike Euro-centrism, cultural chauvinism. It is, as it must be, solidly and fundamentally grounded in the known facts of history, i.e., that humankind and civilization began in Africa. These truths are demonstrable and verifiable; all other historical premises must proceed therefrom. The Nile Valley Conference did indeed proceed from these truths.

FOREWORD

Mayor Andrew Young

As Mayor of Atlanta, I am pleased to have this opportunity to address the readers of the *Journal of African Civilizations* in this "Nile Valley Civilizations" issue.

Recently, Atlanta, through the Martin Luther King, Jr. International Chapel at Morehouse College, was host to the Nile Valley Conference. This four-day conference brought together sixteen leading scholars from varied disciplines to present in a public forum the latest research in the study of Nile Valley civilizations.

Seldom has such a group of scholars gathered for the purpose of presenting and documenting a critically important historical period. The proceedings of this conference will leave a lasting impression on the future historical understanding and development of African peoples in the United States and throughout the world.

I was particularly happy to see the Nile Valley Conference taking place in this city, because it became part of the continuum of African-American history that has been shaped in Atlanta.

W.E.B. DuBois, for 10 years a professor at Atlanta University at the beginning of this century, laid the groundwork for the development of African-American thought in this country. *Souls of Black Folk*, one of the seminal pieces of African-American writing, was written while DuBois was a resident of Atlanta.

William Leo Hansberry, the "Father" of African Studies in this country, initially enrolled at Morehouse College before pursuing his studies at other institutions.

Benjamin E. Mays, one of the towering figures in African-American higher education, was President of Morehouse College for more than 30 years.

Martin Luther King, Jr., Nobel laureate, apostle of peace, and one of the greatest Americans of all, was born and raised in Atlanta. The headquarters of the great movement he led was, under the umbrella of the Southern Christian Leadership Conference, based in Atlanta. Dr. King's church, the Ebenezer Baptist Church in Atlanta, was a spiritual center of the civil rights movement.

The Nile Valley Conference is for us, then, a continuation of a hallowed tradition in this city.

There were other vitally important factors which recommended Atlanta as the site for the Nile Valley Conference. Atlanta is the financial, transportation and cultural center of the South, a region in which 60 percent of all black people in this country still reside. Peoples of African descent compose almost 70 percent of the total population of Atlanta. The city is vigorous, dynamic and growing, and

Atlanta is a national leader in the development and expansion of black-owned businesses. The Atlanta University Center institutions—Atlanta University, Clark College, The Interdenominational Theological Center, Morehouse College, Morehouse School of Medicine, Morris Brown College, and Spelman College—contain the largest concentration of black students and scholars in private institutions anywhere in the world.

The international character of Atlanta is growing daily as international business representatives, scholars and visitors are finding Atlanta a congenial place to live, work, and study.

For all of these reasons, it seemed only natural that the Nile Valley Conference should be held in the setting of Atlanta at the King Chapel.

I salute the Nile Valley Conference organizers, presenters and participants for an outstandingly successful program. The work you started here will have ramifications into the next century and beyond. This issue of the *Journal of African Civilizations*, under the fine editorship of Dr. Ivan Van Sertima, is a fitting testament to the enduring value of the work of the Nile Valley Conference. You have all my best wishes and high hopes for your continuing success.

Address to Readers of the *Journal of African Civilizations*

Hugh M. Gloster

As President of Morehouse College, I wish to express my respect and gratitude for the work of the "Nile Civilizations" issue of the *Journal of African Civilizations*. The dozen papers printed in this issue were first presented at the Nile Valley Conference, September 26-30, 1984, hosted by the Martin Luther King Jr. International Chapel of Morehouse College. As one of the co-sponsors and as the site of the conference, Morehouse was pleased to help shape what was undoubtedly one of the outstanding conferences in African-American history.

The Nile Valley Conference was the inaugural event in our 75th anniversary celebration of the founding of Sale Hall Chapel by Dr. John Hope, the first African-American President of Morehouse. Morehouse has been in the business of building Black men for service in the greater African-American community for over a century. A look at a list of the most important African-American leaders over that period would reveal the names of many Morehouse men including Mordecai Johnson, Howard Thurman, John W. Davis, Martin Luther King, Jr., Julian Bond, Maynard Jackson, and Lerone Bennett, to name just a few. William Leo Hansberry, the Father of African Studies, was originally enrolled at Morehouse before continuing his studies at Harvard and other institutions.

Morehouse has always been a repository of African-American history and culture. *The Journal of Negro History*, founded by Carter C. Woodson, is now housed at Morehouse. The first African-American presidential candidate, Jesse Jackson, launched his campaign at the King Chapel at Morehouse. Morehouse has played host to men such as Kenneth Kaunda, President of Zambia, Robert Mugabe, Prime Minister of Zimbabwe, and Bishop Desmond Tutu, the Nobel laureate. Morehouse, like other important African-American centers of higher learning, has been instrumental in keeping the spirit of African-American group identity, and hence group unity, alive.

It was a matter of historical destiny that such a momentous event as the Nile Valley Conference was held in this place at this time. We like to think of Morehouse as "the Great House"; and, as it is well known, the Egyptian translation of "Great House" was "per aa," and this was the origin of the name "pharaoh."

While we wish that all the thousands of readers of the *Journal of African Civilizations* could have been at Morehouse to share this remarkable experience, we take comfort and satisfaction in the fact that this new and vitally important knowledge that came to light during the conference is being preserved in this "Nile Civilizations" issue. A light has been struck in the darkness surrounding the history of African peoples, and neither we nor the world can ever be the same again. Now that the torch has been lit, we must all labor to keep it burning.

AFRICAN CIVILIZATIONS AS CORNERSTONE FOR THE OIKOUMENE

Lawrence Edward Carter

The Nile Valley Conference was dedicated to the celebration of the 75th anniversary of the founding of the Morehouse College Chapel and to Dr. Benjamin Elijah Mays who was President of Morehouse College for twenty-seven years. In his 1925 University of Chicago Master's thesis, Dr. Mays wrote, "The mysteries of Egypt were in the Greco-Roman world in pre-Christian days, for the cult of Isis and Osiris spread extensively over the Mediterranean world from the beginning of the third century, B.C. and they had reached Rome before the rise of Christianity." The most important temple found in the buried city of Pompeii on the bay of Naples in Italy was a temple to Isis. There were many temples to Isis in France, Hungary, Italy, Spain, and beyond. These temples later became Christian shrines and Black Isis with her child Horus became the Black Madonna and Child in each of these shrines. According to Dr. Martin Bernal of Cornell University, the Greeks and Romans believed that their religion came from Egypt; and they turned to Egyptian religion up until about 100 A.D. Furthermore, Egyptian religion survives in Christianity itself. It is more accurate to view Christianity as a Judaeo-Egypto religion, rather than a Judaeo-Greek religion, though the New Testament was written in Greek and was influenced by Greek culture.

A yet unacknowledged debt is the dependence of Christian Church history and theology on ancient Africa, especially on its classical civilization of Egypt. I think it is important to explain to the readers of this "Nile Civilizations" issue of the *Journal of African Civilizations* why it was most appropriate for the Nile Valley Conference to be held in the Martin Luther King, Jr. International Chapel. The Chapel's two cornerstones acknowledge the dependence of Christianity on ancient Egypt. The monumental cornerstone's time capsule contains one hundred and nineteen separate items. Among these is the so-called Egyptian *Book of the Dead*, more correctly called *The Book of Coming Forth By Day*. It is the 704-page Hieroglyphic transcript of the Papyrus of Ani, translated into English by E.A. Wallis Budge. The second cornerstone has on it the word "OIKOUMENE" which is an aspect of the most universally accepted Christian logo of the World Council of Churches. This is also the logo for the world's most prominent religious memorial to Martin Luther King, Jr.—the King International Chapel at Morehouse College in Atlanta, Georgia. The logo has been the world-wide Christian symbol of the ecumenical movement since 1948. This logo is derived from Ancient Egyptian sources, which may be clearly traced. It consists of the word "OIKOUMENE" depicting the curvature of the earth, showing a boat beneath it with a Latin cross serving as the mast of the boat, while the boat floats upon turbulent waves.

The Greek word oikoumene means "ecumene," "the inhabited earth." Oikos means "house." Ecumene, in the time of the Roman Empire, meant the "inhabited earth" within the limits of the empire. It also meant "the civilized world" as opposed to the world outside of the empire. This "outside world" was identified as the land of Scythians or barbarians, the uncivilized world, which included the Germanic tribes.

Oikonomia (economics, economy, finances) is "house management" (from Oikos-"house" and nomos-"law, law of the house"). "Divine economy" means "God's house management", i.e., "the plan of salvation as conceived, manifested, and fulfilled by God the Father, through the missions of the Son of God and God's Holy Spirit in the world." All of this is derived from what the Ancient Egyptians called the MDW NETERW or what the Greeks called "hieroglyphics." In either case the term means "sacred writing of God", "words of the gods", or "Holy Scripture." Oikoumene may be spelled as follows: (Greek) OI–KOU–MENE; (Egyptian)UA–KHUI–MEN (E). In *The Egyptian Hieroglyphic Dictionary* by E.A.W. Budge, the "UA" in UA-KHUI-MENE has various meanings, including "one or oneness", "governor or warden", "to seek after", "the Supreme One", i.e., "Ra", "Osiris", or "Amen." "KHUI" means variously, "protection, earth, state, spirit." "MENE" means, "to lead a boat into port"; "a form of things of the world", or "the world"; "to be permanent, stable, fixed, to abide, to continue." Hence, the word UA-KHUI-MENE can mean "abiding in one earth or Spirit"; "the many in one abiding in one Spirit"; "the protection of the earth or its estate"; and "to lead the things of the world into a safe port, Amen."

The Greek word, plus the logo image of boat, cross, and turbulent waves is interpreted internationally today in the Christian Church to mean Christ came for the whole inhabited earth that there might be good economic and moral management in the whole earth or family or world as it sails through these turbulent times. In Christian symbolism the boat is feminine and the cross is masculine. These are prototypes of the Church as bride and Christ as groom. The waves are the Nile River. It was crossed by all divine-kings (Pharaohs) in a boat sailing toward the safe harbour (70 days after their deaths) where their eternal possessions lay. This is the ancient origin of the first verse of the Christian hymn by Samuel Sternett, "On Jordan's stormy banks I stand, and cast a wishful eye to Canaan's fair and happy land, where my possessions lie."

This point is strengthened by Margaret A. Murray in her book, *The Splendour That Was Egypt* when she says:

> In religious beliefs and the ritual of the gods, boats played a large part. The sun crossed the sky in a boat, and passed through the countries of the Night in a boat. Amon had a boat-shaped shrine and went in a boat on his great festival. Boat-shaped shrines were a common form of shrine for many of the

> gods; and the sacred lakes which were made within the precincts of the temples seem to have been intended for the deity of the temple to take his pleasure in a boat. Even at the present day the boat of Abu Haggag is kept at the mosque in the temple of Amon at Luxor and is carried in procession at midsummer. (pages 65-66)

As the First Dean of the King International Chapel and as a member of the Governing Board of the National Council of Churches of Christ, U.S.A., I am very pleased to identify one of the Egyptian connections to contemporary Christianity and to the ecumenical and interdisciplinary ministry of the Chapel. We were most pleased to host the Nile Valley Conference. It is generally felt that the conference was on the same historical continuum as the Niagara Conference and the first Black Power Conference in its significance for African-American people. An appropriate followup to this historic event might deal with the dependence of the world's great religions on Ancient Africa, and the images of African Christianity before the historical Jesus.

Lawrence Edward Carter is Dean of the Martin Luther King, Jr. International Chapel, and Member of the Governing Board of the National Council of Churches of Christ, USA.

Editorial

We are indeed proud to present this issue on Nile Valley Civilizations, the published proceedings in part of the Conference held in Atlanta from September 26 to 30, 1984. What happened in Atlanta must rank as one of the turning points in the great struggle to revise the early history of the world in general and the history of Africa's classical civilizations in particular. It is the first conference on African history that drew as many as two thousand, five hundred people to one of its sessions, witness to a new and profound interest in Africa's past, a new and profound effort to illuminate the dark and forgotten rooms in which the mummies of our ancestors lie.

For five days people came from far and wide to file past the body of an Africa that seemed to breathe again because of the transmitted vitality of their awakened memory and interest. The shadows of our greatest men and women walked among us again so that we could hear the muffled thunder of their footfalls, the whisper of their voices in the great hall of the Martin Luther King International Chapel. We could feel connected again to the flow of an ancient electricity that still runs to us, it seems, from the currents of that time.

We felt for a moment a sense of loss when we learnt that Dr. Cheikh Anta Diop, the pharoah of African studies, would not be able to sit among us in person to celebrate this event. According to Diop's own words, the plane taking him from Dakar, Senegal, had been forced to return after the discovery of a fractured wing one thousand miles out from base. It had almost crashlanded on its return to Dakar, blowing out all the tires. The shock of this experience, perhaps, kept Dr. Diop home. News of this, however, cast but a temporary chill over the proceedings. It soon became clear to us all that we had gathered there because of his presiding spirit, because of the essence and purpose of his work, which it was our duty to continue even as we would be forced one day to continue without his physical presence. His spirit was the real catalyst. And even if the wings, upon which his body flew, were broken, his spirit had already flown to us.

Diop submitted a major paper, which I had the honor to read to the Conference in his absence. Originally entitled "Africa's Contribution to World Civilization" it attempts to deal with the three major movements of civilization from Africa to the world, in general, and Europe, in particular. First, the movement of *homo sapiens sapiens* and his less advanced predecessors (Neanderthal man etc.) from their cradleland in Africa to other continents, and the possible emergence of Cro Magnon man (the Caucasoid) as a mutation of Grimaldi man (the Africoid). Second, the movement from the Nile Valley cradle of civilization of many major and seminal scientific developments to Europe, via the Greeks, who studied them and stole them, especially after their invasion of Egypt under Alexander. Third, the movement of equally significant contributions to world science and civilization, not only from Africa but from Asia, to Europe, during the nearly eight centuries of the Muslim domination of the Iberian peninsula.

Because this issue is arranged into thematic sections, Diop's paper has been cut into two parts. The first is the natural opening chapter of this work, dealing as it does with man's earliest beginnings in the land the Egyptians called *Af-ruika* (birthplace) while the second, a brilliantly detailed examination of Egyptian scientific contributions, is a perfect complement to the essays by John Pappademos and Beatrice Lumpkin on the impact of Nile Valley physics and mathematics on the world. The third part of the Diop paper is omitted from this volume since it bears only peripherally on Nile Valley civilizations. Diop's main contribution to the science section is his rare ability to establish, in the most precise and thorough way, based on first-hand knowledge of the mathematical papyri, that Egyptian mathematics was not a mere aggregate of empirical "recipes" but a highly elaborate and theoretical body of science.

John Pappademos shows how Newton, perhaps the greatest figure in European science before Einstein, drew directly and indirectly upon the early sciences of the Nile Valley. Newton achieved a synthesis of three lines of development - astronomy, mathematics and mechanics - and this success rested directly upon his predecessors Kepler, Copernicus, Descartes and Galileo. Pappademos contends that the work of these scientists would have been impossible without the foundation laid centuries earlier in Egypt. He traces the influences of these men upon Newton and the influence of Egypt, both in the classical and later Muslim period, upon these men. Even Newton himself admits on several occasions his debt to the ancient Africans. He attributes for example the first atomic theory to the Egyptians and the Phoenicians. "That all matter consists of atoms was a very ancient opinion . . . I think the same opinion obtained in the mystic philosophy which flows down to the Greeks from Egypt and Phoenicia, since atoms are sometimes found to be designated by the mystics as monads". Newton also admits that his law of universal gravitation had been anticipated two thousand years earlier by the Pythagorean philosophers and that this was the real meaning of their doctrine of the "harmony of the spheres." Pythagorus spent twenty-two years in Egypt studying Egyptian science and it was there, according to Newton, that the Greek mathematician learnt this doctrine. Newton also saw an Egyptian anticipation of his own heliocentric theory (theory of the rotation of the earth and other planets around the sun). In addition to this study of the roots of the Newtonian laws, Pappademos lists all the discoveries of the Egyptians in the field of astronomy, many of which are deliberately ignored by the historians of science.

Mathematician Beatrice Lumpkin highlights Nile Valley pre-eminence in mathematics for four millenia and the leading role this played in building the foundations of modern science. The first cipherization of numbers took place in Egypt where hieroglyphic numerals used special symbols for the powers of 10. Fractions also became necessary very early in Africa because of the vast construction of pyramids, irrigation works, temples and obelisks, which required accurate measurements of lengths, areas and volumes. These fractions were at the heart of Egyptian arithmetic. They enabled the scribes to perform complex operations and they were used by scientists for thousands of years, right up to the modern period. Lumpkin demonstrates, from the surviving papyri, Egyptian breakthroughs in trigonometry, algebra (the *aha* calculus) and geometry. She reclaims Euclid for African mathematics and wonders how a man born and raised in Africa, showing no evidence of an alient parenthood, feeding upon all the mathematical texts available to him in Egypt at the time, could be represented as fair and Greek in all the textbooks. Euclid's *Elements,* containing 13 books and 465 propositions, has dominated the teaching of geometry for 2000 years. She also spotlights the Moorish period when inferior European mathematics was lifted to the level of the African and the Asian by Muslim arithmetic and algebra, the transfer from India of the Hindu numerals (at first resisted by European superstitions about numbers) and the works of the great Egyptian mathematicians like Abu Kamil.

In our section on Nile Valley as source of world philosophy, we have provocative essays by Na'im Akbar, Richard King, and Asa Hilliard. Akbar attempts to outline the nature of the Egyptian contribution to the science of psychology. The Greek word *psyche* is derived from the Egyptian in which *khe* is the soul and *su* is she, hence, the feminine nature of the Greek *Psu-khe.* Omitting the initial Greek P, we have the root of the word — *sakhu.* This, in Egyptian, means the understanding, the illuminator, the eye or soul of being. Akbar points up the difficulty of trying to identify a psychology of ancient Egypt in any explicit sense but he focuses on the doctrine of self-knowledge, wherein lies, in a simplified form, the initial psychology of consciousness. The seven dimensions of the self or soul *(Ka, Ba, Khaba, Akhu, Seb, Putah* and *Atmu)* are discussed. These constitute the natural form of the human being's psychology as well as his evolution. "The challenge of man," says Akbar "was to become knowledgeable of these souls [or forms of the self] and achieve a crystallization of them into an Eighth or Divinely permanent form." This eighth form, according to Gerald Massey, was the Horus or the Christ.

Richard King in his essay "The Symbolism of the Crown" sees the study of the crown, the jewels and the tableau found in the tomb of the 18th dynasty pharoah Tut as excellent examples of symbolic reference to a historical stream of ancient African philosophical thought that runs through classical Egyptian civilization. His analysis of that symbolism and its underlying philosophy leads to more than an introduction to an African psychology of the unconscious. He touches on controversial issues that relate to the pineal gland and melanin with clarity and certitude. He cites items of physical evidence of "the African knowledge of biological psychiatry and depth psychiatry thousands of years before the rediscovery of the same bodies of knowledge by Europeans." Egyptians, he claims, had knowledge of the location and function of the pineal gland. They knew it was located anatomically at the posterior end of the third ventricle of the brain. The pineal gland is a modified eye. It is an actual eye in lower forms, like the lizard, but it withdrew into the head of mammals like man and became a light converter, whose hormonal signals can actually change levels of consciousness. He shows that the black pupil in the eye of Horus, through which rays of light are made to enter in certain Egyptian representations, corresponds to the black dot or pineal eye, the *locus coeruleus,* the uppermost in a chain of twelve pigmented black nucleii in the brain stem.

Asa Hilliard discusses the classical expression in ancient Egypt of the African system of education which was "the parent of other systems of education, especially early European education in Greece and Rome." He selects for his study of this system a peak period of Egyptian development — the eighteenth dynasty — and a major center of government in that dynasty - Thebes (today's Luxor) where stand two gigantic temples that contain the most highly developed education system on record from ancient times. One of these great temples of Luxor housed an elite faculty of priest-professors and at one time catered to an estimated 80,000 students at all grade levels. Temples were at the center of religion, politics and education.

This temple-university had a huge library and its faculty, called "teachers of mysteries," were divided into five major departments: astronomy and astrology; geography; geology; philosophy and theology; law and communication. Hilliard introduces us to the steps in this process of education, which is not seen simply as a process of acquiring knowledge but the transformation of the learner, who progressed through successive stages of rebirth to become more godlike. Hilliard underlines the fact that this education was a blend of the theoretical and practical, a holistic education. The educational concepts of Egypt did not die when the last college at Philae was closed by Justinian in 527 A.D. Some remained in disguised form in the educational systems of the European conquerors.

In our review of the Egyptian dynasties we have reprinted two essays from an earlier issue of the Journal — *Egypt Revisited* — which is now out of print. We have done this because Bruce Williams, author of "The Lost Pharoahs of Nubia" and Legrand Clegg II, who dealt with the greatest dynasty in Egyptian history in "Rulers of the Golden Age" did excellent presentations but did not make formal submissions of their papers. These studies of dawn and noon dynasties are critical to an understanding of early Nile Valley history and the Williams paper is the only report on record in the world at the moment on the kingdom of Ta-Seti, the first monarchy in the Nile Valley. This precedes the Egyptian first dynasty by about 200 years and influenced the early Egyptian dynasties. I had requested Bruce Williams, however, to write me about his latest work, which attempts to go a lot further in its claims for Nubian pharaonic kingship, although it is still tentative and incomplete. In his letter to me he suggests that it was not only in the dawn that the Nubian developed a pharaonic kingship but that there was some pharaonic-type civilization developing parallel to Egypt through the ages. What he stressed in his presentation to the Conference, therefore, was the thesis that a Kushite continuity sustained the pharaonic impulse through the ages, from A-group (3,300 B.C.) right through to X-group (550 AD). This, to put it in his own words, "represents a new departure in the examination of Egypt's place in the African context."

In our section on the Nile Valley as background to the Judeo-Christian heritage we have two major essays, both of which should prove as disturbing as they are revealing. One of them deals with the relationship of the early Hebrews-Israelites-Judahites-Jews to Egypt and Ethiopia on the basis of an examination of *all* the references to these places and their peoples in the Bible. Charles Copher points out that, of the 740 references to Egypt in the Bible, most are of a negative nature. Of the few exceptions there is a passage in Deuteronomy which warns the Jews against their feelings of abhorrence for Egypt since they had sojourned in that land for a long time. These feelings, however, should come as no surprise since Egypt was seen at one time as an oppressor of this sect (sect, *not race*, since blacks also belonged to the early Judaic sect) and the memory of this difficult period in Egypt lingered, in fact was kept alive throughout the generations. Ethiopia is never mentioned until the 25th dynasty and some of the first references are positive. The Ethiopian king Taharka marched into Jerusalem circa 700 B.C. to save the Jews, under King Hezekiah, from the Assyrians. It is important too to consider what Copher calls "the love-hate relationship" between the Jews and the Egyptians. Egypt, from which they had fled, remained, ironically enough, their haven of refuge so that even Jesus (according to Matthew) escaped to Egypt and it was out of Egypt (according to Hosea) that he was recalled to begin his ministry.

Charles Finch, on the other hand, demonstrates that the way for the establishment of historical Christianity was paved for millenia in Egypt. The universal Christ, which was to transcend tribal or sectarian Judaism, did not burst suddenly upon the world. While Finch accepts the individual phenomenon of Jesus, he tries to show that what became Christianity was largely an elaboration and reworking of Kemitic religious and symbolic ideas. He goes into these in painstaking detail and provides astonishing parallels for episodes in the life of the later Christ in his physical manifestation as Jesus. Even the word Christ comes from the Egyptian word *krst (karast)* the Anointed. His conclusion, therefore, is that around the person of an historical figure (Jeshu ben Pandera?) the vast savior mythology of previous generations coalesced.

We leave Egypt to trace its branches in other worlds — Asia and America. Runoko Rashidi pursues the thread of the black presence in Asian antiquity which is one of the least known aspects of the Black experience. It covers a period of more than half a million years. "As the first hominids, simple hunters and gatherers, primitive agriculturists, warriors and civilizers, gods and goddesses, servants and slaves, the Black race has known Asia intimately from the beginning." Rashidi tracks them down in places like South Arabia. Sumer and Elam, the Indus Valley, China and Japan, from one end of the Asian landmass to the other. It is no easy task and he is fast becoming one of the leading scholars in this field. He will co-edit the special issue of the *Journal* devoted to the *African Presence in Asia* in the spring of 1985. He is to be commended for his meticulous and assiduous scholarship in a field which is still fairly virginal and where the hard factual data and visual materials are sparse and scattered.

This volume concludes with an essay on the Egyptian-Ethiopian presence in ancient America. I have done a considerable amount of new research into Olmec civilization, the first major American civilization, after the publication of my book *They Came Before Columbus* in 1977. This essay, first published in the February-March 1983 issue of *Dollars & Sense,* restates the case for African voyages to the New World but with a new clarity and focus. It concentrates on a particular geographical region, (the Gulf Coast of Mexico) a particular culture complex or civilization (Olmec) and a particular period of history (circa 948-680 B.C.) My book dealt with about half a dozen contacts, both accidental and designed, between Africa and America. This essay touches on the most important and earliest of these. It was the most important because it was to affect all other culture complexes in America. It also proceeded from the heartland of ancient African civilizations because of very special military and commercial developments in the last phase of the Bronze Age. The bibliography, which is vast, is omitted. Those who are reading of this theory for the first time are asked to refer to the original book, which was published by Random House and is now in its tenth printing.

Something very unusual has begun to happen both in this field and in the field of African civilization studies as a whole. One cannot travel around this country any more, go to conferences like the one held in Atlanta, visit the ancient archaeological sites of Mexico, as I did in the summer of 1984 with half a hundred African-Americans, without feeling a sense of pilgrimage, a sense of something even more exciting, such as early explorers felt as they set out for new lands or such as quivered in the heart of warriors as they embarked on new crusades. This book is a testament to that pilgrimage to the ancestral shrine, that crusade for a change in consciousness through the revision of history, that we began in Atlanta.

Ivan Van Sertima

AFRICA: CRADLE OF HUMANITY

Cheikh Anta Diop

Africa is the continent which Hegel and the modern ideologues who came after him excluded from history. Even Karl Marx did it. Friedrich Engels thought that if whites were more intelligent than blacks, it was only because they were shepherds and ate meat and drank milk! As a result of innumerable distortions of the truth, the continent of Africa—Mother of Civilization—is seen today as having made no significant contributions, As a result of numerous recent works, her once amnesic sons are finding their memory for history again.

As it happens, Africa has produced a great many of the treasures of civilization. Three times, from the earliest prehistory to the dawn of modern times, civilization (the sciences, technology, and philosophy) has flowed out of Africa into Europe, in particular, and on to the rest of the world in general. These are the three stages we wish briefly to characterize here, all the while resting on strict scientific ground. We must avoid at all cost falling into the ideological shortcomings that we so often criticize.

From Early Prehistoric Time to the First Writing: 5 Million Years to 4,000 Years B.C. — Africa, Cradle of Humanity.

Following the discoveries of Arambourg, it has often been said that the "cradle of civilization" is a cradle on wheels, destined to move from continent to continent as research progresses.

Nothing could be further from the truth. This cradle was first placed in Asia for three reasons: (1) the very ancient presence of three races (black, white, and yellow), (2) the discovery of the pithecanthrope in Java (at a time when African soil had just become the subject of archeological excavation), and (3) the Biblical tradition which puts the cradle of humanity in Palestine with the creation of Adam and Eve from clay.

As new discoveries were made, the cradle slid from Asia to Africa where it seems it will remain.

Despite the very prudent positions taken by some scholars (Darwin in the 19th century, Dart in South Africa, Abbé Breuil, Arambourg, Teilhard de Chardin, L.S.B. Leakey and the intuition of ancient writers), just 30 years ago it took great temerity, as a scientist, to take seriously the idea that Africa might be the birthplace of mankind.

To be credible, to be taken seriously, to be in step with the music, it was necessary to be careful not to become wed to any such opinion. If an African should hold such an opinion, this could only be interpreted as a wild claim and the result of a complex created by colonization.

Hominoids and Hominids

There are two large groups of monkeys: the platyrrhine or new-world monkeys and the catarrhine or old-world monkeys (Africa, Asia, Europe). The first group, the platyrrhine (varieties of which have been seen particularly in South America), is excluded from the evolutionary process which has resulted in man. Therefore, it was not the new world (the three Americas) that gave birth to man; he came to the Americas by way of the Bering Straits during the Upper Paleolithic already having the characteristics of *homo sapiens sapiens,* as we will see below. Only the catarrhines figure in hominid evolution. It is to be remembered that the hominoids group together man and the great apes while the hominids include man and his cousins, *australopithecus, homo habilis* and *homo erectus.* It was only a few years ago that paleontologists were able to fix the separation between hominids and the great apes at a time approximately 15 million years ago.

But the staggering progress of molecular biology in giving us a new science, fossil genetics, has made it possible to delve into the most diverse questions relating to the process of hominid evolution. Humanity's family tree can now be drawn with precision. Due to the results of biochemical analysis, using immune reactions or the hybridization of DNA, it is now considered given that the apes of Africa—those without tails, the gorilla and especially the chimpanzee—are closer to man than the apes of Asia such as the orangoutan and the gibbon. These last two also do not figure (or figure very little) in the process. They began to diverge from the common trunk some 16 million years ago, well before the gorilla and the chimpanzee. The chimpanzee shows a 99% genetic similarity to man.[1] It can be deduced from this biological relationship that the last common ancestor of the gorilla, the chimpanzee and man lived roughly half as long as the last ancestor common to all hominoids.[2] Contrary to what had been believed, the same analyses place the ramapithecus among the primitive apes typified by the sivapithecus orangoutang, thus far removed from man.[3]

The separation of the hominids from the apes was complete approximately 7 million years ago. The series of hominids was introduced by the australopithecus who had a massive skeletal structure and a cranium resembling an arrowhead. It has, no doubt, been in existence for 3.5 million years. This is the age attributed to australopithecus afarensis, called "Lucy" (Ethiopia).

The footprints, or "Laetoli tracks" in Tanzania, which were discovered by Mary Leakey and which attest to the existence of the biped, belonged to the same period. The origin of the australopithecus is probably even further back in time since a fragment of a mandibule dating back 5 million years has recently been discovered in Kenya, though this age must be confirmed by radiometric dating.

Two and a half million years ago, three hominids were in existence: the australopithecus robustus; the australopithecus gracile who had a larger cranium than the former and a more developed bone structure; and *homo habilis,* decidedly more evolved than the australopithecus, with a still larger cranium (700 cubic centimeters). The relationship between these three hominids is far from being clear.

The research to date indicates that these three specimens never achieved a potential for expansion sufficient to move beyond Africa. Perhaps this was only transitional.

In 1982 an English American and Canadian team[4] made a discovery at Chesowanja, Kenya, which would be of great importance if it were verified. These writers allege that *australopithecus robustus,* the most primitive of the nominids would have made fire 1.4 million years ago. In addition, they had a lithic industry which was surprising, although rudimentary, and a fired clay pottery which was equally surprising. Up to the present, the first fire has been attributed to the Peking Man of the Chonkontien cave (500,000 years ago).

The three hominids referred to above were followed by *homo erectus* (formerly called *Pithecanthropus*) during the period 1,800,000 to 100,000 years ago. *Homo erectus* must have lived during a short period of time with *homo habilis* and perhaps even with australopethicus if his origin dates back as far as 4,000,000 years as certain specialists claim.

The average volume of his brain was 800 cm^3. He was the first hominid to go out of Africa at different periods to people Asia and Europe: Java pithecanthropus, Tautavel Man, etc. The tools that he manufactured were the biface and the hatchet which he brought to Southern Europe in particular.

In the morphological evolution toward modern man, *homo erectus* is followed by the Broken Hill Man (Zambia) who is a typical neanderthaloid dating back 110,000 years as indicated by methods using amino acids. If these dates were combined, then the geographical origin of the Neanderthal Man would be seriously challenged. Indeed, the age which is commonly considered to be the oldest is 80,000 years, that is the beginning of the Würm glaciation for the European specimens. These ages are not determined by radiometric methods. The new C.14 methods, based on mass spectrometry, making it possible to push back the C.14 ages considerably—to some 70,000 to 80,000 years—would be of tremendous help. In fact, the method of fixing the date by the amino acids must be measured by the C.14 method in order to obtain reliable results. There is some doubt then as to the accuracy of the date of the Broken Hill fossil. But it has become indispensible to test, as far as can be done, all the African, European, Palestinian, Neanderthaloid fossils according to the strict criteria of radiometric dating. The new C.14 method is not destructive because it requires only a few milligrams of organic or carbonated matter. It is conceivable that a sample can be taken from the fossil even though the bones are not the ideal material for fixing a date because of pollution factors in hot and humid climates.

Opinion is almost unanimous at the moment that the Neanderthal Man is of European origin. It is quite possible but this idea needs to be scientifically verified. If this is true, the oldest European neanderthal fossils will necessarily be older than all the neanderthalian fossils in the rest of the world. This, then, is the only really scientific criterion to determine the geographical origin of the Neanderthal Man.

An American mission has just discovered Neanderthal Man in Egypt. As a result, we now have two datable fossils. From the results of these analyses, the origin of the Neaderthalian will be known. In the meantime, the African fossil seems to be older than the European and Palestinian fossils. If we follow strictly this criterion for dating fossils we observe that Palestine could not have been the starting point for the peopling of Europe neither at the stage of the Neanderthal Man nor at the stage of the *homo sapiens sapiens.*

In fact the species which follows the Neanderthal Man is *homo sapiens sapiens* who has the same morphology as modern man. This has been in Africa with the Omo I skull which is 130,000 years old.[5] A skull found at Laetoli seems to represent an intermediate specimen between *homo erectus* and *homo sapiens;* in other words, an archaic *sapiens sapiens* like Omo II. It is highly probable that it was in fact this African *homo sapiens sapiens* with Grimaldian negroid features who left Africa about 40,000 years ago to people Europe.[6]

If the Grimaldian came to Europe with his Aurignacian industry completely developed and if he came from the east as it is believed, the age of industries should decline from east to west but we have observed that the opposite took place.

There were three possible routes with different levels of difficulty that the Africans could have taken when they left the Great Lakes region: (1) The Nile Valley, the Suez Isthmus, Palestine, and from there Asia, Oceania, Europe. It is in the light of the first route that the first human presence in Palestine can be considered. No one was born there. They came from elsewhere. (2) The Straits of Gibraltar, Spain, France, Asia, Oceania and the Americas through the Bering Straits. Since the IX IUSPP Congress in Nice, we have known that Australia was peopled during the Upper Paleolithic period; therefore, navigation could not date from the neolithic period, and the Straits of Gibraltar could have been crossed because the seas had been reduced by glaciation. (3) Cape Bon, Sicily, Southern Italy and Europe.

Thus the chain of hominids is made up of six species. The first three never left Africa. The last three reached such a level that they could not only spread over Africa but leave Africa with their industries to people other continents. Therefore after verification it appears that the African species were always older than those on other continents and other parts of the world. In point of fact even the physiology of man demonstrates he was born, not in a temperate climate but in the warm and humid climate of a tropical region.

The man born in Africa was necessarily dark-skinned due to the considerable force of ultraviolet radiation in the equatorial belt. As he moved toward the more temperate climates, this man gradually lost his pigmentation by process of selection and adaptation. It is from this perspective that the appearance of Cro-Magnon Man in Europe must be seen. In the Solutrean he is seen after 20,000 years of adaptation and transformation from the Grimaldian negroid in the condition of the final Würm glaciation.

Therefore, Cro-Magnon Man did not come from anywhere. He is rather the product of the mutation of the Grimaldian negroid where he was found and no pre-historical archeology has provided any other explanation for his appearance.

Richard Leakey even thinks that *homo erectus* must have been dark-skinned for the reasons I have just indicated with respect to the Grimaldian *homo sapiens sapiens,* and that the skin of this homo erectus must have become lighter as he moved to the northern regions. This is even more true in the case of *homo sapiens sapiens.*

Since man has existed for such a long time in Africa we argued that art must have existed in the Upper Paleolithic. This has now been proven: the carvings in the Apollo II cave in Namibia have been dated at 28,000 by the C.14 method. This makes them almost twice as old as the Ascaux painting in the south of France. The dancing sorcerer in the Afvallingskop and the dancing sorcerer in the grotto of the three brothers are remarkably similar. Richard Leakey reports that, in Tanzania, some carvings date back as far as 35,000 years. Leo Frobenius found paintings of an elk in the Khotsa grotto in the Basuta country of South Africa which dates to the Upper Paleolithic. The same could be said of paintings found in Sahara.

It must be noted that *homo sapiens sapiens* is responsible for this art wherever it is found, and the *homo sapiens* (or Neanderthal Man, as he has been renamed) never reached any level of artistic creation as such. There is a noticeable anatomical difference between him and *homo sapiens sapiens* in that he has no frontal lobe in the brain which is the seat of imagination.

It can be concluded from the foregoing, that from 5 million years ago to the glacial thaw 10,000 years ago, Africa almost unilaterally peopled and influenced the rest of the world.

Notes

1. Jerold M. Lowenstein: "Genetics in Fossils," in *Research,* no. 148, October 1983, pp. 1266-1270.
2. David Pilbeam: *From Primates to Man in For Science,* May 1984, pp. 34-44.
3. Jerold M. Lowenstein, *op. cit.*, p. 1269.
4. Members of the team: J.W.K. Harris, University of Pittsburgh (USA); J.A.J. Cowlett, Oxford University (GB); D. Walton, MacMaster University, Hamilton, Ontario (Canada); and B.A. Wood, Middlesex Hospital School, London (GB).

5. Yves Coppens, F. Clark Howell, Glynn Li, Isaac and Richard E.F. Leakey: Earliest Man and Environment in the Lake Rudolf Basin, *Pre-historic Archeology and Ecology* series, ed. Karl W. Butzer and Leslie G. Freeman, pp. 19-20.
6. According to molecular biology, the negroid branch became autonomous 120,000 years ago while the caucasoids and mongoloids separated 55,000 years ago. cf. J. Ruthie, *Biology:* Flammarion (Paris), p. 398. This is the opposite of assertions made by certain anthropologists who, preoccupied by ideological concerns, date the origin of negroids to the Neolithic. For them, man's oldest ancestor is actually his youngest!

Editor's Note: The second part of the Diop essay appears under the section "Nile Valley Civilizations as Source of Science"; the third part is omitted from this volume since it is peripheral to Nile Valley Civilization studies.

THE LOST PHARAOHS OF NUBIA

By Bruce Williams

A newly discovered ancient kingdom is always a matter of intense interest, but when it precedes the earliest known monarchy, the unification of Egypt in the fourth millennium B.C., then history itself is reborn. The place is anient Nubia at Qustul, where the investigation of archaeological materials recovered during the great 1960's rescue effort has recently unveiled a birthplace of pharaonic civilization several generations before the rise of the first historic Egyptian dynasty. This finding is rendered even more startling by the fact that advanced political organization was not believed to have come to Nubia, or anywhere south of Egypt, for another 2,500 years.

Transforming prehistory into history is always an enormously complex task, even in Egypt whose earliest written records rival those of ancient Mesopotamia. The firm progression of contemporary records from pharaoh to pharaoh trails off rapidly into obscurity just before the beginning of the First Dynasty. The establishment of this dynasty in about 3200-3150 B.C.—marking the political unification of Upper and Lower Egypt—is believed to have been achieved by the first pharaoh of both lands, Aha, in the conquest virtually completed by his predecessor Narmer. Much of the evidence for this period at the edge of history stems from great tombs dated to Aha and his successors in the First Dynasty. They were found with tombs of their predecessors, Ka and Karmer, at Abydos, the ancient holy city of the god Osiris, located 100 miles down the Nile from Luxor, and at Saqqara outside of Cairo. Farther upstream at Hierakonpolis in Upper Egypt, another great find was made in the beginning of this century—a major cache that included large stone palettes and maceheads associated with both Narmer and yet another predecessor, Scorpion, and some of even earlier times. The most important of these was the great stone Narmer Palette. Although shaped like other smaller stone palettes then used for grinding cosmetics, this one was inscribed with representations and symbols in bas relief that told of a triumph of the Upper Egyptian king over part of Lower Egypt, with the king's name, Narmer, spelled out at the top. In addition to this all important evidence, other monuments of Narmer and Scorpion document aspects of the unifying thrust northward. New excavations now in process at Hierakonpolis should add even more evidence.

Otherwise, there are only frustratingly enigmatic fragments from the Pre-

Reprinted from *Archeology Magazine*, volume 33, no. 5.

dynastic period—serekhs, palace façades symbolic of royalty, that were scratched on pottery, as well as a small group of other seemingly royal palettes showing evidence of warfare, and an earlier group depicting animal struggles. Since none of the palettes and maceheads were found in their original contexts, no precise chronological relationship for the various fragments can be established. Later king lists refer to whole dynasties before the unification of Egypt, but the names cannot be connected to any specific monuments, events or people. They are dynasties without substance preceded by the entirely mythological kingship of the gods. Until now, the lack of direct evidence has made the study of these early sovereignties largely speculative.

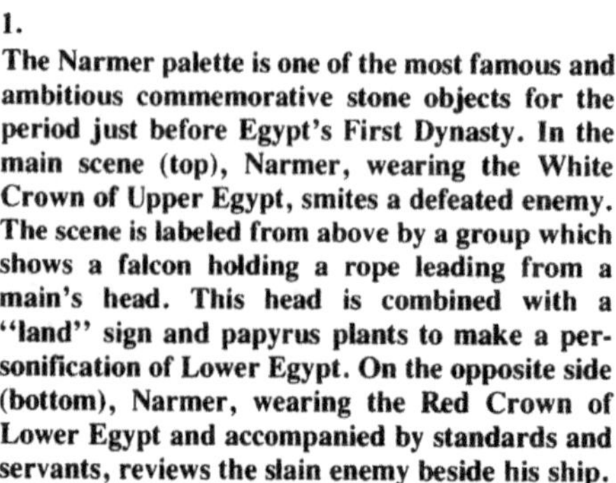

1.
The Narmer palette is one of the most famous and ambitious commemorative stone objects for the period just before Egypt's First Dynasty. In the main scene (top), Narmer, wearing the White Crown of Upper Egypt, smites a defeated enemy. The scene is labeled from above by a group which shows a falcon holding a rope leading from a main's head. This head is combined with a "land" sign and papyrus plants to make a personification of Lower Egypt. On the opposite side (bottom), Narmer, wearing the Red Crown of Lower Egypt and accompanied by standards and servants, reviews the slain enemy beside his ship.

In the last few years all this has sudenly changed. Direct evidence for kings in the Nile Valley before the reign of Narmer has finally emerged in context, but in a place and culture that no one had expected—Qustul in Lower Nubia, very near the present-day border of Egypt and the Sudan. The inhabitants of Lower Nubia in this period, whose cultural remains are called A-Group by archaeologists, were long thought to have had too simple a culture and too small a population to establish and support the complex political institutions and centralization implied by the presence of pharaohs. How could they possibly have achieved some "first dynasty" of their own? Even though the A-Group culture was substantially derived from that of Upper Egypt in the early Predynastic period, called Naqada I or Amratian after major sites in Egypt, by middle and late Predynastic times (the Naqada II and III or the Gerzean period), native objects are not Egyptian and many reveal characteristic traits from the Sudan. Based on the poverty of the country and the mixed character of the culture, archaeologists have concluded that A-Group Nubia was at most a scattered group of chiefdoms or, more likely, a loose collection of kin groups.

In an ironic twist, the startling evidence that reverses this thinking entirely was retrieved just when excavation at Qustul was all but doomed. In 1962, when an eleventh-hour international archaeological team set out to rescue ancient remains threatened by the rising waters of the Aswan Dam, the area of Qustul near the river was considered to be unworthy of further excavation. Keith C. Seele, then director of the University of Chicago's Oriental Institute Nubian Expedition, decided otherwise. After clearing sites and cemeteries of all pre-Islamic periods, in the last months of the last possible season, the expedition found a cemetery of A-Group tombs as large as those of Ka and Narmer at Abydos. Seele was immediately impressed with the importance of this site, which he designated Cemetery L, although every tomb in it had been plundered and the contents were mostly smashed and burnt. The immense bulk of material recovered put off any systematic consideration of Cemetery L, so only a preliminary partial assessment could be made on the basis of the 33 tombs and the registry of special objects in them. As a result, and because no explicit evidence of royalty could immediately be detected, Seele's early suggestion that these tombs might be those of Predynastic Nubian "princes" or "kings" was totally ignored—neither Qustul nor Cemetary L is mentioned in recent major discussions of A-Group or Predynastic civilization.

But by 1977—sadly, only a few years after Keith Seele's untimely death—the project of publishing the materials recovered by the Oriental Institute's Nubian Expedition turned to the systematic investigation of the remains from Cemetery L. The first and most daunting task was to make sense of the piles of sherds and fragments of stone vessels. Several years earlier these had been searched for "joins" but, for lack of time, had not been compared with one another to isolate the unconnected fragments from single vessels. A necessary process in even roughly determining the original number of objects in the tombs, distinguishing the fragments of one vessel from another was facilitated both by the distinctive designs on the numerous A-Group painted bowls, and by the variable texture of the "alabaster" calcite of which most of the stone vessels were made. Although the dedicated volunteer who had searched the collection for joins years before, Elizabeth Tieken, had warned that many sherds matched no others, no one even remotely expected the large numbers of objects that would appear; painted vessels are uncommon and stone vessels are rare in other A-Group sites. During weeks of comparing, counting and cross-checking, it became increasingly apparent that the Qustul collection contained greater numbers of both kinds of vessels than had ever been found before in Nubia—all told, more than 1,000 complete and fragmentary painted pots, and over 100 stone vessels. The range of these and other fragments from the plundered cemetery began to indicate a wealth and complexity that could only be called royal.

The pottery falls into five major groups distinguished by manufacture and decoration. By far the most numerous vessels, the painted pottery bowls, are sometimes decorated with elaborate overall patterns reminiscent of ripple burnishing, a practice that apparently had been abandoned earlier in Egypt and was reintroduced to Lower Nubia from Sudan. Most of this painted pottery is decorated with geometric or linear patterns in horizontal bands that resemble no other painted pottery of the period. It may be modeled after the well-known band incised pottery from Sudan to the south, or perhaps was inspired by the patterns of net slings used to carry the vessels. One smaller group of vessels may actually have been of Sudanese origin or may have been made at Qustul, copying a specifically Sudanese style with broad bands of incised decoration and zig-zag rocker-stamp patterns so well known in the south.

Thick, soft, poorly fired shallow bowls with incised and stamped decorations on a burnished surface represent another tradition. Some of these bowls are decorated with serpents in reserve, outlined against the impression-filled background, a motif strikingly similar to serpents found on black-incised bowls of the C-Group—the name for the culture that occupied Lower Nubia from the Late Old Kingdom to the start of the New Kingdom (ca. 2300-1500 B.C.). These bowls so closely resemble their C-Group counterparts, they must be considered part of a long-standing, unbroken tradition. The entire manufacturing technique and style is so different from any other A-Group material that they must have been imported from the home of the later C-Group, probably in the west.

After the A-Group painted vessels, Egyptian pottery is the most common. Distinctive pieces clearly match pottery from the Naqada III period, the last phase of Predynastic culture in Egypt. These pieces include small to monumental bowls; miniature lentoid flasks; narrow-necked bottles; cylindrical jars with incised wavy bands, including one from a late tomb with painted lattice decoration; spouted jars; and large heavy storage jars, 23 of which were found intact in the trench of one monumental tomb. Four of these great storage jars—which have a modified shape found in the latest Predynastic royal tombs of Abydos—were in-

2. The central portion of a seal from Siali in the northern part of Lower Nubia clearly shows a man saluting a serekhor palace façade with a falcon above it, labeled by a bow over a rectangle as the Horus of Ta-Seti. This indicates that Nubia was a territorial state. It is assembled from three sealings and was corrected by eliminating a probable crack in the original seal down the center of the palace façade. The falcon and the palace façades above the man are partially restored.

cised with inscriptions that clearly represent an early form of hieroglyphic writing. A substantial number of the Egyptian vessels are painted, mostly with groups of wavy lines that characterize late Predynastic vase painting. A few of these pots are decorated with groups of figures that proved to be extremely significant.

The last group came from the Levant and was made in the tradition of Syro-Palestinian vessels dating to the Early Bronze I period (before ca. 3200/3150 B.C.). Almost all of these were found in a single early Cemetery L tomb and represent a type that has never been found in Egypt—although close parallels have been found on the Asiatic coast.

In addition to the large group of pottery and 100 stone vessels, other badly damaged objects of local A-Group, Egyptian and Sudanese origin give eloquent testimony to the thorough plundering of the cemetery. Their special quality and unusual number tell a story. Some of the small stone A-Group palettes, for example, were made of highly polished, hard, colored quartz. Large mortars were generally carved to precise shapes from an extremely hard quartzite; sometimes simple spiral decorations were added. But most important are the distinctively A-Group incense burners—cylindrical objects made of local sandstone or a mixture of clays and sepiolite (meerschaum)—found at Qustul in numbers several times greater than ever before in all of Nubia. Several of these incense bur-

3. The preserved part of a bowl from Qustul shows the typical late prehistoric motif of two giraffes flanking palm trees. The crowns of the trees have been replaced with representations of historic significance. Vultures tear at fallen enemies, here partly obliterated. On the right, the enemy, who has fallen forward, is labeled Upper Egypt, the first mention of this region as a political entity. On the left, the victim appears to be Libya. This scene, together with the label on another Qustul jar, which shows a vulture attacking Hierakonpolis, links the more allegorical representations of cultures attacking serpents on slightly earlier objects to specific scenes of royal victory.

ners were incised and carved with the representations and symbols of Egyptian royalty—a decisive indication of the true meaning of the size and wealth of the Qustul tombs.

A number of small objects reflect a third tradition, and one that stems from a most interesting source. The most common of these are small hooklike objects carved from seashells, with tapered heads and pointed shanks that varied from a short spike to a long, curved semicircle. Hooks, studs and tokens of this type are relatively rare in Egypt and occur only in a few poor graves. They are almost entirely missing from any excavated A-Group tomb in Numia. Early forms of these same objects, however, mostly in stone, are common farther upstream at Shaheinab in Sudan where they probably originated. Although many of these small pieces were found throughout Cemetery L, the only totally unlooted pile of shell objects contained more than 1,650 as well as 2,600 other objects of unknown purpose usually called "lip plugs," which were also common at Shaheinab but rare in Egypt and Lower Nubia. Although no clear evidence for the purpose of the small plugs or tokens is known, they could hardly have been intended for use in very large numbers. It is clear that the more than 4,000 objects found in this pile may be tokens of wealth in other materials.

Tombs of this size, wealth and date in Egypt would have been immediately recognized as royal. Their extraordinarily varied contents would have been taken as evidence of a complex culture exposed to wide outside connections. But be-

4. The Archaic Horus Incense Burner (*bottom*), named after the Horus clearly present in the last ship, shows two royal processions of three ships, but most of the passengers are difficult to locate in the badly crumbled surface. The presence of Horus emphasizes the development of official religion at Qustul of a type later characteristic of dynastic Egypt. Preserved measurement, 7.5 by 15.3 centimeters.

cause the discovery was made in Nubia at a time and a place when kingship was thought impossible, further proof of royalty is necessary. Fortunately, such crucial supporting evidence was on hand in the form of the incense burners incised with serekhs, the representations of paneled palace façades. Definitive symbols of Egyptian royalty, serekhs appear in late Predynastic times often surmounted by a falcon-Horus symbol of the Pharaoh; later they are used to enclose Horus names of Egyptian pharaohs, the major royal name used during the first and Second Dynasties. The palace façades on the incense burners are similar to the simplest examples found incised on Predynastic pottery in Egypt. Some of these façades are associated with ship processions, and in two cases are especially elaborate. In fact, the most interesting and precious object found at Qustul, the largest, finest and most elaborately decorated of all the A-Group incense burners, has the best example of such a scene incised in a sunk silhouette style related to rock drawing. It was found in one of the earliest and richest tombs of Cemetery L, dating to about four generations or more before the time of the Egyptian King Ka, six or seven generations before the start of the First Dynasty. The Oriental Institute researchers quickly recognized that this incense burner showed a procession of three ships with their tall sterns and bent prows going toward a palace façade. Investigators also noted both the curious concentric design of the serekh and possible Mesopotamian connections for it and the ships. But because only one occupant of the three ships was known, and the passengers of the other two seemed unrestorable, the Qustul incense burner remained an enigma. Later, however, when the incense burner was reexamined in the light of the obviously royal stature of the people buried in Cemetery L, the essential restoration of the missing elements was immediately clear.

In the first ship, a prisoner is kneeling on a palanquin or litter held by a rope in the grasp of a guard with a mace. Although the figure in the middle ship is almost completely destroyed, the white crown of Upper Egypt clearly stands out above the ship. In front of it is the tail of a falcon—another sign of kingship. The crown indicates that the figure is a king, and the falcon should be seen as perched on a serekh, together a characteristic representation in early dynastic Egypt. In front of the falcon is a rosette, a symbol of royalty before the First Dynasty. The pair, bound prisoner and pharaoh, are well known in early Eygptian iconography, but are represented somewhat unusually here. During the First Dynasty, scenes of the two are static with the king and prisoner both firmly placed on dry land—but on the incense burner from Qustul, generations before, they are transported by ship. The early date of the Qustul incense burner is further reflected by other figures that have important connections to middle and later Predynastic art—an unnamed feline deity (determined by a falcon on a standard); a man saluting in a pose and style typical of Naqada II vase painting; and two animals, an antelope and carnivore, cavorting around the central royal ship. They pose in the characteristic manner of early palettes which show groups of struggling animals; this type precedes those with scenes of historical events. Its date provided by context, style and composition, the Qustul burner furnishes the earliest definite representation of a king in the Nile Valley or anywhere. This conclusion is further supported by several other incised incense burners depicting a combination of ships and palace façades in royal procession. However, their designs are so simple or poorly preserved that they were difficult to recognize until the Qustul incense burner was deciphered.

As the weeks and months wore on, the continued reevaluation of the Qustul objects began to indicate a sequence that led generation by generation from Cemetery L to the time of the last pre-First Dynasty tombs at Abydos. The people buried at Qustul were obviously kings with the full wealth expected of royalty, and had even far wider cultural contacts than has ever been thought possible for such a remote place. But what is known about this new kingdom? What relationship did these first pharaohs have with their subjects and surrounding political entities? Perhaps the most troublesome question was why nothing of this kingdom had been known until now. Actually, the truth is that evidence, other than the cemetery at Qustul, has been known for some time but it has been either ignored or wrongly interpreted and dated. The greatest example is the large Gebel Sheikh Suleiman monument located south of Qustul. Originally, this inscription was thought to have been made by the Egyptian pharaoh Djer, the second king of the First Dynasty, identified by his Horus name in a serekh. But the incisions across the lower body of the falcon perched on the serekh, which have been taken to be Djer's name, are actually part of an animal common in rock graffiti if Nubia. In fact, there is no room for a name on this serekh, and it must be dated with other unlabeled ones to the Predynastic period. The nameless serekh presides at a battlefield scene including fallen enemies, two bound prisoners and a

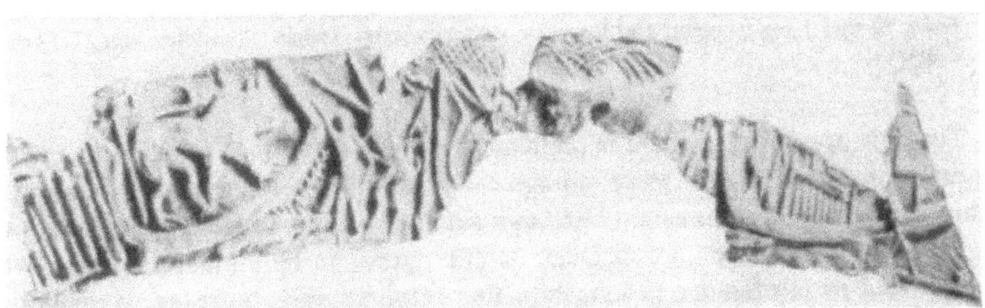

5. The incense burner from Tomb L24 is the most vivid evidence of kingship at Qustul (*top, bottom and opposite page, top*). Made of a mixture of fine clay minerals, it is an ancestor of the slate palettes and monumental maceheads that show royal events and ceremonies in Egypt. The scene shown here is a royal sacrifical procession of three ships going toward a palace façade. The completed restoration (*opposite page, top*) shows a bound prisoner held by his guard in the forward vessel: a pharaoh, indicated by the White Crown of Upper Egypt and the falcon, in the middle ship; and a feline deity with a falcon standard in the third. About 8.5 by 15.5 centimeters.

royal ship. Interestingly, these enemies have labels that do not seem to be associated with Nubia. In addition, one is being physically bound, rather than labeled, by a bow, which is significant because the "Land of the Bow" is the earliest hieroglyphic name for Nubia and, later, is the actual name for the southernmost nome or province of Egypt. By acting as agent of the pharaoh, the bow marks the ruler as one of Nubia, and makes this an A-Group rather than an Egyptian monument.

6. Pottery from the A-Group royal tomb at Qustul includes large amounts of fine painted pottery (*left*), with one large bowl decorated with rows of palace façades; a Syro-Palestinian Early Bronze I jug (center); and Egyptian pottery (*right*). Height of handled jug, 17.7 centimeters.

The bow appears elsewhere in prehistoric monuments—for example, on a seal impression found in a A-Group storage cache at Siali far to the north of Qustul. This sealing had been misinterpreted as a result of a crack in the original ivory or wood seal, which made a concentric serekh appear to be a plant and thus was overlooked as a reference to kingship. Its central subject, however, is undoubtedly a concentric serekh surmounted by the familiar falcon symbol. Although a number of aspects of this seal are still difficult to verify, certain features of the iconography are fairly certain, including representations of incense burners in use; D-shaped altars or pylons associated with the Heb-Sed festival, the jubilee celebrated by a pharaoh first in his thirtieth year and periodically thereafter; and a man seated in a chair saluting the bow symbol. This time, however, the bow hovers over a shortened rectangle which in this period represents land. The obvious interpretation is that the man is saluting the name for Nubia—Ta-Seti, or "Land of the Bow"—as a kingship and territorial state. Obviously, Nubia was a sophisticated political order of an actual and not embryonic rule.

Three objects from Cemetery L relate even more directly to the history of the kingdom of Ta-Seti. The first is a large Egyptian bowl from tomb L23 which has an elaborate painting of a processional scene leading to a shrine made of poles. Three vultures appear, two of them holding serpents in their talons and attacking

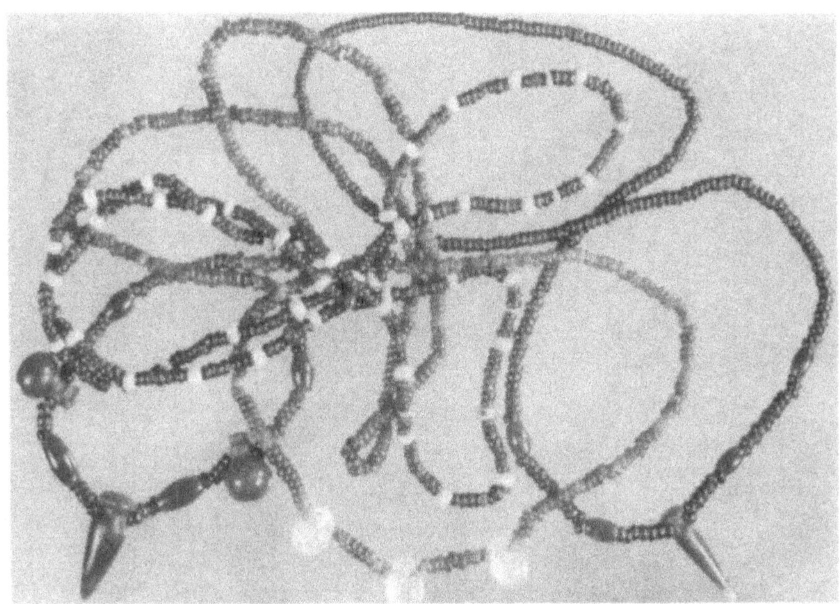

7. Little jewelry remained in the plundered royal cemetery at Qustul, but what did survive was of high quality, including carnelian, amethyst, faience and rock crystal.

them with their beaks. An identical motif is found on other vessesl and occurs in simplified form on a series of famous Predynastic Egyptian ivory objects decorated with elaborate rows of animals. Aside from this connection, the specific occurrence of this motif on the Qustul bowl allows us to follow a chronological progression in the development of this motif on two other important objects. One of these is also a large bowl; the other is an Egyptian storage jar with a faded black ink label on its shoulder from tomb L6, an animal sacrifice burial contemporary with L23. Because this label was applied after firing, it was most likely done locally and could hardly have referred to an Egyptian event. It shows a vertical pole with an oval object on it that is being attacked by an elongated, vulture-like bird. The back and neck of the bird are stretched in an exaggerated arc, like that made by the tails, backs and necks of the vultures on the bowl from L23. The oval under attack contains two diagonal lines, clearly the sign for Nekhen or Hierakonpolis, the late prehistoric site that has yielded so much evidence for the rise of the Egyptian pharaohs.

The third piece of evidence, from tomb L19, is a large bowl somewhat smaller than the example from L23. Painted on the sides are static heraldic groups, consisting of two giraffes facing a tree with at least one animal above and behind them. Groups of this kind are already well known from two monumental palettes, one depicting the early animal hunt group, and the other from the later historical series. Both the shapes of the giraffes and the roots of the tree indicate that this

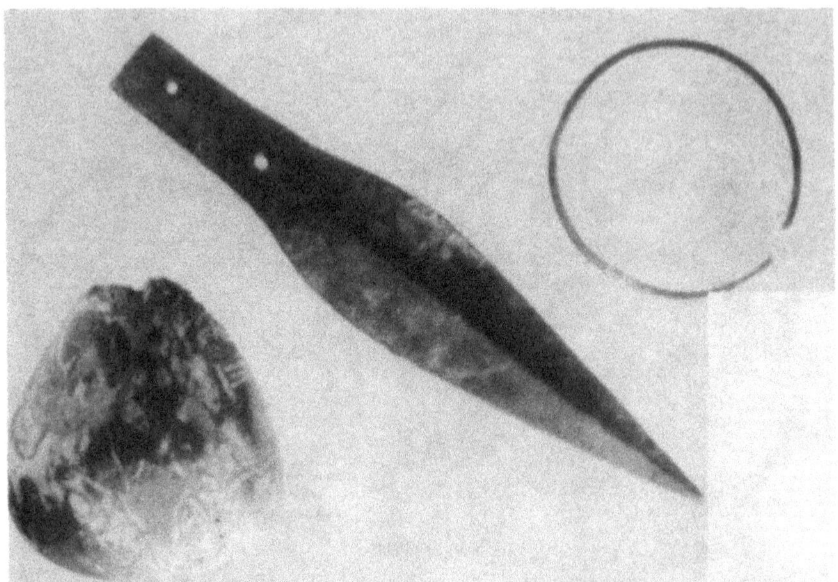

8. Few weapons remained in the robbed tombs at Qustul, but they included this spearhead and macehead. The bracelet is made of gold or electrum. Length of spearhead, 15.5 centimeters.

representation belongs to the early group. It seems that the paint was applied after firing, for much of it has been removed and what remains is vulnerable to contact with water. Since the paint was so delicate, it could hardly have been put on anywhere but in the immediate vicinity of Qustul because it would not have been able to stand the rigors of travel. In fact, so much of the paint has disappeared that the design could not have been followed if the background around the painted areas had not faded, leaving a traceable shadow of the original design.

The most striking feature of this decoration is the crown of the palm tree between the giraffes which has been supplanted by an animal group including the now familiar vulture. Here, the bird tears not a serpent or symbol, but a fallen man, a group seen elsewhere on the "Lion Palette" in England, one of the later palettes which show historical events. On the L19 bowl, the fallen man is labeled below his knee with the familiar oval land sign—without the two diagonal marks. Instead, a plant extends at an odd angle from the left end of the oval, presumably because it had been displaced from the vertical by the man's torso which can no longer be seen. The plant has three opposed pairs of short leaves (now partially obliterated) and a broad stalk that curves sharply to a point. Although the leaves are short and the stalk broad, this plant is clearly an early form of the symbol for Upper Egypt. The plant, together with the land oval, can plausibly be read one way only—the fallen enemy is labeled Ta-Shemau or Upper Egypt. Although the second group remaining on this bowl is fainter than the first, it can be seen that

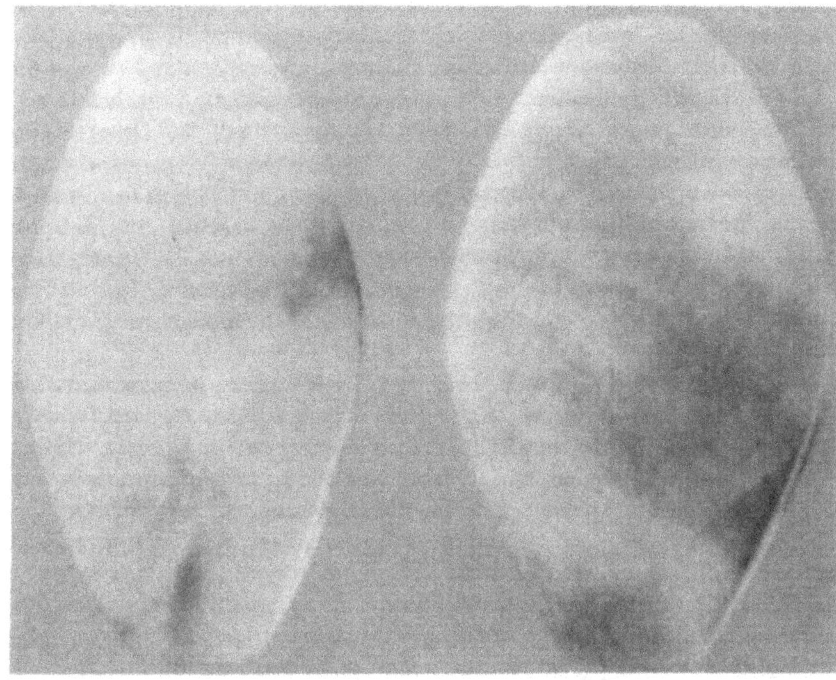

9. Some of the palettes from Qustul used to grind malachite for eye paint were made of special colored quartz and were given a jewel-like polish. Average length, eight centimeters.

"the enemy" has fallen on his back rather than forward. The long flat sign (land) extends from the enemy's knee and the unimpeded vertical identifying sign appears to make a kind of question mark above—this, in all probability, is the label Ta-Tjemeh or Libya.

All of these complex parts comprise the great legacy of the cemetery at Qustul—the eloquent remains of a remarkable civilization that rose out of both Egyptian and Sudanese heritages and had contacts as far away as Libya and western Asia. For nine generations or more, according to the sequence of tombs in Cemetery L, some twelve kings at Qustul participated with other kings in Upper Egypt in the creation of a unified culture. For Egypt, they helped fashion pharaonic civilization and thus a legacy for the First Dynasty which the world has marveled at for millennia. For Nubia, they established an early political unity and led that country to its first cultural distinction. Sifting through the individual artifacts, one can recreate the grand chain of events from the broken fragments.

In the first and second generation, the seal from Siali shows a king ruling Ta-Seti even before the unification of Upper Egypt. The actual king appears in the "third generation" figure on the Qustul incense burner, and is a link in the successive royal monuments both in Nubia and Egypt that culminate in the rise of the First Dynasty as shown on the Narmer Palette. The faded ink label of the Qustul storage jar, by describing the conflict with Hierakonpolis in Egypt, takes us to the fourth generation and, most important, the earliest known recorded event. In the fifth generation, this conflict grows ominously to include a now possibly united Upper Egypt. At about the same time, the Gebel Sheikh Suleiman monument seems to specify the places and/or people against whom the pharaohs of Ta-Seti fought. Whether it refers to actual events or is merely propaganda, the records of their victories are repeatedly asserted, and A-Group tombs, including one of royal size and design, have been found at Hierakonpolis itself. In the sixth generation, perhaps due to reverses in battle, the tombs at Qustul diminish sharply in size, possibly reflecting a reduction in stature of those buried in them.

The next generation, finally, appears to be contemporary with the first great royal burials at Abydos and the last Egyptian pharaohs before the First Dynasty. At Qustul, the royal cemetery continued for another two generations with the tombs growing ever smaller until no more were made, and the sepulchres were pillaged and burned. Apparently, the demise of Qustul coincides with the campaign of Aha in Nubia, the first king of the Egyptian First Dynasty, who recorded the smiting of Ta-Seti. Afterward, the A-Group culture ceased to exist in Lower Nubia. It may be that the remarkable adventure in political organization that began at Qustul and had such fateful consequences for human history was also terminated at this time. But striking parallels between the much later royal cemetery at Kerma, just south of the Third Cataract, and Cemetery L show another possibility: perhaps the survivors of the A-Group went south, beyond the reach of First Dynasty conquerers to the area even south of modern Lake Nasser. Although the chronological gap between the A-Group and Kerma is great and needs to be filled in by systematic field research, the present lack of evidence by no means rules out this possibility. After all, the kingdom at Qustul was not thought possible at that time or place. Given such a sudden and complete reversal of assumptions, there is reason to believe that knowledge of the achievements that created and sustained Egyptian civilization penetrated even further south than Qustul at a very early time. There must be a new search.

Bibliography

FOR FURTHER READING on Nubian kingship in general: William Y. Adams, *Nubia, Corridor to Africa* (Princeton University Press, Princeton 1978), for a current reconstruction of social organization in A-Group Nubiam this is a large-scale discussion of all periods of history in the region; A.J. Arkell, *A History of the Sudan to A.D. 1821* (Athlone Press, University of London 1961, second edition), a thoughtful work, but based on a much smaller body of evidence; Hans-Ake Nordstrom, *Neolithic and A-Group Sites* (Scandanavian Joint Expedition to Sudanese Nubia Vol. 3, Uppsala, Sweden 1972); Boyce Rensberger, "Nubian Monarchy Called Oldest" (*The New York Times*, March 1, 1979, A1 and A16), except for other short notices in the press, no other publication available to the public refers to the possibility of kingship in Nubia during the A-Group; Bruce G. Trigger, *History and Settlement in Lower Nubia* (Yale University Publications in Anthropology, No. 69, New Haven 1965), discusses A-Group culture generally.

On the "new chronology for the Egyptian Predynastic period: Elise J. Baumgartel, "Predynastic Egypt" (Cambridge Ancient History, Vol. 1, Chapter IXa, Cambridge 1970); *Die altorientalischen Reiche I: vom Paläolithikum biz zur Mitte des 2. Jahrtausends* (Fischer Bucherei K.G., Frankfurt A.M. and Hamburg 1965), accepts an alternative reconstruction which recognizes late predynastic (Naqada III or Late Gerzean): Werner Kaiser, "Stand und Probleme der ägyptischen Vorgeschichtsforschung" (*Zeitschrift für ägyptische Sprache* 81 (1956): 87-109 and "Zur inneren Chronologie der Naqadakultur" (*Archaeologia Geographia* 6 (1957): 69-77, propose this alternative reconstruction; "Einige Bemerkugen zur ägyptische Frühzeit," parts I-III, *Zeitschrift für äyptische Sprache, vols.* 84 (1959), 85 (1960), 86 (1961) and 89 (1964), discusses pharaonic culture in late predynastic and early dynastic times.

LATEST RESEARCH ON NUBIA:
A Letter to the Editor

Dear Editor:

In answering your request for remarks on new evidence to extend our knowledge of Nubia into uncharted ages, I will begin by indicating some of the foundations being laid by recent research.

As indicated by my talk at the Nile Valley Civilizations Conference, the present status of knowledge and probably the actual occupation along the river between the Neolithic and the Christian periods is episodic. Occupations appear, last for some centuries and disappear, often separated from each other by long ages with little or no identifiable settlement. The longest traceable continuities are those of the Kushite kingdom of Napata and Meroe that last from ca. 750 B.C. to 350 A.D. Before that time, several gaps interrupt our knowledge. About 16 years ago, an Austrian, Manfred Bietak, developed criteria for distinguishing specific cultures in the C-Group phase, ca. 2300-1500 B.C. in Lower Nubia. By re-examining published sites and exploring new ones, we can begin to trace the appearance of some of these specified traits in earlier and intervening times. In my talk, I concentrated on certain specific themes that reappear, a pharaonic kingship that differs in many details from that of Egypt, a V-shaped beaker, a bed burial, the ring tumulus (and its easy transition to the pyramid), and the southward-facing chapel built to the north of the normal approach to the tumulus.

A complex professional discussion with complete discussion or citation of key published evidence would be necessary for any serious presentation of the thesis that some continuous pharaonic-type civilization existed parallel to Egypt and I hope to do this in appropriate detail elsewhere. For now, I can only point out some major outlines.

As discussed in the *Archaeology* article, I believe that A-Group Nubia developed a pharaonic kingship as the late prehistoric Egyptian institution was forming to the north. Its full role in that formation has not been specified, but it was distinct enough to be creative. It also had: a. an early version of the V-shaped beaker; b. the bed burial—though this was rather rare; c. the ring tumulus. It also had a ocal form of the building with the panneled facade specifically associated with earliest pharaonic representations as the *serekh*. The Siali sealings give the name of this kingdom as Ta-Seti, the most ancient name for Nubia in written documents. Its first well-identified king appeared on the badly destroyed Qustul Incense Burner.

A-Group was uprooted, apparently by Egyptian military action, and the succeeding period, Egypt's greatest age, is poorly known in Nubia. About 2300

B.C., in the Sixth Dynasty, new occupation appears in the area, documented by the records of trade and political interference by Egyptian governors of Aswan, execration texts that curse over 180 Nubians, and major archaeological remains in Lower Nubia and at Kerma south of the Third Cataract.

The archaeological remains can loosely be called C-Group, and they belong to a prosperous cattle culture based on an economy that can often be seen in modern Africa. In the First Intermediate Period, we actually have the names of three individuals who seem to have ruled in Lower Nubia, names repeatedly inscribed on the rocks south of Aswan. The date and local character of these rulers was pointed out by Torgny Save-Soderbergh over a generation ago, with the clearly pharaonic nature of their names in cartouche. The third of these rulers has a personal name that compares very closely with those in the recently-published Old Kingdom Execration Texts, and it would appear that we have a short-lived C-Group Nubian dynasty. Whatever its origin, the Eleventh Dynasty that reunited Egypt also pursued the interests of Egypt by campaigning in Nubia, probably to suppress this potential rival. In the succeeding twelfth Dynasty, Lower Nubia was conquered and garrisoned, though the C-Group population was left to itself. Quite probably, the real motive was control of access to the south for trade and security. The real opponent was Kush.

It would appear that Kush raised a truly serious threat, for Senwosret III in the nineteenth century made major campaigns against that power and, at the same time, erected an enormous complex of fortresses to control the frontier, along with carefully maintained apparatus of communication, such as a long slipway around the cataract, and a systematic program of patrolling the desert with large detachments. Since no such mighty complex protected the northeastern frontier against Asiatics, we can only infer that Kush was a great power at this time.

In Kush, the early culture at Kerma developed into a major state by 1750-1700 B.C. Between 1660 and 1550, under the control of Kush, Upper Nubia with at least two peoples, and Lower Nubia with the Egyptian fortress-garrisons left over from the Middle Kingdom, Medjay from the Eastern Desert, and C-Group all took part in Kush's first empire. The capital at Kerma is once again being excavated, by a Swiss, Bonnet, and its extraordinary success as a center of trade and industry, especially in copper, faience, and pottery, is being clearly documented. Here, too, the features we have been tracing, V-Shaped beakers, bed burials, ring tumuli, and north-south chapels were characteristic. In addition, stone stelae from Buhen with specialized figures of pharaohs and a winged sun disc painted in the most important burial chamber at Kerma, among other evidence, indicate that the Kushite empire was pharaonic.

At the end of the Second Intermediate Period, the Egyptian Pharaoh Kamose recorded a letter sent by the last Asiatic ruler in the Delta to Kush urging him to attack Egypt's southern frontier now made vulnerable by Kamose's northward advance. The threat this represented stalled Egypt's northward thrust and led to a long series of campaigns that culminated in the conquest of Kush by 1500. Although the old renegade Egyptian garrisons were destroyed and replaced by fresh troops and the rulers of Kush were removed, the area continued to be ruled as a single political unit by the King's son of Kush, virtually as a parallel subject kingdom.

New details were introduced from Egypt at this time, such as the pyramid, which was adopted as a direct equivalent of the ring tumulus of old Kush.

The last phases are well known, first as the empire of Napata and Meroe and then as X-Group. The Kushite kingdom and civilization of Napata and Meroe have been studied extensively over the last fifty years and more, an enterprise whose general results have been summarized extensively in such works as W.Y. Adams' *Nubia, Corridor to Africa* and P.L. Shinnie's *Meroe*. The early appearance of the beaker, the ring-tumulus, and the bed burial accompanied the appearance of the distinct version of pharaonic kingship, but these early Kushite features were soon masked by an overlay of imported northern practices.

Our last era to be considered occurred between 350 and 550 A.D., when the so-called X-Group culture flourished in Lower Nubia. This culture combined numerous features of Meroitic official culture with some key revivals of early Kushite practices, especially the tumulus (often with a ring-trench), long rows of chapels on the north sides of Royal Tumuli opening to the south, and bed burials, as well as distinctly Meroitic pharaonic regalia.

Tracing these few criteria through widely separated ages hardly serves to more than illustrate the thesis that a Kushite continuity sustained the pharaonic impulse through the ages from A-Group to X-Group. The details will have to be examined with great care before any such thesis can be considered verified, but a beginning has been made in many quarters, by many researchers working over a long period.

Despite the incomplete state of its formulation and verification, it was only fitting that this thesis be stated first in the Dr. Martin Luther King Chapel at Morehouse College. While it is based on the work of many scholars, many features will have to be examined with a critical eye before it can be stated decisively. However, this thesis may represent a new departure in the examination of Egypt's place in the African context, and we can hope for much new light on this context in future.

Please accept my best regards and thanks for your kindness.

Bruce Williams
The Oriental Institute,
October 1984

BLACK RULERS OF THE GOLDEN AGE

By Legrand H. Clegg II

> *When Asia overwhelmed Egypt, Egypt sought refuge in Ethiopia [Nubia] as a child returns to its mother, and Ethiopia then for centuries dominated Egypt and successfully invaded Asia.*
>
> —W.E.B. DuBois, *The World And Africa: An Inquiry into the Part Which Africa Has Played in World History*, New York: International Publishers, 1961, p. 117.

Over the past quarter of a century during which Americans and Europeans have gradually lost their total monopoly on the study and interpretation of world history (and such allied fields as anthropology, archaeology and paleontology), there have emerged two distinct positions on the racial identity of the ancient Egyptian people. One view, which was introduced by Nineteenth Century Egyptologists and has dominated Western scientific thinking ever since, is that "the people who lived in Ancient Egypt were 'white,' even though their pigmentation was dark, or even black, as early as the predynastic period. Negroes made their appearance only from the XVIIIth Dynasty onwards."[1] Little evidence has ever been presented in support of this position, but it has survived largely, if not entirely, on the strength of the reputation, power and influence of the scientists and scholars who espouse it. The opposing view, which holds that "ancient Egypt was peopled, 'from its neolithic infancy to the end of the native dynasties,' by Black Africans,"[2] appears to have been the only opinion on the subject from the time of the ancient Hebrews[3] and Greeks[4] until the birth of the science of Egyptology in Europe over a century ago.

During the 20th Century the latter view has been resurrected in the writings of such African-American scholars as W.E.B. DuBois, William L. Hansberry, J.A. Rogers, Carter G. Woodson, Chancellor Williams, Yosef Ben Jochanan and John Henrike Clark and a number of African scholars, including Cheikh Anta Diop and I. Obenga. One of the major periods in Egyptian history that these scholars have considered in support of their opinion is that of the Seventeenth and Eighteenth Dynasties (Egypt's "Golden Age") which is the focus of this paper.

Undoubtedly because of their defensive position in the face of the awesome might of Western scholarship, the advocates of a Black Egypt have been most meticulous in proving their case as they seek to change prevailing opinion. Chief among these scholars is Diop, probably the world's greatest living historian and certainly the foremost contemporary authority on African History and culture. He relies on anthropology, iconography, melanin dosage tests, osteological measurements, blood groupings, the testimony of classical writers, self-descriptive Egyptian hieroglyphs, divine epithets, Bibical eyewitnesses, linguistics and various cultural data in support of his opinion regarding the ethnicity of the ancient Egyptians.[5]

We enter this controversy as proud disciples of Dr. Diop and the other distinguished scholars who have relied on evidence rather than passion in their pursuit of the truth with respect to the racial identity of the ancient Egyptians. While we understand why the advocates of a Black Egypt have persisted in pressing for the overall acceptance of their position by the moguls of Western academia, we are disinclined to follow this course. It is clear to us that Western authority, as a whole, has conspired to suppress, distort or ignore African history with the intent of perpetuating white historical supremacy; and that this deeply entrenched practice will not give way to the truth simply because the truth is right, just or supported by solid evidence. Therefore, this paper is not intended as another debate with Western scholars over whether the ancient Egyptians as a general rule were blacks. In our opinion, this issue has been settled in the affirmative.

Nevertheless, all points of view should be periodically updated and refined in order to maintain their scientific accuracy. Hence, in further support of our opinion that the ancient Egyptians were essentially a Black people, we hereby propose that a new, comprehensive ethnic examination be undertaken of the general Egyptian population during the Old, Middle and New Kingdoms, the First and Second Intermediate Periods, the Nubian Renaissance (Twenty-Fifth Dynasty) and the period of decline. We also recommend that a similar analysis be made of every possible ruler of each dynasty from the time of Menes in the First Dynasty to the conquest of Egypt by Alexander of Macedonia. This will probably require years of research and it is made difficult by the paucity of available evidence; yet the task must be undertaken if we intend for our work to supplant the lies and inaccuracies of prevailing opinion in African history.

In keeping with the above proposal, our specific intent in this brief paper is to undertake a scientific evaluation of the racial characteristics of the rulers of Egypt's Seventeenth and Eighteenth Dynasties. We have chosen this period because of its significance in African history and world affairs. The Seventeenth Dynasty began a major war of liberation which ended victoriously in the founding of the Eighteenth. This succeeding royal family brought Egypt to new heights of technical achievement and military might, and marked the first time that any nation expanded its borders to encompass a vast world empire. We believe that our scrutiny of the familial ties of the rulers of these two great dynasties will establish a concrete and verifiable genetic continuum that may well remove the ethnicity of these royal families from the realm of speculation.

Background

But in order to lay the foundation for our case here, we must look beyond both the Seventeenth and Eighteenth Dynasties into the Twelfth Dynasty of the Middle Kingdom (circa. 2000-1780 B.C.) at which time Egypt had lapsed into confusion, contention and internal strife that ultimately led to what is called the Second Intermediate Period (i.e., the Thirteenth through the early Seventeenth Dynasties, c. 1786-1567 B.C.). Manetho, an Egyptian priest (ca. 300 B.C.), wrote an historical treatise on Egypt which includes this period, but it has perished. Fortunately, however, Jewish historian Flavius Josephus quotes a portion of Manetho's account of the Hyksos invasion which was the most significant event of the Second Intermediate Period and which transformed Egyptian History. "[A] blast of God smote us," Manetho states, "and unexpectedly from the regions of the East, invaders of obscure race marched in confidence of victory against our land. By main force they easily seized it without striking a blow; and having overpowered the rulers of the land they then burned our cities ruthlessly, razed to the ground the temples of the gods, and treated all the natives with a cruel hostility, massacring some and leading into slavery the wives and children of others . . . Finally, they appointed as king one of their number whose name was Salitis."[6]

Manetho designated these invaders as "Hyksos," which he interprets to mean "king-shepherds" in the Egyptian language.[7] Today the word Hyksos is more generally interpreted as "rulers of foreign lands."[8]

These invaders were largely Semitic foreigners driven from Western Asia into Africa by instability and famine. They appear to have established themselves in Lower Egypt and may have extended their influence, if not their actual rule, over much of the remainder of the country.[9]

Although Manetho holds that the Hyksos dominated Egypt for 511 years, [10] modern scholars generally believe that they ruled for no more than about two centuries.[11] During this period their cultural impact was most unremarkable. "The Hyksos left no literary evidence of their occupation of Egypt. Indeed, they left practically no large monuments at all. What we know about them has been painfully gleaned from a host of scarabs . . . . cylinder seals, and few other isolated objects . . ."[12]

The Hyksos are of particular significance to us here, however, because they appear to have expelled the native African royal family from Egypt and to have driven its members far to the south. How far southward this family was driven and what ultimately became of its members and their descendants are critical issues.

A number of scholars believe that during the Hyksos period (i.e. the Fifteenth through the Seventeenth Dynasties), "the members of the [Egyptian] royal family retired to Kush [i.e. Nubia] where they lived as guests and wards of the Kushites for many years."[13] In other words, the native rulers were expelled from Egypt entirely and then "sought refuge in Ethiopia [Nubia] as a child returns to its mother"[14] until Egypt could be liberated from foreign domination.

Other authorities hold, however, that Hyksos domination was not nearly so pervasive as had been reported. Diop, for example, insists that the Hyksos "occupied only the eastern region of the Delta, with Avaris as their capital'' and that ''the Black dynasty'' remained strong in upper Egypt.[15]

What appears to be relatively certain is that during the period of Hyksos occupation the peoples of Upper Egypt and Nubia (the country immediately south of Egypt) grew close together in the apparent recognition of a common enemy—the Semitic invaders. From this Black interdependence appears to have come much ''cross-breeding,'' cultural interchange, trading and the forging of strong political alliances. Redford has commented on the special relationship between Egypt and Nubia at this time:

> During the Seventeenth Dynasty a good deal of contact took place between the peoples of Nubia and the Egyptians of the incipient Theban kingdom. Egyptian freebooters and adventurers drifted south out of Upper Egypt into the wilds of the transcataract region to hire themselves as soldiers to the king of Kush [Nubia] while an opposite movement brought Nubian mercenaries of Medja extraction into the service of the Seventeenth Dynasty. In numbers the latter migration far outweighed the reverse movement of Egyptians. At numerous sites in Upper Egypt as far north as Asyut the Medja have left behind the remains of their settlements and their shallow pan-graves. So large was the body of Medja mercenaries present in Egypt at this time that they formed a whole contingent of the army Kamose led north against the Hyksos.
>
> It is inconceivable that so sizeable a settlement of Nubians inside the narrow confines of the 'head of the south' should have left the culture of the tiny Theban state unaffected. Although the extent of the influence will probably never be known correctly, not a few of the distinctive features of New Kingdom society and religion may have appeared through contact with Nubia.[16]

This prolonged contact between the Egyptians and Nubians also resulted in considerable intermingling between the two royal houses. So much so that scholars do not know whether the actual founders of the Seventeenth Dynasty were pure Nubians or Egyptian nationals of Nubian lineage.[17] The emphasis here on the Nubian origin of the Seventeenth and Eighteenth Dynasties should not be taken to suggest that the Nubians and Egyptians were of separate racial stocks. Both appear to have been Black people—the Egyptians having become hybridized by Asian immigrants, while the Nubians retained the physical characteristics of the old Egyptian (i.e., African) stock. Therefore, when scholars speak of Egyptians with ''Nubian features'' or ''Nubian admixture,'' they are referring to Egyptians of ''unmixed'' African type. The ''purity'' of Nubian ancestry provides a strong case for unmistakable Black lineage, while references to Egyptian roots alone—at this time in history—leaves some room for ethnic speculation.[18]

Historian William Hansberry quotes British Egyptologist Flinders Petrie as stating that ''the Kushite [Nubian] characteristics of so many members of the 18th Dynasty stemmed from the fact that many of their ancestors had 'mingled their blood with the natives' of Nubia during the period of Hyksos domination.''[19] Redford adds that ''[i]t is not unlikely, in view of the heavy influx of

Nubians into Upper Egypt, that the family of the Seventeenth Dynasty could boast of a large admixture of Nubian blood.''[20]

The Seventeenth Dynasty

Is there solid evidence on which to base Petrie and Redford's opinions as to the Black roots of the 17th and 18th Dynasties? In search of such evidence, one must focus attention on each of the rulers of this period. As has been noted, the Second Intermediate Period was a time of great confusion. So much so that few details have survived concerning events that transpired during the Thirteenth, Fourteenth, Fifteenth, Sixteenth and early Seventeenth dynasties—all of which fell between 1786 and the late 1500's B.C. Scholars are generally agreed, however, that about 1600 B.C., around the time of the late Seventeenth Dynasty, there arose a family in Upper Egypt that would be strong enough to expel the Hyksos and ultimately consolidate Egypt. Two commoners, Senakhtenre Tao and his wife Tetisheri, became rulers of Upper Egypt at this time. No one is certain how they achieved this power, but James Harris and Kent Weeks note that ''[Senakhtenre] Tao may have been related to an earlier king of the Seventeenth Dynasty, Antef V, or he may have usurped the throne. In any case it is clear that he and his wife founded the most powerful line of rulers Egypt was ever to know. Their descendants reigned for three hundred years.''[21]

While no mummy has been brought to light that can be identified as that of Senakhtenre Tao, Tetisheri's mummy has been found; unfortunately, however, nothing has been said about its racial characteristics. This royal couple, nevertheless, were the direct forebears of each of the other rulers of the Seventeenth Dynasty; and it has particularly been noted that ''Tetisheri's role as mother of the line was strengthened because both males and females of the next several generations could trace their ancestry directly to her.''[22] It may be reasoned, then, that evidence of the racial type of the descendants of Senakhtenre Tao and Tetisheri will shed light on the ethnic category into which these founding parents should be placed.

Senakhtenre Tao was succeeded by his son Seqenenre Tao who married his full-blooded sister Ahhotep I. This royal couple began the great war of liberation against the Hyksos people. As a matter-of fact it is believed that Seqenenre Tao died in battle[23] and, following his death and the death of his son Kamose,[24] Ahhotep I ''rallied the Upper Egyptian soliders to continue to fight the enemy and rid the land of them in order to clear the way for this native dynasty to rule over a united Egypt.''[25]

The mummy of Seqenenre Tao has been found and a number of authorities have commented on it. ''From the Berber type of [Seqenenre],'' writes Petrie, ''it seems probable that the [Seventeenth] dynasty had come from Ethiopia . . . and the earlier part of it . . . of which we have no names, may have dwelt in Nubia, and only harassed the Hyksos from thence.''[26] Hansberry has commented on the "obvious Kushite [Nubian] traits" of the remains of "Seqenenra III" [Seqenenre].[27] And Harris and Weeks have taken special notice of this pharaoh's mummy:

> Of particular interest and importance are the physical features revealed by [Seqenenre] Tao's mummy . . . His entire lower facial complex, in fact, is so different from other pharaohs (it is closest to that of his son Ahmose) that he could be fitted more easily into the series of Nubian and Old Kingdom Giza skulls than into that of later Egyptian kings. . . . Various scholars in the past have proposed a Nubian—that is, non-Egyptian—origin for Seqenenre and his family, and his facial features suggest this might indeed be true. If it is true, the history of *the family that reputedly drove the Hyksos from Egypt, and the history of the Seventeenth Dynasty, stand in need of considerable re-examination*.[28]

The mummy of Seqenenre Tao's wife Ahhotep I has been found, but, as in the case of her mother's remains, no direct mention has been made of Ahhotep I's racial characteristics. This, too, can be inferred, however, from the description given the mummies of two of the children of Seqenenre Tao and Ahhotep I. The royal couple had at least six children, of whom three survived childhood; and it was these offspring, according to most scholars, who succeeded in driving the Hyksos from the Nile Valley.[29] Kamose, the eldest surviving son, followed his father into battle and died shortly thereafter. "How he died is not known, since his mummy was in extremely poor condition when found; it crumbled to dust in the excavator's hand."[30]

Ahmose I, the youngest son of Seqenenre and Ahhotep, continued the war of liberation and finally drove the hated Hyksos out of Egypt. According to Petrie:

> The history of the war of independence then seems to have been, that perhaps for twenty or thirty years before 1600 B.C. the *Nubian princes of Thebes* had been pushing their way northward against the decaying power of the Hyksos. Active warfare was going on at about 1600 B.C.; and a sudden outburst of energy, under the active young leader Aahmes [Ahmose I], concluded the expulsion of the foreigners, and the capture of their stronghold, within a few years, ending in 1582 B.C.[31]

Harris and Weeks have noted similarities between the remains of Ahmose I and those of his father Seqenenre: "Ahmose [I] and Seqenenre Tao shared many general physical features that were strikingly different from those of later Egyptian rulers. . . [O]ne wonders if both were not genetically influenced by peoples of the south [Nubia]."[32]

The only surviving daughter of Sequenenre Tao and Ahhotep was Ahmose-Nefertari, whom Petrie has described as "the most venerated figure of Egyptian history."[33] While we shall give considerable attention to this queen at a later point in our paper, it is important at this time to consider some observations that have been made regarding her mummy. British anatomist Grafton Elliot Smith was one of the first scientists to examine the great queen's remains. He reported in part that "Nofritari [Ahmose-Nefertari] had very little hair on her head and the vertex was quite bald. Elaborate pains had been taken to hide this deficiency. Twenty strings, composed of twisted human hair, were placed across the top of her head . . . *The appearance of these plaits is not unlike that of the modern Nubian women's hair*."[34] Hansberry has noted that "the queen's teeth were large and healthy, her nose rather short and broad, her mouth wide, her lips full, and her jaws—particularly her upper jaw—tended toward marked prognathism."[35]

The foregoing observations regarding Ahmose-Nefertari's mummy are critical because of her direct familial ties to her predecessors, particularly in the female line. Harris and Weeks have noted the similarity in the physical types of the three queens who stand at the head of this extended family:

> Her head [the head of Tetisheri], broken from the badly damaged body, was one of the first studied. X-rays showed the same prominent dentition, the same type of malocclusion, and the same shape of the skull as the women found in the royal caches of the next four generations. The moderate wear on her teeth and even an impacted third molar, which lay at a very disfunctional angle in the jaw, were the same sort of problems found among her descendants. A comparison of this mummy, now confidently called Tetisheri, with those of her daughter Ahhotep and her granddaughter Ahmose-Nefertiry [Nefertari] showed how well she fit this family group.[36]

It would appear logical to conclude that the physical similarities of the three queens do not end with the observations recorded by Harris and Weeks. In other words, one can infer from their published reports that the mummies of Ahmose-Nefertari's female predecessors bear the same marked Nubian physical features that Hansberry noted in the mummy of Ahmose-Nefertari. As a matter of fact, Harris and Weeks clearly imply this in their references to the possible Nubian origin of this entire family—including patriarch Senakhtenre Tao and his male descendants—on the basis of the mummified remains of the family members whom the two scientists have examined.[37]

While the Nubian origin of the Seventeenth Dynasty is strongly suggested by the remains of the rulers of that period, there is additional evidence that may be even more persuasive. First, the female rulers of the dynasty wielded great power vis-à-vis their husbands and children.[38] This has been a strong characteristic of royal houses in Nubia from ancient through modern times, but it was rather unusual in ancient Egypt.[39] Secondly, there is evidence in the Seventeenth Dynasty of personal names compounded with *I 'h, k3* and *Ghwty*. "These theophorous names," writes Redford, "presuppose a strong attachment to a lunar cult, and there is no reason to believe that it was a Hermopolitan or a Theban one. The moon cult flourished in Nubia, too, and personal names of the Second Intermediate Period compounded with lunar elements are found in Nubia."[40] Redford further notes that "the early Eighteenth Dynasty image of the royal family as carrying on the traditions of the Twelfth Dynasty finds no explanation if the Seventeenth Dynasty was of Theban origin—the connexions of the Twelfth Dynasty were all with the Faiyum area. But if the [Senakhtenre] Ta'o's were in whole or in part of Nubian origin, an explanation could easily be found in the strong impression left by the Amenemhet's and Senwosret's [rulers of the Twelfth Dynasty] in Nubia, where the forts they had built continued to be used during the Hyksos period, and where their deified persons were already ranked alongside the local pantheon."[41]

On the basis of the foregoing evidence it seems probable that the uninterrupted Seventeenth Dynasty, which appears to have been founded by Senakhtenre Tao and his wife Tetisheri, was of Nubian origin—and it is almost certain that each member of this royal family was black. This conclusion is critical to any discussion of the ethnicity of the Eighteenth dynasty—Egypt's new kingdom; because, as Redford points out, "the royal family of the two dynasties is the same: Ahmose [I], the king who in Manetho's list stands at the head of the Eighteenth is a full-blooded scion of the Seventeenth."[42]

The Eighteenth Dynasty

While Ahmose I may indeed have founded the Eighteenth Dynasty, it was his wife-sister, Queen Ahmose-Nefertari, whom the Egyptian people deified as the great ancestress of this family line. We have noted on the basis of their mummies that this royal couple were most probably of Nubian lineage. In the case of Ahmose-Nefertari, this assumption would appear to be reinforced by the fact that in most pictorial representations she is depicted as a woman with black skin. She is so represented in the tomb at Deir el-Medineh and on walls in ruins at Nibnu-tiru, Unnofir and Sheikj Abd el-Qurnah. A statue in the Turin museum portrays her with Black skin, a wide mouth, full lips, a rather thick nose and more or less prognathous jaws. She is depicted in a similar manner in a bust molded in relief on her mummy case discovered at Dier-el-Bahari.[43]

A number of Egyptologists and historians have taken note of Ahmose-Nefertari's black complexion. "At the Eighteenth Dynasty," writes Samuel Birch, "the negress mounts the throne."[44] Rawlinson observes that Ahmose-Nefertari "is represented on the monuments with pleasing features, but a complexion of ebon (sic) blackness."[45] Osburn speaks of the queen as being "an Ethiop (sic) in complexion and descent."[46] DuBois has stated that "this queen with a black skin has . . . been regarded as a Negress;"[47] and Maspero has noted that Ahmose-Nefertari is generally "painted black."[48]

Ironically, some scholars hold that the fact that Ahmose-Nefertari is generally depicted with black skin is not necessarily conclusive evidence that she was indeed Black. Egyptologist Jules Taylor, for example, has noted that frequently Black Egyptians "are not represented black, but brown, red or yellow . . .;" while the color black is often used to depict "individuals regardless of their own personal coloration, in ritualistic black guise."[49]

Plate 1. Queen Ahmose-Nefertari (chief queen of King Ahmose I).

The foregoing is of particular significance in the present case when we note that Ahmose-Nefertari appears to have been the fullblooded sister of Ahmose I;[50] yet she is always painted black, but he is depicted in the traditional reddish-brown of the Egyptian male. Historian Lester Brooks has offered some very interesting insight into this whole question:

> [Ahmose-Nefertari] is often shown in pictures of the court with a dark, almost black skin. This is highly unusual, for Egyptian tradition always assigned a fair skin to females, whatever their actual color, and a reddish-brown skin to males. One explanation for the unusual treatment of [Ahmose-Nefertari] by artists is, of course, that because she was so highly regarded, they painted her in her 'true colors', faithful to her real skin tone. Another is that as she became more and more venerated she was assigned divine status and was shown as one of the gods of the Underworld, represented in blueblack colors.[51]

Whatever one believes about the significance of the pictorial representations of Ahmose-Nefertari, when all of the evidence is taken as a whole it is apparent that both she and her husband-brother, co-founders of the Eighteenth Dynasty, were Blacks. And, as we shall see, the evidence also suggests that they were succeeded by rulers of the same racial stock.

Ahmose I, whose name, according to Rawlinson, signifies "child of the moon,"[52] ruled from 1570-1546 B.C. His Chief Queen, Ahmose-Nefertari, bore for him at least four sons—of whom all but one predeceased their father—and two daughters. The surviving son, Amehotep I (1546-1526), continued the reorganization begun by his father following the expulsion of the Hyksos.

The "badly battered" mummy of Amenhotep I was found in the Deir el-Bahri cache where it had been placed by priests of the Twenty-First Dynasty.[53] Unfortunately, nothing has been said about the mummy's racial characteristics, but it would stand to reason that Amenhotep I inherited the African features of his parents.

A painting of Amenhotep I and his mother was found by an early Prussian Expedition on the wall of a tomb at Gournon, "the burial place of Thebes."[54] It is now in the Berlin Museum. Noting the pharaohs's racial characteristics as depicted by the ancient Egyptian artist, Osburn states that "he [Amenhotep I] has himself a noble countenance, but his complexion has the sickly, pallid tint which denotes a mulatto."[55] This is a curious observation since there is no evidence whatsoever that either of the pharaoh's parents was Caucasian.

While Amenhotep I probably had several children by one or more of his sister-wives, none of them survived. The pharaoh was therefore forced to designate his brother-in-law, Thutmosis, to succeed him.

The ascension of Thutmosis I (1526-1512) to the throne represents the first break in the royal family line since the Seventeenth Dynasty co-founders Senakhtenre Tao and Tetisheri. But even here the Black genetic continuum appears to remain intact. While Thutmosis' origin is unknown, his mummy has been examined and has been described by Hansberry as presenting "a noticably Negroid or Kushite cast."[56] The remains of the great pharaoh's two wives, Ahmose and Mutnofret, have not been found, but their parentage leaves little doubt as to their ethnic origin. Both were daughters of Ahmose I and Ahmose-Nefertari and sisters of Amenhotep I.

Thutmosis I also had a number of children, but only two are of significance here: Hatshepsut, the daughter of Thutmosis and his Chief Queen Ahmose; and Thutmosis II, the son of Thutmosis I and his lesser wife Mutnofret.

When the elder pharaoh, a great militarist who revived Egypt's glory, died, his sickly son, Thutmosis, ascended the throne and ruled as Thutmosis II (1512-1504). Here, again, we have a pharaoh whose mummy has been described as "noticably Negroid" and whose ancestry is clearly black.[57] His wife and half-sister, the famous Queen Hatshepsut (1503-1482), who succeeded him to the throne and ultimately ruled as pharaoh, bore for Thutmosis II at least two daughters, Neferure and Meryetre-Hatshepsut.

Plate 2. Queen Hatshepsut.

Although Hatsheput's mummy has not been found, it is clear that she is the granddaughter of Ahmose and Ahmose-Nefertari and the daughter of Thutmose I and Mutnofret. From this one can readily infer that she, too, in Hansberry's words, "was neither a blond nor a brunette but rather a person who was in all liklihood either dark-brown or black."[58]

Thutmosis III was the son of Thutmosis II and his lesser wife Isis. Scholars believe that, upon his father's death, little Thutmosis ascended the throne with his step-mother/aunt, Hatshepsut, serving as co-regent. However, "during the second year of her stepson's reign she took over all authority from the young ruler and was crowned King of Upper and Lower Egypt."[59]

Following Hatshepsut's death, Thutmosis III finally achieved independent power. This pharaoh, who earned the reputation of being Egypt's "greatest and most powerful ruler," reigned from 1504-1450 B.C. His roots also appear to have been black. According to Diop, Isis, the mother of Thutmosis III, was from the Sudan.[60] DuBois has stated that the pharaoh's "granite head in the British Museum has distinct Negro features."[61] And Maspero has commented on the great king's mummy: "His [Thutmosis III] statues, though not representing him as a type of manly beauty, yet give him refined, intelligent features, but a comparison with the mummy shows that the artists have idealized their model. The forehead is abnormally low, the eyes deeply sunk, the jaw heavy, the lips thick, and the cheekbones extremely prominent; the whole recalling the physiognomy of Thutmose II [Thutmosis II], though with a greater show of energy. Thutmose

Plate 3. Temple of Queen Hatshepsut at Luxor.

III [Thutmosis III] is a fellah of the old stock, squat, thickset, vulgar in character and expression, but not lacking in firmness and vigour.''[62]

Thutmosis III was succeeded to the throne by Amenhotep II, a son borne for him by his half-sister Meryetre-Hatshepsut, the daughter of Queen Hatshepsut. Amenhotep II's uneventful reign extended over a period of about twenty-five years. From his mummy it has been noted that this pharaoh was ''taller than both his father and his son [Thutmosis IV];''[63] but nothing has been said regarding the king's racial characteristics. However, both of the pharaoh's parents appear to have been black or ''Negroid'' and the same may be confidently said of him. The surviving statues of Amenhotep II seem to confirm this hypothesis.[64]

Amenhotep II's chief queen, about whose origin little is known, was Tia. She bore Thutmosis IV, who succeeded his father to the throne. This pharaoh ruled from 1425-1417 B.C. His emaciated mummy has also been found and Harris and Weeks have noted its strong ''resemblance to Amenhotep II, a fact that helps confirm the known order of royal succession.''[65] Just as in the case of his father, nothing has been said regarding the racial characteristics of the mummy of Thutmosis IV. As the grandson of Thutmosis III and his Chief Queen Meryetre-

Plate 4. Queen Tiye (chief queen of Amenhotep III).

Plate 5. King Akhenaton (son of Amenhotep III and Queen Tiye).

Hatshepsut, however, it may be inferred that Thutmosis IV inherited considerable African genetic material.

The final rulers of the Eighteenth Dynasty were the descendants of Thutmosis IV. At this time a new infusion of Nubian "blood" appears to have entered the royal family through Mutemwiya[66]—the wife of Thutmosis IV; and through Yuya and Thuya, the parents of Queen Tiye and the pharaoh Ay.[67]

Amenhotep III, "the magnificent" (1417-1379 B.C.), was the son and successor of Thutmose IV and Mutemwiya. This king married the beautiful Queen Tiye and, according to early scholars, she bore for her husband the successive rulers of Egypt—Amenhotep IV (Akhenaton), Smenkhare and Tutaṇkhamun.[68]

A number of scholars have described Amenhotep III as Black. "The features" of this monarch, writes British Egyptologist John Wilkinson, "cannot fail to strike everyone who examines the portraits of the Egyptian kings [as] having more in common with the Negro than those of any other pharaoh."[69] Massey notes that the sculptures of Amenhotep III "show the Aethopic [Nubian] type."[70] DuBois adds that the king "inherited his mother's Negroid features."[71] And Rogers concludes that "[t]he Eighteenth Dynasty was of almost unmixed Negro strain; in fact, its two principal representatives, Amenophis III [Amenhotep III] and his son, Akhenaton, seem to have had no 'white' blood."[72]

Much the same has been written of this great pharaoh's chief queen, Tiye. Desroches-Noblecourt has noted, for example, that during this period "the Nubians played a part about which too little has been said. They enjoyed exceptional privileges at the court of Malkata. It was ruled by a queen almost certainly of their own race, as some portraits of Tiye, such as the little ebony head now in the Berlin Museum show her to have been.''[73] Tiye's ''sourthern looks are even more pronounced on a pendant (the *Menat* counterpoise) . . . and another similar portrait found at Tell El Amarna. Finally there is little room left for doubt when one studies the small sardonyx tablet, now in the Metropolitan Museum, which depicts the queen as a female sphinx. The face clearly betrays her origins; it was recently compared with another image of her still to be seen at Sedeinga in Northern Sudan in the ruins of the temple, dedicated to Tiye. Even the wigs of the royal ladies at Malkata as well as Tell el Amarna were inspired by the short neat coiffures of the Nubians.''[74]

Rogers has described Tiye as a ''full-blooded African;''[75] anthropologist Ivan Van Sertima refers to the queen as ''the Negroid mother of Tutankhamen;''[76] historian Alexander Von Wuthenau states that Tiye was of ''pure black stock.''[77] But it is probably Brooks who has provided the most graphic portrayal of this great queen; ''Any Sunday morning you may see her modern counterpart proudly entering America's Negro churches across the land.''[78]

The mummy of Amenhotep III has been found, but nothing has been recorded regarding his racial characteristics. In 1978, a team of scientists reported that a ''royal'' mummy, whose identity had been in dispute for over seventy years, was thought to be the remains of Queen Tiye. Regrettably, this team has also failed to publish any information regarding the racial characteristics of this mummy.[79] At least one authority contends that the mummys of Tiye's alleged parents, Yuya and Thuya, have Nubian traits,[80] while another strongly disagrees.[81] It would appear that, whatever one's opinion may be with regard to existent mummys, whose identities may justifiably be questioned,[82] the iconographic evidence with respect to the racial characteristics of Amenhotep III and his chief queen Tiye are most persuasive, and serve to strengthen our position that the Eighteenth Dynasty was essentially Black and largely of Nubian origin.

Amenhotep IV, who later changed his name to Akhenaton (1379-1362), succeeded his father to the throne. This great reformer of Egyptian art, literature and religion inherited his parent's African racial features. Egyptologists Cyril Aldred and A.T. Sandison note that Akhenaton's ''face is shown to be elongated with a prominent prognathous or progeniac jaw, large full lips, a coarse nose, large ears, and oblique eyes.''[83] Another Egyptologists, Edward Wente, speaks of Akhenaton's ''elongated skull, protruding jaw [and] thick lips;''[84] while Osburn observes that the pharaoh's ''dusky complexion, high cheekbones, projecting jaws and thick lips, call forcibly to mind the features of the true Negro;''[85] and Rogers adds that Akhenaton's ''skull . . . is what some scientists call that of a typical Negro. The jaw is exceedingly prognathous. His lips, as seen in profile, are so thick that they seem swollen.''[86]

The skull to which Wente and Rogers refer is apparently that associated with the mummy once thought to be Akhenaton's, but which is now identified as that

Plate 6. King Tutankhamun (ebony statue).

Plate 7. King Tutankhamun and Queen Ankhesenamon.

of his immediate successor, Smenkhare (1364-1361).[87] This ruler, whom traditional scholars believe to have also been the son of Amenhotep III and Tiye, inherited the racial characteristics of his parents. Harris and Weeks have noted that his "skeleton and broken skull . . . reveal a man who resembles the Thutmosid line,"[88] which, as we have seen, was decidedly "Negroid." Moreover, the paintings and sculptures of Smenkhare clearly depict his African features.[89]

Upon Smenkhare's death, his younger brother Tutankhamun (1361-1352 B.C.) ascended the throne. Events of the life and death of this king are so widely known that we need not recount them here. If we accept the traditional view, that King Tutankhamun was the son of Amenhotep III and Queen Tiye, his ethnic affinity is obvious and requires no further elaboration. Even if we adhere to the theory that Tutankhamun was the son of Akhenaton by one of his lesser wives,[90] it is still most probable that the boy-king was Black. As a matter of fact, given Tutankhamun's immediate and distant ancestors, his surviving mummy and the valuable relics that depict his facial features, one cannot escape the conclusion that Von Wuthenau has reached: "The features of this Egyptian king, whose mother was of pure black stock, are almost as Negroid as the ones of his captured Nubian enemies."[91]

The great royal wives of the successors of Amenhotep III also played prominent roles during the reigns of their consorts. However, no mummies of these queens were found. Nevertheless, a persuasive case can be made for the opinion that they too were either Black or "Negroid." Nefertiti, Chief Queen of Akhe-

Plate 8. Queen Nefertiti (chief queen of Akhenaton).

Plate 9. Daughters of Akhenaton and Nefertiti .

naton, appears to have been the granddaughter of Yuya and Thuya and the daughter of their son Ay.[92] We have mentioned the possible Nubian affinities of Yuya and Thuya. One Egyptologist, William Osburn, claims to have observed, or at least to have knowledge of, the physical characteristics of the mummy of Nefertiti's father. Speaking of the pharaoh's tomb, Osburn says, "The Negro countenance of the King was the most remarkable thing in it."[93] Unfortunately, nothing is known about the mother of Nefertiti.

Most paintings and sculptures of Nefertiti depict her as having decidedly African features—often with the same elongated skull, protruding jaw and thick lips that characterize her husband Akhenaton.[94] All of the couple's daughters, including Meryet-Amon, who was the Chief Queen of Smenkhare, and Ankhesenamun, the Chief Queen of Tutankhamun (and later, following his death, the wife of King Ay) also appear to have had African physical features. Proof of this is found in full detail in the large collection of photographs published in Cyril Aldred's *Akhenaton* and *Nefertiti*.[95]

The final rulers of Egypt's Eighteenth Dynasty were Ay (1352-1348 B.C.) and Horemhab (1348-1320 B.C.). Ay was an old man upon ascending the throne and his reign lasted only four years. Horemhab, who had once served as a general under Akhenaton and Tutankhamun, returned Egypt to its traditional and formerly stable ways. While we have mentioned Ay's mummy and his ancestry, little is known of Horemhab's family except for the fact that he married Mutnodjme, the sister of Nefertiti. Nevertheless, it must be pointed out that the published depictions of Horemhab suggest that he too falls within the ethnic spectrum of his predecessors of the distinguished Eighteenth Dynasty.[96]

Conclusion

The evidence presented in this paper tends to indicate that the Seventeenth and Eighteenth Dynasties of ancient Egypt were of Nubian origin and that each of the rulers of these extended families was either Black, ''Negroid'' or of Black ancestry. We believe it most probable that any newly discovered evidence will support our general premise and will probably also shed more light on the Black (and perhaps Nubian) origin of the first several dynasties, the Middle Kingdom and, of course, the Twenty-fifth Dynasty or renaissance period.

We therefore urge objective scientists to take a new, hard look at Egypt from an African perspective and to discover a whole new universe which the arrogant giants of Western scholarship have grown too blind to see.

Notes

1. Symposium on ''The Peopling of Ancient Egypt And The Deciphering of the Meroitic Script'' by the International Scientific Committee For The Drafting of a General History of Africa (United Nations Educational Scientific And Cultural Organization), Cairo, January 28 through February 3, 1974. Transcript of symposium distributed in limited numbers: SHC - 73/CONF. 812/4, Paris, June 28, 1974, page 3.

2. Ibid. We are well aware that the new anthropological party line is that ''there is no such thing as 'race,''' and that it is now unscientific to delimit mankind on the basis of ''race.'' We do not accept this point of view for the following reasons: First, three major subspecies of the human family, i.e., the Africoid (''Negroid''), Caucasoid and Mongoloid are readily distinguishable and can be scientifically defined without the absurd assumption that racial ''purity'' is widespread in either category. Secondly, it appears that the abandonment of the study of ''race'' by modern science is not so much an attempt to stress the unity of the human species as it is to focus away from the inevitable conclusions that such study has forced upon the academic community. Eighteenth century scientists embarked on the study of human subspecies in order to prove the superiority of the white race and it is no accident that, as their modern disciples come to the startling realization that the human family was born in Africa, that the first homo sapiens were probably Black and that Caucasians probably sprang from prehistoric Black people as a genetic mutation to albinism, these scientists are eager to suppress this information. Finally, as long as the world is dominated by White people, as long as those White scientists—who now claim that there is no validity to the study of race—continue to practice racism socially and academically; and, most important, as long as the Black race bears the universal badge of inferiority forced on it by scientists who have distorted or suppressed Black history, we shall not only include race as an integral part of our historical writings, but we shall prominently focus on it whenever and wherever the truth can be told until sincere men of science return the Black race to its former position of respect and reverence on the earth.

As for the Black or ''Negro'' race, we accept the definition of Cheikh Anta Diop: ''Anticipating the agreement of all logical winds, I call *Negro* a human being whose skin is black, especially when he has frizzy hair.'' Cheikh Anta Diop, *The African Origin of Civilization: Myth Or Reality?* New York, Lawrence Hill & Co., 1974, p. 136. We also agree with DuBois' position that ''[t]here was and is wide mingling of the blood of all races in Africa, but this is consistent with the general thesis that Africa is predominantly the land of Negroes and Negroid peoples, just as Europe is a land of Caucasoids and Asia of Mongoloids. We may give up entirely, if we wish, the whole attempt to delimit races, but we cannot if we are sane, divide the world into whites, yellows and blacks, and then call blacks white.'' W.E.B. DuBois, *The World And Africa: An Inquiry Into The Part Which Africa Has Played In World History,* New York, International Publishers, 1961, p.119.

Finally, we are aware that there is an intermediate view (between the two extremes presented in the text) regarding the racial type of the ancient Egyptians—i.e., the Egyptians were neither Black nor White, but a mixed type. We have omitted this position from our discussion mainly because it is generally presented as nothing more than a variation of the first point of view, i.e., the Egyptians were ''mixed Caucasoids.''

3. Diop, *The African Origin of Civilization*, pp. 5-9.

4. Ibid., pp. 1-5.

5. Cheikh Anta Diop, ''Origin Of the Ancient Egyptians,'' *General History of Africa*, Ed. G. Mokhtar, UNESCO 1981 Vol. 11, pp. 27-55.

6. *Manetho*, Edited by T.E. Page et al., with an English translation by W.G. Waddell, Cambridge, Harvard University Press, MCMXL, pp. 79-81.

7. Ibid., p. 85.

8. George Steindorff and Keith C. Seele, *When Egypt Ruled The East*, Chicago, the University of Chicago Press, 1942, p. 24. This appears to be the more correct translation of the Egyptian *heku shoswet*.

9. Ibid., p. 26.

10. Manetho, pp. 85-87.

11. Steindorff and Seele, *When Egypt Ruled The East*, pp. 30 & 274.

12. Ibid.

13. William L. Hansberry, ''Africa's Golden Past,'' *Ebony,* November, 1964, p. 37. The names Nubia and Kush (and sometimes Ethiopia) are often used interchangeably to describe the region south of the Nile's First Cataract and sometimes known as Wawat, a land rich in gold. To the east of Nubia, extending along the Red Sea in what today is the coast of Sudan, Ethiopia and Somalia, was the land which the ancients referred to as Punt. The word Ethiopia, which is Greek for ''land of burnt faces,'' was also once used to designate all of Africa.

14. W.E.B. DuBois, *The World and Africa*, p. 117. DuBois was one of the earliest modern scholars to resurrect the ancient view that Egypt was originally a colony of Ethiopia. Also see W.M. Flinders Petrie, *A History of Egypt During the XVIIth and XVIIIth Dynasties*, London, Muthen and Co., Ltd., 1896, p. 4.

15. Cheikh Anta Diop, *The African Origin of Civilization*, p. 209.

16. Donald B. Redford, *History and Chronology of the Eighteenth Dynasty of Egypt*, University of Toronto Press, 1967, p. 67. Kamose, who is mentioned in this quotation, was the third ruler of the Seventeenth Dynasty.

18. Chancellor Williams, *The Destruction of Black Civilization: Great Issues of A Race From 4500 B.C. to 2000 A.D.*, Chicago, Third World Press, 1974, pp. 62-124. Also see Ivan Van Sertima, *They Came Before Columbus*, New York, Random House, 1976, p. 111. We shall not here indulge in the silly argument over whether the ancient Nubians were actually Black people anymore than present-day scholars feel compelled to defend the foregone conclusion that the Greeks and Romans were white Europeans. For a discussion on the racial identity of the ancient Nubians, one may consult *They Came Before Columbus*, pp. 123-138.

19. Hansberry, ''Africa's Golden Past,'' p. 38.

20. Redford, *History and Chronology of the Eighteenth Dynasty of Egypt*, p. 68.

21. James E. Harris and Kent R. Weeks, *X-Raying The Pharaohs*, New York, Charles Scribner's Sons, 1973, p. 120.

22. Ibid.

23. Steindorff and Seele, *When Egypt Ruled The East,* p. 29.

24. Ibid., p. 31.

25. Barbara S. Lesko, *The Remarkable Women of Ancient Egypt*, Berkeley, Scribe Publications, 1978, p. 4.

26. Petrie, *A History of Egypt During The XVIIth And XVIIIth Dynasties,* p. 17. Petrie's reference

to Seqenenre as being of the "Berber type" should not be cause for confusion. He apparently believed the Berbers, Ethiopians and Nubians to have been Black people and, on page 337, he specifically refers to Seqenenre as Black.

27. Hansberry, "Africa's Golden Past," p. 37. Professor Hansberry refers to a Seqenenre III. At one time it was believed that three pharaohs of the Seventeenth Dynasty bore the name Seqenenre. Scholars are generally now agreed that there was only one Seqenenre and his father bore a similar but different name, Senakhtenre.

28. Harris and Weeks, *X-Raying The Pharaohs,* pp. 123-124. Emphasis added. We would take the two scientists' position a step further and say that the history of the Eighteenth Dynasty is also in need of reexamination.

29. Ibid., p. 125.

30. Ibid.

31. Petrie, A History of Egypt During the XVIIth And XVIIIth Dynasties, p. 23. Emphasis added.

32. Harris and Weeks, *X-Raying The Pharaohs,* p. 127.

33. Petrie, *A History of Egypt During the XVIIth And XVIIIth Dynasties*, p. 41.

34. Grafton Elliot Smith, "The Royal Mummies," *Catalogue General Des Antiquités du Egyptiennes du Musée du Caire,* nos. 61051-61100, Cairo, Service des Antiquites de l'Egypte, 1912, p. 13. Emphasis added.

35. Hansberry, "Africa's Golden Past," p. 37.

36. Harris and Weeks, *X-Raying The Pharaohs,* p. 121.

37. Ibid., pp. 123, 127 & 135.

38. Lestor Brooks, *Great Civilizations of Ancient Africa,* New York, Four Winds Press, 1971, p. 49. Also See Redford, *History And Chronology of the Eighteenth Dynasty of Egypt.* pp. 65-69.

39. Brooks, Great Civilizations of Ancient Africa, p. 49. Also see Redford, *History And Chronology of the Eighteenth Dynasty of Egypt,* pp. 65-69.

40. Ibid., pp. 68-69.

41. Ibid., p. 69.

42. Ibid., p. 28. According to this author, Manetho placed Ahmose at the head of a new dynasty "only because he put an end to Hyksos rule in Egypt and inaugurated a period of independence."

43. Hansberry, "Africa's Golden Past," p. 37.

44. Samuel Birch, *Ancient Egypt From The Monuments, Egypt From The Earliest Times to B.C. 300*, New York, Scribner, Armstrong & Co., 1875, p. 83.

45. George Rawlinson, *History of Ancient Egypt*, New York, American Publishers Corp., 1880, Vol. II, p. 114.

46. William Osburn, *The Monumental History of Egypt*, London, Trubner & Co., 1854, p. 175.

47. DuBois, *The World And Africa*, pp. 126-127. DuBois also refers to the now outmoded view to which many early scholars subscribed, i.e., that, because of her color, Ahmose-Nefertari was not Egyptian by birth, but the daughter of a Nubian monarch with whom Ahmose I had entered an alliance for assistance in expelling the Hyksos rulers. The young princess, according to this view, was married to Ahmose I in order to strengthen the Egypto-Nubian alliance.

48. Gaston Maspero, *The Struggle Of The Nations,* New York, D. Appleton & Co., 1877, pp. 98-99.

49. Jules Taylor, "The Black Image In Egyptian Art," *Journal Of African Civilizations,* April, 1979, Vol. I, p. 27. It should be noted that, while many Egyptologists might object to any consideration of iconographic material to verify the racial characteristics of the ancient Egyptians, J. Vercoutter and N. Blanc have stated that "[t]he incongraphic material available . . . has extremely significant characteristics from the XVIII Dynasty onwards." Symposium on "The Peopling of Ancient Egypt And The Deciphering Of The Meroetic Script," p. 3.

50. For an opposing view, i.e., Ahmose-Nefertari may have been the half-sister of Ahmose I, see Petrie, *A History of Egypt During The XVIIth And XVIIIth Dynasties*, pp. 9 & 337; and Harris and Weeks, *X-Raying The Pharaohs,* p. 128.

51. Brooks, *Great Civilizations of Ancient Africa,* p. 50.

52. Rawlinson, *History of Ancient Egypt*, Vol. II, p. 112. This in itself, according to Redford, strongly suggests that Ahmose I was of Nubian origin. *History And Chronology of The Eighteenth Dynasty*, pp. 68-69.
53. Harris and Weeks, *X-Raying The Pharaohs*, p. 129.
54. Osburn, *The Monumental History of Egypt*, p. 175.
55. Ibid.
56. Hansberry, "Africa's Golden Past," p. 38.
57. Ibid.
58. Ibid.
59. Harris and Weeks, *X-Raying The Pharaohs*, p. 134.
60. Diop, *The African Origin of Civilization*, p. 12.
61. DuBois, *The World And Africa*, p. 128.
62. Gaston Maspero, *The Struggle Of The Nations, Egypt, Syria And Assyria*, London, Society for Promoting Christian Knowledge, 1910, p. 289.
63. Harris and Weeks, *X-Raying The Pharaohs*, p. 138.
64. Cyril Aldred, *New Kingdom Art in Ancient Egypt*, London, Alex Tiranti, Ltd., 1951, figs. 49, 50 &51.
65. Harris and Weeks, *X-Raying The Pharaohs*, p. 139.
66. Rawlinson states, "Born, as it would seem, of an Ethiopian mother, Mutemua [Mutemwiya], Amenophis [Amenhotep III] had a somewhat foreign physiognomy." *History of Ancient Egypt*, Vol. 2, p. 261. Also see Gerald Massey, A Book of The Beginnings, Secaucus, New Jersey, University Press, Inc., 1974, Vol. II, p. 405.
67. Christiane Desroches-Noblecourt, *Life And Death of A Pharaoh*, New York, Graphic Society, 1963, p. 116.
68. Ibid., pp. 120-121. Many scholars no longer accept this view. Wente, for example, and a number of others, now hold that both Smenkhare and Tutankhamun were sons of Akhenaton by minor wives.
69. John G. Wilkinson, *The Ancient Egyptians*, London, 1878, Vol. I, p. 42.
70. Massey, *A Book Of The Beginnings*, Vol. II, p. 405.
71. DuBois, *The World And Africa*, p. 129.
72. J.A. Rogers, *Sex And Race, Negro-Caucasian Mixing In All Ages and All Lands*, New York, published by the author, 1944, Vol. 1, p. 54.
73. Desroches-Noblecourt, *Life And Death of A Pharaoh*, p. 121. Also see Grafton E. Smith, *Tomb of Queen Tiyi*, London, Constable & Co., 1910.
74. Ibid.
75. J.A. Rogers, *World's Great Men of Color*, New York, Collier Books, 1972, Vol. II, p. 63.
76. Van Sertima, *They Came Before Columbus*, p. 29.
77. Alexander Von Wuthenau, *Unexpected Faces in Ancient America*, 1500 B.C.–A.D. 1500, New York, Crown Publishers, 1975, p. 136.
78. Brooks, *Great Civilizations of Ancient Africa*, p. 58.
79. Jamės E. Harris et al., "Mummy of the 'Elder Lady' in the tomb of Amenhotep: Egyptian Museum Catalog Number 61070," *Science*, June 9, 1978, vol. 200, p. 1149.
80. Desroches-Noblecourt, *Life And Death of A Pharaoh*, p. 116.
81. Barbara Mertz, *Red Land, Black Land*, New York, Dodd, Mead & Co., 1966, 1978, pp. 11-17.
82. The mummified remains of the kings and queens of the New Kingdom of Egypt (c.1575 B.C. to 1070 B.C.) were first examined by the French Egyptologist Gaston Maspero in 1889 and the English anatomist Grafton E. Smith in 1912. The mummies had been deposited in two hiding places at Thebes. In 1881 the first cache was discovered in the reused tomb of Queen Inhapy at Deir el-Bahari. The second find, reportedly made in 1898, was in the tomb of King Amenhotep II of the middle Eighteenth Dynasty. "From these two caches were recovered the mummies of most of the kings of

the New Kingdom and a number of the queens. The mummies had been hidden in these two tombs about 3000 years ago after robbers had plundered the original tombs of the kings and queens in the Twentieth Dynasty. During the Twenty-First Dynasty, the mummies were collected and restored or rewrapped, since for the most part they had been badly damaged by tomb robbers looking for treasures placed on the mummies beneath the wrappings

"In a number of cases no identification whatsoever was found on the wrappings or coffins of these mummies. This should not be completely surprising since the grave robbing had occurred over a long period of time, and the royal mummies, after having been badly damaged at the hands of the grave robbers, had been moved from place to place for safety. The priests of the Twenty-First Dynasty were rewrapping mummies some of which were even then as old as 500 years." Harris, "Mummy of the 'Elder Lady'...," vol. 200, p. 1149.

Certain scientists have raised questions concerning the integrity of the white Egyptologists who exhumed the ancient mummies and thereafter indentified them. In this vein, Dr. Diop has written:

> It is customary to mention the straight hair of certain carefully chosen mummies, the only ones found in museums, to affirm that they represent a prototype of the white race, notwithstanding their prognathism. These mummies are displayed conspicuously in an attempt to prove the whiteness of the Egyptians. The very coarseness of their hair precludes acceptance of that contention. When such hair exists on the head of a mummy, it merely indicates the Dravidian type, in reality, whereas the prognathism and black skin—pigmented, not blackened by tar or any other product—excludes any idea of a white race. The meticulous selection process to which they have been subjected ruled out any possibility of their being a prototype. In fact, Herodotus told us, after seeing them, that the Egyptians had wooly hair... [One] may well wonder why mummies with such characteristics are not exhibited. Those that should be most numerous are currently the least discoverable, and when we are lucky enough to stumble upon one, we are assured that it represents a foreign type. *The African Origin of Civilization,* p. 165.

83. Cyril Aldred and A.T. Sandison, "The Pharaoh Akhenaton, A Problem in Egyptology and Pathology," *Bulletin of the History of Medicine,* XXXVI (1962), p. 305. We should point out here that Aldred, Sandison and a number of others have speculated that Akhenaton's "grotesque," "appalling" and "frankly hideous" facial features as rendered by Egyptian artists are a "distortion of the human form," or on the other hand, may be an accurate depiction of a pharaoh who suffered some physical malady. Most scholars explain away the king's apparent "Negroid" features in this manner. We reject this in its entirety because we do not believe that science must resort to conjecture in order to explain Akhenaton's features. He was a black African who chose to be depicted "true to form" rather than to be represented in the traditional nondescript Egyptian fashion. It is highly possible that other pharaohs had physical characteristics similar to those of Akhenaton but chose, for whatever reasons, not to be portrayed as they actually appeared. Even if we accept the far-fetched theory that Akhenaton was truly "deformed," this still need not carry him out of the Black race. Is it not possible for him to have been a Black man with "exaggerated" facial characteristics?

84. Edward F. Wente, "Tutankhamun And His World," p. 23.

85. Osburn, *Monumental History of Egypt*, Vol II, p. 329.

86. Rogers, *World's Great Men of Color*, vol. I, p. 63.

87. Harris and Weeks, *X-Raying The Pharaohs,* p. 146.

88. Ibid., pp. 146-147.

89. Cyril Aldred, *Akhenaton And Nefertiti,* New York, Brooklyn Musuem in association with Viking Press, 1973, pp. 98 & 101.

90. Edward F. Wente, "Tutankhamun And His World," p. 26.

91. Von Wuthenau, *Unexpected Faces in Ancient America,* p. 136.

92. Harris and Weeks, *X-Raying The Pharaohs,* p. 189.

93. Osburn, *Monumental History of Egypt*, vol. II, p. 341.

94. Cyril Aldred, *Akhenaton and Nefertiti*. We are aware that a number of scholars believe that the art of this period was stylized and therefore the representation of the ruling family with "exaggerated

Negroid'' features was a distortion of its actual appearance. Here, as in our reference to Akhenaton, we find it quite possible to believe that the artists were simply depicting Black people in an accurate manner. But, even if we assume that the artwork was stylized, is it not possible for Black people to have stylized art? Does stylized Greek art mean that the people generally depicted were not White Europeans?

95. Ibid.

96. Cyril Aldred, *New Kingdom Art in Ancient Egypt*, fig. 174. Also see Maspero, *Struggle of Nations*, p. 348.

AFRICA'S CONTRIBUTION TO WORLD CIVILIZATION: THE EXACT SCIENCES

Cheikh Anta Diop

Since Struve edited the mathematical papyrus of Moscow, the world scientific community knows that Egyptian mathematics was not a mere aggregate of empirical "recipes" but was rather highly elaborate and theoretical. In fact, this papyrus raises two particularly difficult problems involving the surface area of the sphere (problem 10), and the volume of the pyramid's frustrum (problem 14), respectively. Those who have dealt with mathematics, even minimally, know how delicate the treatment of the curved surface is. But the "formula" found by the scribe 1,700 years before Archimedes is rigorously accurate: $S = 2\pi R^2$ for the surface area of the hemisphere. Indeed, to solve the problem it was necessary to calculate what the surface area of the hemisphere was and then multiply the result by two to obtain the surface area of the whole sphere.

The sphere and the circumscribed cylinder, having the same height as the diameter of the sphere are theoretically two inseparable bodies. Their two surface areas are identical and equal to $4\pi R^2$. Being as shrewd as they were, the Egyptians could not have missed this fact. He who can do more can do less. That is why, it was this body of figures that Archimedes considered to be his most remarkable discovery and chose as an epitaph; and it is indeed this epitaph which authenticated the discovery by Cicero of Archimedes grave in Syracuse, Sicily.

But Archimedes could not have been unaware that prior to him the Egyptians had discovered the very same theorem that he probably used, arranged and presented in his own way.[7] His other dealings with Egyptian science testify to that. Speaking exclusively of what is certain, one must say that the Egyptians have passed down to posterity the formula of the exact surface area of the sphere and the exact "formula" of the volume of the cylinder, calculated with the value of π=3.16.[8] Archimedes did not mention these results at all in his treatise entitled *On the Sphere and Cylinder* written about two thousand years after the Egyptian mathematical papyri.

Problem 50 of the Rhind papyrus provides the exact surface area of the circle having a diameter equal to 9 and a value of π=3.16 in the following formula:

$$S = \frac{(8 \,.\, d)^2}{9} = \frac{\pi \,.\, d^2}{4} = R^2$$

Archimedes made no mention of this formula in his treatise entitled: *Measurement of the Circle.*

He did the same thing for the calculation of the value π for which he gave the lower and upper limits.

Finally, in his treatise entitled *On the Equilibrium of Planes or Centres of Gravity of Planes,* nowhere did Archimedes show that the Egyptians had already mastered the theory of levers of all kinds, as well as that of the inclined plane, before he did. The scales with annular slides which made it possible to weigh more accurately is the proof of this and it has been confirmed by the works of G. Davies.[9] A further proof is that of the Chadouf[10] which is the current application of the lever with uneven arms. Because he could use this device, Archimedes could say: "Give me a place to stand and I will move the earth."

What was the research method of Archimedes who is regarded as the most ingenious representative of Greek mathematics and intellectualism? Archimedes described it in a letter to his friend Eratosthenes who was a geometrician. Archimedes did not hesitate to tell him how he proceeded. Indeed he first weighed the geometrical figures and only when they were equal did he use mathematics to demonstrate that they were equal. He advised his friend to follow the same method.[11] But Paul Ver Ecke suspects that Archimedes was dishonest and simply wanted to hide the real sources of inspiration and very carefully cover his tracks.[12]

Could this hidden source by anything else than Egyptian? It certainly could not. Indeed, like all the Greek scientists, Archimedes went to study or to further his studies in Egypt. It is only when he came back from Egypt that he "invented" the endless screw that Egyptians had been using for centuries before he was born for the extraction of percolated water.[13]

And so, the method of the most important representative of Greek mathematics is forgotten when gratuitous mention is made of Egyptian empirical methods and scientific recipes.

In studying the method that, in all likelihood, the scribe followed to find the surface area of the sphere, Struve shows that the scribe must have associated the sphere to the circumscribed cylinder of a same surface, of a height equal to the diameter of the big circle of the sphere (as Archimedes did later on). This made it possible for the scribe to deduce a general empirical/theoretical method for the study of curved surface areas and volumes and establish the relationship between the surface area and the volumes of these two bodies. In this way, Struve adds, problem 10 of the Moscow papyrus provided both the formula for the surface area of the sphere and that for the length of the circumference.[14]

In order to understand the significance of this last remark, it is important to remember that the formula $C=\pi D$ is attributed to Dinostratus. This formula which gives the length of the circumference is believed to have been established by the Egyptians 1,400 years before its alledged Greek author. Quoting the works of L. Cron, Struve also points out that in the field of mechanics, the Egyptians had a much wider knowledge than was ever acknowledged. Their planes were as accurate as those of modern engineers.[15]

He concludes that it therefore stands to reason that the Greeks explicitly admitted that the Egyptians were their masters in the field of geometry which came to

Greece from Egypt and not from Babylonia. Struve also insists on the accuracy of Egyptian geometry.

Indeed, an empirical geometry using "recipes" like the Babylonian geometry for instance could never have come to establish formulas approaching the accuracy of Egyptian geometry. This leads us to the second problem, problem 14, of the Moscow papyrus dealing with the volume of the pyramid's frustrum.

The scribe gives the following formula:

$$V = {}^{h}/_{3}\ (a^2 + ab + b^2)$$

where a = the length of the side of the square of the bottom; b = the length of the side of the square at the top; h = height separating the planes of the two squares.

Even Peet who was one of the most vocal detractors of Egyptian mathematics acknowledges the fact that for 4,000 years researchers in the field of mathematics have not been able to improve on that formula.

In fact it is a rigorously accurate formula.

For the same figure Mesopotanian geometry gives the following formula:

$$V = {}^{h}/_{2}\ (a^2 + b^2)$$

This formula which does not even come close to the Egyptian one is wrong. The same situation is observed for the volume of the cone's frustrum:

$$V = {}^{h}/_{2} = (S + S')$$

S and S′ being the surface areas of the circles at the bottom and at the top. Mesopotamian geometry calculated the volume of a cylinder with the value of $\pi=3$ by likening it to a prism, whereas, as was shown above, the corresponding formula in Egyptian geometry is rigorously accurate: In actual fact the whole corpus of Egyptian mathematics does not include a single erroneous formula be it in geometry, in algebra, in trigonometry, in arithmetic or in mechanics: therefore, it can only be a highly theoretical science.

If Egyptian mathematics were simply empirical, one would have to conclude that empiricism outclasses theory, because for centuries mathematicians have been trying in vain to figure out the so-called empirical recipes which resulted in Egyptian mathematics: popular empiricism would then be less accessible than theory.

The So-Called Pythagorean Theorem

Some elements of Egyptian mathematics make it possible to affirm that Pythagoras did not demonstrate the theorem that is attributed to him and a large number of mathematicians who know anything at all about the Egyptian data are conscious of this fact.

Indeed, going back to Plutarch (Isis and Osiris) and to Plato (Politics) one would already know that of all the right triangles, the one whose sides are 3,6,5, respectively, is sacred (problem 6 of the Moscow Papyrus).[17]

And it is readily admitted that the Egyptians certainly had a knowledge of particular cases of the so-called Pythayorean Theorem. But no one wanted to admit that they also demonstrated this knowledge in the general case.

However, it is known that this theorem was certainly discovered along with the irrational numbers, in the general case, without specific numeric value. This can be shown in the case involving the duplication of the square starting from a diagonal.

There exists in relation to this an Egyptian unit of length, the accurate definition of which leaves no doubt that the Egyptians had cognizance of the theorem of the hypothenuse as well as the existence of irrational numbers. This unit of length was known as the "double-remen." The double-remen is the length of the diagonal of a square whose side = a = one (royal) cubit. So $d=a\sqrt{2} = 20.6 \times \sqrt{2} = 29.1325$ inches.[18]

We know that $\sqrt{2}$ is the irrational number *par excellence* but the Egyptians even knew how to extract the square root of fractions. Indeed the Egyptians used this unit of length to draw squares having a surface which was the double of that of the initial square whose side = *a*, or to divide into two an initial double square. It is not possible to find a more obvious application of the theorem of the square of the hypothenuse in the most general case and this was done without mechanical value at least 2,000 before Pythagorus was born.

It also appears that the Egyptians had a thorough knowledge of irrational numbers. This is typically confirmed by the geometrical (not the arithmetical) definition that the Egyptians had for the square root; the phrase was: "to make the (right) angle of a number. For instance: To make the (right) angle of 9=3. Three is the hypotenuse of the isosceles right triangle whose side is *a:* for instance, to make the (right) angle of $(2a^2) = A\sqrt{2}$; To make the right angle of $(20.6\sqrt{2})^2 = (20.6)^2 \times 2 - 20.6\sqrt{2}$. This geometric definition of the square root is sufficient to show that the Egyptians had mastered the theorem of the square on the hypothenuse and had already made several applications of that.

Quadrature of a Circle

In the history of mathematics, problem 48 of the Rhind Mathematical Papyrus (RMP) is the first one ever to state the problem of the quadrature of a circle. The surface area of a square with a side = 9 was compared to that of a circle whose diameter was also equal to nine.

Trigonometry

The Egyptians were the first to invent trigonometry. Problems 56 and 60 of the RMP all deal with the calculations of trigonometric lines: sine, cosine, tangent, cotangent. Each time, two trigonometric lines are given and the third one is to be determined. Problem 56 involves the calculation of the incline of a pyramid, which is the same as calculating a tangent.

The scribe likened the light of the pyramid to the axis of the sine and, the cosine to half of the parallel of the side of the square at the bottom which passes through the center of the square.

$$\sin = 250 \text{ cubit}$$

$$\text{ws} = {}^{360}/_{2} = 180 \text{ cubits}$$

$$\tan = {}^{250}/_{180}$$

Then the scribe reversed this relation to determine the cotangent:

$$\cot = {}^{250}/_{180} = {}^{1}/_{2} + {}^{1}/_{5} + {}^{1}/_{50}$$

He multiplied this result by 7 to express the final result in palms. Indeed a cubit equals 7 palms. The final result is

$$\cot \alpha = 7 \times ({}^{1}/_{2} + {}^{1}/_{5} + {}^{1}/_{50}) = 5 \text{ palms } {}^{1}/_{25}$$

For the scribe this result had the value of an angle because it enabled him to affirm that the displacement of 5 palms along the axis of the cosine corresponds to a rise of a cubit along the axis of a sine.

It is much later that modern mathematics invented the trigonometric unitary radius.

The Surface Areas of Elementary Figures

Problem No. 49 of the *RMP* deals with the surface areas of the rectangle, $S=1\times1$. Problem No. 5 deals with the surface areas of the triangle, $S = {}^{b\times h}/_{2}$. No. 52 deals with the surface area of the trapezoid, $S = {}^{A+B\times h}/_{2}$. We have already seen that problem 41 deals with the volume of the cylinder, and problem 44 with the volume of the cube. Problem 46 deals with a parallelepiped whose base is square. The volume is given and the three faces must be determined. It is likely that the problem on plate VIII of the Kahum papyrus deals with the volume of the half-sphere with a diameter = 8 units, as Borchardt postulated.[19]

Mathematical Series

The Egyptians were masters when it came to geometric and arithmetic progressions. They knew how to add them or how to find the sequence of terms.

Problem 79 of the RMP deals with a geometric progression whose ratio is $r=7$ and the scribe applied the formula accurately:

$$S = a \frac{R^n-1}{R-1}$$

Problem 40 deals with an arithmetic progression. The problem deals with the proportional division of 100 loaves among five people in such a way that the shares would be in arithmetic progression and the sum of the two lowest shares is equal to $^1/_7$ of the sum of the three highest shares.[20]

Problem 64 deals with distributing differences, that is, distributing 10 loaves to 10 people in such a way that the difference between the shares each person and his neighbor is $^1/_8$ of an hekat. One comes to the same result as the scribe by applying the classical formula of an arithmetic progression:

$$l = a + (n-l)d \text{ with}$$
$$l = \text{the last term}$$
$$a = \text{the first term}$$
$$d = \text{the common difference } ^1/_8$$

The Rhind papyrus shows that the Egyptians did invent the arithmetic and geometric progressions. It is interesting to note that the most famous "alleged" discoveries of Pythagoras deal with geometric and arithmetic series. All the operations that he made—summations in particular—were commonly made by the Egyptians. For instance, the summation of the terms of the simplest arithmetic progression corresponding to the series of natural numbers (and in which the relation of or difference between the term is equal to the unit) gives the *trigonal* or *triangular* numbers.

In order to find out the tetragonal or square numbers that are 1,4,9,16, and 25, one had to find the summation of the terms of a progression in which the difference of terms was 2, that is a progression of odd numbers like 1,3,5,7,9. Pythagoras believed that the soul was tetragonal and we will come pack to this fact to emphasize that the ideas attributed to Pythagoras are without any doubt of Egyptian origin.

The progressions in which the difference of terms is 3 gives the pentagonal number 1,5,12,22,35. When the difference is 4, one obtains the hexagonal numbers 1,6,15,28. With the same process heptagonal, octogenal and enneagonal numbers can be obtained.

Let us come back to the tetragonal or square numbers. According to Pythagoras they characterize the shape of the soul. They can all be found by means of a series of successive rectangles called "gnomons", from a square unit. One then obtains, as described above, the series of odd arithmetic numbers: 1,3,5,7, etc.

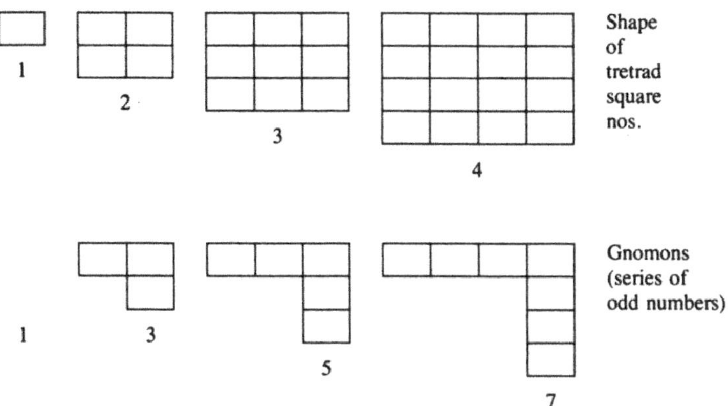

All this explains the importance of the tetrad and the gnomon in Pythagoras' philosophy.

Pythagoras and his disciples have been sò much influenced by Egypt that, in spite of the fact that they spoke a different language and had a different writing, they did use the Egyptian hieroglyphic signs in their pre-algebraic mathematical notations. For instance, they used the hieroglyphic sign for water to symbolize the progression of numbers.

The series of odd numbers was represented by a right-angle shaped gnomon (7). The series of even numbers was represented by the sign (=) of the scale. The circle, which was the sign of the Ra, the Egyptian sun God represented eternal motion (O).[21]

We cannot show in a more convincing way that the whole of Pythagoras' philosophical doctrine as well as his theory of numbers were extremely indebted to Egyptian thought.

Algebra

The Egyptians invented algebra. The series of the *RMP* problems described by the Egyptian "Aha," that is, quantity in its most general meaning, are algebra problems in which the unit plays exactly the same role as the unknown factor x is found in modern algebra. The reasoning of all these problems is essentially algebraic as admitted by Eisenlohr, Canton Revillov and even by a detractor like Neugebauer.

The problems studied in the Rhind Papyrus belong to three categories:

1. Problems 26-27 are solved by the method of false assumption. Problem 24. "A quantity and its $^1/_7$ added together become 19. What is the quantity?" Obviously this comes down to the first degree equation:

$$X + {}^x/_7 = 19$$

2. Problems 28 and 29. Problem 28: "A quantity and its $^2/_3$ are added together and from the sum $^1/_3$ of the sum is subtracted, and 10 remains. What is the quantity?" The corresponding first degree equation is:

$$X + {}^{2X}/_3 - {}^1/_3 \,.\, (X + {}^{2x}/_3) = 10$$

3. Problems 30-34.[22] Problem 30: "What is the quantity of which $^2/_3$ $^1/_{10}$ will make 10?" The first degree equation is:

$$X\ ({}^2/_3 + {}^1/_{10}) = 10$$

Second Degree Equations

Two problems of the Berlin papyrus deal with a system of simultaneous equations and one of them is a second degree equation. Written in modern form they would be:

$$\text{I}\quad \begin{array}{rcrcr} X^2 & + & Y^2 & = & 100 \\ 4X & - & 3Y & = & 0 \end{array}$$

$$\text{II}\quad \begin{array}{rcrcr} X^2 & + & Y^2 & = & 400 \\ 4X & - & 3Y & = & 0 \end{array}$$

Here is a second degree equation: "How do you divide 100 in two parts in such a way that the square root of one part equals $^3/_4$ of the square root of the other part?" One must write:

$$X^2 + Y^2 = 100$$

$$\text{but } Y = {}^{3X}/_4$$

$$\text{So, } X^2 = {}^9/_{16}\ \ X^2 = 100$$

Gillings thinks that problems 28 and 29 of the Rhind papyrus are the oldest examples recorded in the history of mathematics. They existed well before Diaphantes of Alexandria came to be. They belong to the a category of problems called "think of a number" or "find a number such as." The weighting of quantities: Series of problems called the *"Pesu"* problems in the Rhind papyrus.

In the problems dealing with mass and weight, food quantities in particular were accompanied by a coefficient of utility. These quantities were weighted so as to take into consideration only their useful weight. Example: If the "pesu" of a load is 12, it means that the loaf contains $^1/_{12}$ bushel.

Recto Table of the Rhind Papyrus: Arithmetics

The Recto of the Rhind Papyrus contains the result of the division of 2 by a series of odd numbers from 3 to 101. The results are expressed in unit fractions whose numerator is always equal to one.[23] Today, mathematicians still do not know exactly how to determine the use of this old table. Moreover, they do not know how to figure out the method of decomposition used by the ancient Egyptians. (For further study of this a useful work is Professor Maurice Caveing's dissertation which deals with the history of mathematics in antiquity.)[24]

This table is found in 2000 B.C. and in 600 A.D. Gillings observes that the Greek, Roman, Arabic, and Byzantine mathematicians were never able to discover a more efficient technique to treat a fraction as ordinary as $^p/_9$. In their arithmetic the Greeks have kept the old Egyptian fraction notation of 2200 B.C. Indeed, on the Greek papyrus one can read that $^1/_{17}$ of a silver talent equals 352 + $^1/_2$ + $^1/_{17}$ + $^1/_{34}$ + $^1/_{52}$ drachmas.

Modern mathematicians wanted to know whether the ancient Egyptians proceeded empirically (by trial and error) or theoretically. So, in 1967, a computer was programmed in the U.S. to make all the decompositions that were possible and it produced 22,295 figures. If the scribe's divisions were based on theory, then among the tens of thousands of figures, he had chosen only the 49 simplest and most elegant ones. If this is so, then he will not be bested by the 20th century electronic machine, invented 4,000 years later. That is exactly what happened. "We can conclude that, in this division as elsewhere, the computer did not find a decomposition superior to that given by the ancient scribe."[25] The method that the Egyptians used figures in all the laws of elementary arithmetic, a field that it is not possible to deal with in this paper.

It must be said that, traditionally, philosophers and scientists were persecuted in the Greek Athenian state. On the contrary, the Egyptian State has always encouraged the development of science, philosophy, and arts. Up to the end of the history of the Indo-European state, science and philosophy were as antinomical to the state in continental Greece as they were inseparable from the state in Egypt.

Most of the scientists who gave Greece its scientific fame were persecuted and had to flee from Greece to take refuge in Egypt. Almost all of them went to Egypt for training. Anexagoras, Socrates, Aristotle, Plato were persecuted or had to flee to escape persecution. Aristotle did not hesitate to testify to the fact that if the Egyptian priests reached such a high level in theoretical and speculative science, it was because they were free from material worries. And this was because the state supported them.

The Egyptian Calendar

There have been an impressive number of inventions in Africa between 2000 and 3000 B.C. This was the time period in which indigenous domestication of plants and animals occurred, and this was done by means of indigenous techniques.

It was during that time that metallurgy was invented. The Egyptians of the ancient empire no doubt knew the metallurgy of iron.[26] Also, the recent archeological discoveries made by the Belgium in Burundi confirm our challenging ideas concerning the first iron age in Africa.[27]

Moreover, it is now common knowledge that in 4236 B.C., the Egyptians had already invented a calendar based on the heliacal rising of Sothis or Sirius (the brightest star in the sky) which appeared every 1,460 years. Indeed the Egyptians knew the two types of year: 365 days and 365 days + 1/4. The first one contains 12 months and 30 days = 360 + the five epagomenal days which were dedicated to the birthdays of Osiris, Horus, Seth, Isis and Nephthys, the five Egyptian Gods. So, methologically speaking, Osiris was indeed born the night of December 25 as was Jesus Christ who can be compared to Osiris in this case and in many others.

However, the Egyptians know that the civil year of 365 days was 1/4 of a day shorter than the solar year. This meant that their civil year slipped steadily backwards through the solar year, 1/2 a day every two years and one day every four years. Therefore, as early as the fourth millenium B.C., the Egyptians had already created the leap year. However, it is remarkable that they preferred to choose a time-lag of 1,460 years in order to add a whole year instead of adding one day every four years. Indeed, this time period of 1,460 years is the period which separates the two heliacal risings of Sothis. The latitude of Memphis is certainly not the place where the calendar was invented for reasons which will be too long to develop here.

The heliacal rise of Sothis (a star) coincided with that of the sun. Even Neugebauer, who was a great detractor of Egyptian science, said that "this calendar is indeed the only intelligent calendar which existed in human history."[28] And Gillings added, "it is simpler even than the 'perpetual calendar' which though recommended for world wide use by astronomers seems condemned to remain forever in some official pigeon-holes in all countries" (p. 235).

About the two calendars Gillings concludes: "These two calendars (of 365 and 365 1/4 days) existing side by side from, it is thought, the time of the first pharaoh of upper and lower Egypt, was "the most scientific organization of calendar which has yet been used by man."

We said in our book entitled *Civilization or Barbarism* that "until today, with the Egyptian sideral calendar which could very well be reactivated, humanity or at least Africa has a scale of absolute chronology compared with which the Christian era, the hegira and various landmarks, are completely relative.[30]

At the annual congress on Egyptology, held February 24-26, 1984, at Los Angeles Southwest College, Black Americans of the Diaspora reactivated this calendar using 4,236 (give or take 4 years) as the absolute chronological landmark.

Unlike Mesopotamia which never managed to establish a calendar worthy of the name and which, even at its highest period of development had not gone beyond the stage of drawing up "ephemerides." When the chronological gap became very wide the king simply added a thirteenth or fourteenth month to the year.

Because Rome had no scientists or astronomers worthy of the name, he had an astronomer come from Egypt. Similarly when an eclipse of the sun brought widespread panic in the ranks of the Greek army during Alexander the Great's battle against the Persians, it was not Aristotle, the king's tutor, but a priest, an Egyptian astronomer, who restored calm by giving a scientific explanation of the phenomenon.

The Carlsberg papyrus no. 9 describes a method for determining the phases of the moon deriving from more ancient sources and which were in no way influenced by the hellenistic sciences. The same is true of the Carlsberg papyrus no. 1 which proves that there existed treatises on Egyptian astronomy.

In the Denkmaller III, plate 228(b), Lepsius reproduced a figure which represents a real system of coordinates centered on the observatory to locate the position of the stars according to the time of the day or night. The positions are recorded on a graph accurately squared using coordinates.

Egyptian science was well aware of the concept of coordinates. Ivan Van Sertima[31] published a diagram drawn by an ancient Egyptian architect during the third dynasty which is no more and no less than a descending curve. The descending ordinates are given in hieratic writing according to the divisions into equal values of x (abcissa).

We have seen that the two Egyptian calendars were already in use during the first dynasty. This did not prevent Diagenes Laerces, Thales' biographer (6th century B.C.), from writing that he was the first to divide the year into 365 days.

Mechanics

Much could be said about Egyptian mechanics. Ivan van Sertima[32] published in the *Journal of African Civilizations* the model of an Egyptian glider dating from the fourth or third century B.C. This object was in Room 22 of the Egyptian museum in Cairo and bore the no. 6347. It is 14 cm long. The article is signed jointly by Khalil Messiha and Guirguis Messira. "The model attracted my attention," said Messira, "as it was very much like the aeroplane models I used to make some 20 years ago. It was discovered in Sakkara, in 1898, and is made of sycamore wood."[33]

The two authors quoted above are aeronautical engineers. Dr. Gamal Mokhtar, a former Egyptian minister and former Director of Antiquities in Egypt, is associated with this publication. These are the facts: it was a NASA official who collected the documents. Dr. Gamal Mokhtar writes that the discovery was made during a visit to the museum by the members of the International Aerospace Education Commission. Having regard to the credibility of the authors, we relate the fact although we ourselves are unable to authenticate it. We can have no personal opinion on the matter as we have not yet seen the model itself, only a copy of it. In any case, confirmation of the fact would be of vital importance.

We do not have space here to go into statistics and the mathematical bases of Egyptian architecture, using the values of the series (oudjat) $^1/_2 + ^1/_4 + ^1/_8 + ^1/_{16} + ^1/_{32}$ to determine the proportions of the monuments and in particular just how thin to make the columns.

The Egyptians routinely siphoned off liquids using atmospheric pressure and the difference in level.

Again, we do not have the space to speak of the influence of the Egyptian cosomogonies (Heliopolitan and Hermopolitan) on Greek philosophy, particularly pre-Socratic philosophy. However, there is a very close connection between Plato's Timaeus and the heliopolitan cosomogony and the latter would help to clarify many unclear passages in this book.[34] Empedocles merely repeated the theory of the four elements of heliopolitan cosmogny.

Medicine

Opinion is virtually unanimous that in this field, especially in the area of bone surgery, the Egyptians had already achieved the scientific level from the time of the ancient empire. The basis for this belief can be found in the 48 minutely detailed descriptions of cases of brain injury in the Smith papyrus. What we find there is in fact location of the brain functions, 3,000 years before Broca; in fact, the 48 cases of injury all relate to the skull and the neck and in each case to the side effects on parts of the body. Even those furthest away from the brain are noted. "Case 6" describes for the first time the cerebral convolutions that take place when the cranium is pulled away, like "the wrinkles that form on copper when it is being smelted." "Case 8": an injury to the brain causes "an inversion of the eyeballs" and the patient "drags his feet when he walks." "Case 22": a perforated temple causes loss of speech. "Case 31": dislocation of the neck vertebrae causes paralysis of the arms and legs. . . .

For each case, a cure is given if there is one. The Ebers papyrus shows that the Egyptians had discovered blood circulation and the functioning of the heart. The document states that: "the heart speaks in all the organs." the reference is to the heart beat which is reflected in the pulse.

Theophrastus, Dioscorides and Galen all consulted annals of Imhotep in the Memphis Temple Library until the second century A.D. Hippocrates had already done this before them in the fifth century.

The influence of Egyptian medicine on Greek medicine can be observed. For example, the method given in the Carlsberg papyrus no. 4, whether it is true or false, has been copied out verbatim by "the father of medicine": I refer to the clove of garlic method for diagnosing sterility in women.

Like all the other Egyptian sciences, medicine survived in the rest of Africa, but deteriorated as Africa became more and more isolated, and as the continent fell under foreign domination.

Dr. Charles S. Finch quotes the Edinburgh Medical Journal, 1884 where Dr. R.W. Felkin describes a Cesarean operation performed by a Ugandan surgeon using traditional medicine. Both mother and child were saved, something that had never been seen at that time even in Europe, where they were usually content to save the infant at best.[35]

Never has a similar case been recorded in ancient civilizations.

By way of conclusion to this second part dealing with the study of how the values of the civilization of Egypt were transmitted to the rest of the world and to Greece in particular, we can refer to the title of the Rhind Papyrus "Rules for Studying[35] nature, for understanding everything that exists, every mystery, every secret."

Dr. Faustus could have signed this declaration of belief. In fact, it was not until the renaissance that F. Bacon stated a similar lay belief in the almighty power of the number.

The Greeks never went any further in the expression of man's desire or ability to master nature through science and through mathematics in particular. Contrary to a current belief, Egypt was not that land hidebound by a religiosity that prevented it from conquering nature through science. Let it be remembered that it was in fact this country, which through science brought mankind out of prehistory to the real conquest of civilization. The first state organization in the world was in the Nile Valley, in Nubia in Sudan, first at Qustul,[36] then in Egypt with Menes (circa 3,150 B.C.).

Bureaucracy, that is to say, the scientific and scholarly organization of the state, was first of all a tremendous step forward, a technological conquest. It has often been disparaged much more because of Eurocentrism, than because it constituted any real danger: for even today, what State even a revolutionary one has managed to do without it?

It is only true that it was not an invention of the Indo-European city state in the period following the prehistoric era; it was without question an African invention for controlling the organization of the human community on the large scale of the Egyptian nation state from 3,150 B.C.

Furthermore, "the dialogue of a desperate person with his soul" shows that the Egyptians were not satisfied to tame external nature through science but that they made an equally thorough study of human nature.

We perceive the falseness and the danger of the stereotyped opinions advanced by the ideologists of the different schools, who could not accept the idea that civilization began in Africa.

However, this would mean forgetting the opinions that were current until the XIX century. In fact, Lenormant in his study of the first Oriental civilizations reminds us that throughout antiquity the unanimous opinion of the Indo-European and semitic peoples, who were then lagging behind the Blacks, was that the descendants of Kam were particularly adept at taming nature, creating science and material civilization and that they were the first to embark on this course: mankind everywhere owes them its early progress and the first civilizations.

Notes

Since Dr. Diop's paper is published here as two separate articles to fit the thematic structure of this issue, the notes in this, the second article, begin with note 7.

7. V. Struve. Mathematischer papyrus des Staalichen Museums der Schönen Kunste in Moskau (Quellen und Studien zur Geschiste der Mathematik, Abteilung A: Quellen, Band I) Berlin, 1930.
8. $V=\pi R^2$ h: See the Rhind mathematical papyrus, T.E. Peet, ed. no. 41.
9. N de G. Davies. Rekhmire p. 1L IV.
10. N de G. Davies. The Tomb of two Scupltors at Thebes. P. h 28.
11. Archimedes dedicated his treatise *The Method* to his friend E. Ralosthenes and revealed that his mechanical method (of weighing geometric figures) was the hidden source of his main discoveries.
12. Paul ver Ecke: *Les Oeuvres Completes d'Archimede* (Archimedes Complete Works) Albert Blanchard, Paris, 1960. Introduction p. SLIV-SLV.
13. P. ver Ecke, op. cit. p. XIV-SV. Strabon geography translated by Amedee Tardieu Vol. III book SVII p. 433. Diodore de Sicile: *History.* Vol II Book V. Chapter XXXVII, p. 39.
    Also, Albert Slosman writes: "For let us not forget that it was because of the rampant use of plagiarism among the Greeks that Clement of Alexandria said at the time: "A one thousand page book will not be long enough to cite the names of my fellow countrymen who have used and abused the Egyptian science." Albert Slosman *Le livrede l'au-dela de la vie.* (The book of the Life Beyond) Boudouin, Paris, 1979.
14. "Die Aufgabe Nr. 10 hat uns aber zusammen mit der Formel fur die Kugeloberflache auch die Formel fur den Kreisumfang gebracht," Struve; op. cit., pp. 177-178.
15. "Die agyptischen Werkzeichnungen erweisen sich abenso genau wie die der modernen Ingenieure."
16. P. ver Ecke, op. cit. p. XXXI. That is why an Egyptian priest told Diodores of Sicily that once the Greeks returned home they took credit for all the sciences they learned in Egypt.
17. Pythagoras and Plato, who received their training in Egypt, adopted this method of notation.
18. Richard J. Gillings: *Mathematics in the Time of the Pharoahs.* M.I.T. Press, Cambridge, Massachusetts and London, England. Chapter 20, p. 208.

19. Borchardt: AZ, 35, p. 150-152.
20. Peet RMP. p. 78.
21. Ferdinand Hoefer: Histoire des Mathematiques, Librarie Hachette. Paris, 1984 (4th edition), pp. 99, 129-130.
22. R. J. Gillings, op. cit.
    Peet: RMP - Problems 24 to 34 (op. cit.)
23. R. J. Gillings, op. cit. p. 181.
24. Maurice Coveing: Idealite mathematique grecgue. Paris.
25. R. J. Gillings, op. cit. p. 52.
26. Cheikh Anta Diop. "La metallurgie du fer sous l'ancien Empire" (The Metallurgy of Iron in the Ancient Empire) in *Bulletin B. IFAN*, vol. XXXV, Series B, no. 3, Dakar, 1973.
27. Cheikh Anta Diop. "Vers une remise en question de l'age du fer en Afrique" (Toward a Reassessment of the Iron Age in Africa), in *Notes Africaines* IFAN, no. 152, October 1976.
28. O. Neugebauer. *The Exact Sciences in Antiquity.* New York: Harper, 1962, p. 81; quoted by Gillings, op. cit., p. 235.
29. J.W.S. Sewell "The Calendars and Chronology," in *Legacy of Egypt*, S.R.K. Glanville ed., London: Oxford University Press, 1963, p. 7; quoted by Gillins, op. cit., p. 236.
30. Cheikh Anta Diop. *Civilisation ou Barbarie* (Civilization or Barbarism). Paris, 1981: Presence Africaine, p. 356.
31. Ivan Van Sertima, op. cit., p. 77.
32. Ibid., p. 92-99.
33. *Blacks in Science*, Ivan Van Sertima (ed.), p. 92; Qudjat = Eye of Horus.
34. cf. Cheikh Anta Diop: Civilisation ou Barbarie, chapter 17.
35. Charles Finch, "The African Background of Medical Science," in *Blacks in Science* op. cit. p. 152.
36. Bruce Williams, Chicago Oriental Institute.

Bibliography

P. Lenormant, *Ancient History of the East*, vol. III, p. 100.

UNESCO, Seminar at Athens, March 30 - April 3, 1981. Racism, science and pseudo-science-close relationship between the Indo-Europeans, the Blacks and the Boschmen from the viewpoint of the antigones of seplems. Article by Albert Jacquart, "Science and Racism."

M.H. Day, M.D. Leakey and C. Magore, "A New Hominid Fossil Skull," (L.H.18) from the Ngaloba Beds, Laetoli Northern Tanzania in Nature, vol. 284, March 6, 1980.

David Pilbeam, "From Primates to Man," *Pour la Science*, May 1984.

Proc. Nat. Acad. Sci. USA, vol. 78, no. 4, pp. 2638-2642, April 1981. Popular biology. A. Piazza, P. Menozzi and L.L. Cavalli Sforza, "Synthetic Gene Frequency Maps of Man and Selective effects of Climate."

M.J. Johnson, D.C. Wallace, S.D. Ferris, M.C. Baltazzi and L.L. Cavilli Sforza, "Radiations of Human Mitochondria DNA Types analysed by Restruction Endonuclease Cleavage Patterns."

La recherche, no. 148, October 1983.

Beaujouan, C., "Ancient and Medieval Science," PUF, 1957.

Archaelogical Dictionary of Techniques, vols. I and II. Editions de l'Accueil, 1963.

Gimpel, Jean, *The Industrial Revolution in the Middle Ages*, Editions du Seuil, 1975.

Van Sertima, Ivan, *They Came Before Columbus*, Flamarion, 1981.

Y. Al-Hassan, Ahmad, "Islam and Science," *Research*, no. 138, July 1982.

THE NEWTONIAN SYNTHESIS IN PHYSICAL SCIENCE AND ITS ROOTS IN THE NILE VALLEY

John Pappademos

Sir Isaac Newton is conventionally considered today to be the founder of the science of mechanics, the co-inventor of the calculus, discoverer of the binomial theorem, important pioneer in the science of optics, and discoverer of the law of universal gravitation. He has been frequently termed "the greatest scientist that ever lived".[1] Born in England in 1642, he lived there until his death in 1727. His greatest work, published in London in 1867, was the *Philosophiae Naturalis Principia Mathematica*, or "*Principia*" for short. In this treatise, he not only set forth and applied the law of universal gravitation, but stated the now-famous three laws of motion—the so-called Newton's Laws.

In Isaac Newton's work, there was achieved a synthesis of three lines of development,[2] each of which started in ancient times. These were astronomy, mathematics, and mechanics. Newton's success rested directly on his predecessors Kepler, Copernicus, Descartes, and Galileo in the fields of astronomy, mathematics, and mechanics. In this article we will show that the work of Newton's predecessors would have been impossible without the basis laid centuries earlier in Egypt, so that Egyptian science, after a thousand years, indirectly motivated Newton through his European predecessors such as Kepler, Descartes, Copernicus, and Galileo. Furthermore we will show that Newton was, in addition, directly influenced by ancient Egyptian science.

Galileo

First, we should note that the Italian scientist Galileo (1654-1642) exerted a profound influence on Newton, who, in his *Principia*, assigned the honor of discovery of the first two laws of motion to Galileo,[3] and while still an undergraduate student, was led in the course of solving a problem set by Galileo to a proof that gravity was the force holding the moon and planets in their orbits.[4]

It is not difficult to trace the influence of the scientific writings of the ancients on the young Galileo. He, like other Europeans of the 13th through the 17th centuries A.D., would have made far less progress had it not been for the legacy of thought bequeathed to them by the Egyptian, Greek and Muslim authors of various nationalities. As a student at the University of Pisa and later as a professor at the same institution (1589-92), Galileo studied assiduously the works of Euclid, Ptolemy, Archimedes, Pappus, and literally dozens of other Greek,

Muslim, and Egyptian scientists.[5] His knowledge of the ancient philosophers, as evidenced in his notes taken at the time, is remarkable. One of Galileo's particular heroes was Archimedes,[6] who is reported to have spent time at the University of Alexandria.[7] According to Reymond,[8] "Archimedes must have sojourned for some time in Egypt, or he would not have brought out his works in Alexandria, dedicating them to Eratosthenes, Conon, and Dosithenes who lived in that city. . . . It is likewise in Egypt, if Diodorus of Sicily is to be believed, that Archimedes discovered the screw which bears his name. . . . It is doubtful whether such an apparatus had not been used in Egypt before the time of Archimedes".

Another name mentioned many times in Galileo's notebooks[5] was that of the Alexandrian philosopher Philoponus, whose theory of impetus led to Galileo's mechanics.[9] Philoponus, who, like most of the other Alexandrian philosophers, can be taken to be of Egyptian origin, showed by experiment the falsity of the Aristotelean dogma that heavier objects fall more rapidly than lighter objects a thousand years before Galileo, who conventionally gets the credit for proving the dogma false by his reputed experiment of dropping two balls of different weights from the Leaning Tower of Pisa.[10,11]

The influence of the ancient Greek and Egyptian students of mechanics was also effected indirectly through Galileo's university studies of his European 14th and 15th century precursors such as Jordanus, Tartaglia, Bradwardine, Buridan and a number of others. The work of Jordanus and his followers, for example, constituted a discipline known in the later Middle Ages in Europe as the Science of Weights, and belonged to a tradition stemming from texts on mechanics written by Heron, an Egyptian.[12] Furthermore, Stillman Drake has shown[13] how Galileo's famous studies of accelerated motion depended on the theory of proportions developed by Eudoxus, a Greek philosopher trained by the Egyptians.[14]

The influence of Africa also made itself felt in Galileo's experimental work. In his experiments on motion, he used a water clock, an Egyptian invention,[15] to measure time intervals; his measurements of length were based on the Egyptian unit of length (the cubit—braccio in Italian). Although Galileo is commonly credited with the invention of the thermoscope (effectively a thermometer without a scale), it has been noted by Bedini[16] that "the principle of the thermoscope had been noted . . . in the works of Hero of Alexandria (end of first century A.D.), in which the nature of the vacuum and the elasticity of air were discussed. Hero's work as well-known, or at least available, in Italy by the end of the 16th century . . . Galileo was certainly familiar with this work and had studied it . . ."[16] Galileo certainly helped to establish the validity of the heliocentric theory of the solar system by using the telescopes he constructed to observe the phases of Venus as well as the phenomenon of sunspots, but seldom have the prior experiments of Ibn-al-Haytham (Alhazen) of Egypt on lenses been given credit. Alhazen (died in Cairo in 1039 A.D.) was one of the greatest students of optics of all time. The Latin translation of his book *Optics* exerted a profound influence on European science, and included studies of the magnifying power of lenses.[17]

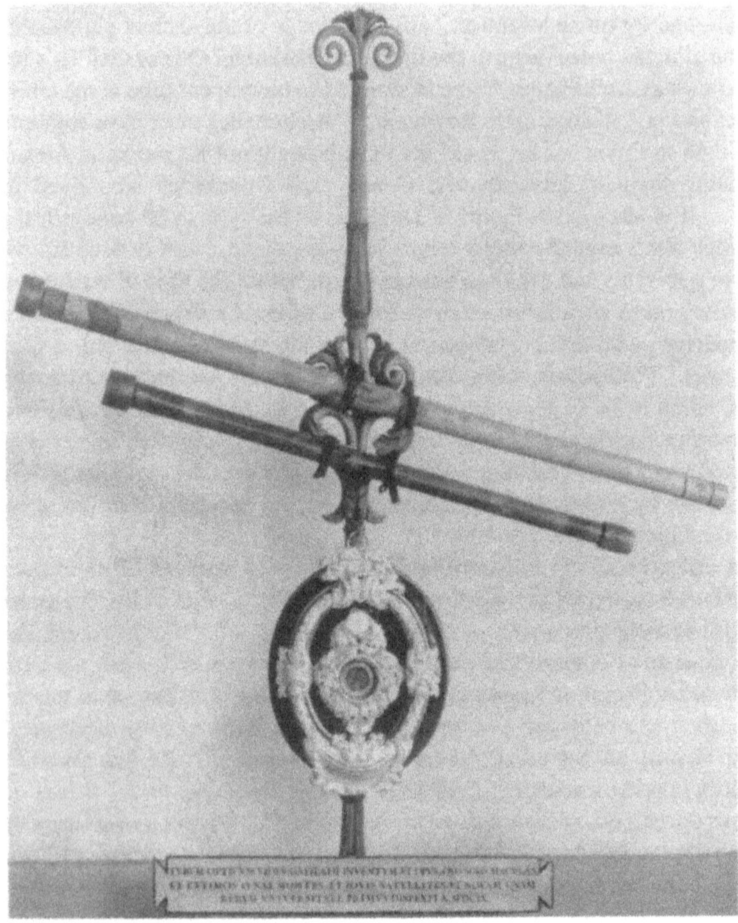

Figure 1. Galilean telescopes.

Copernicus

Nicholas Copernicus, astronomer, was born in Poland in 1473 and died in 1543, 21 years before Galileo was born. His major work, *De Revolutionibus Orbium Coelestium*, published the year of his death, is generally credited with causing a revolution in science, and which led through Kepler to Newton's *Principia*. *De Revolutionibus* was modelled on Ptolemy's *Almagest*, which was published in Alexandria, Egypt, 13 centuries earlier.[18] In *De Revolutionibus* Copernicus set forth the heliocentric theory of the sun and planets. (In the *Almagest*, on the other hand, the sun, stars, and planets were taken to rotate about the earth as center.) The notion that the earth moves and is not the center of the universe was

Figure 2. Archimedean screw for raising water. A whole series of such hollow screws could be geared together and used for delivering water up a considerable incline.

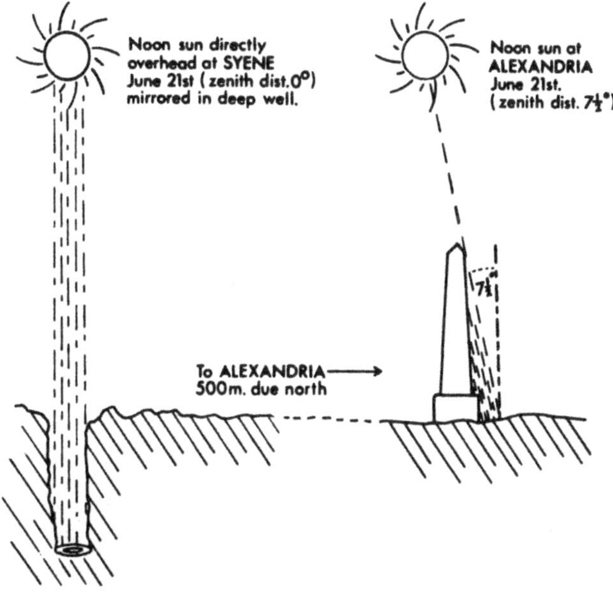

Figure 3. Erasthothenes method of measuring the Earth. He noted that at Syene the sun was directly overhead on Midsummer's Day, while at Alexandria the sun's rays were 7½° from the vertical, a value calculated from the length of a shadow cast by a column of known height. From this, and knowing the distance between the two places, he calculated the circumference of the Earth to be 250,000 stades (about 24,000 miles).

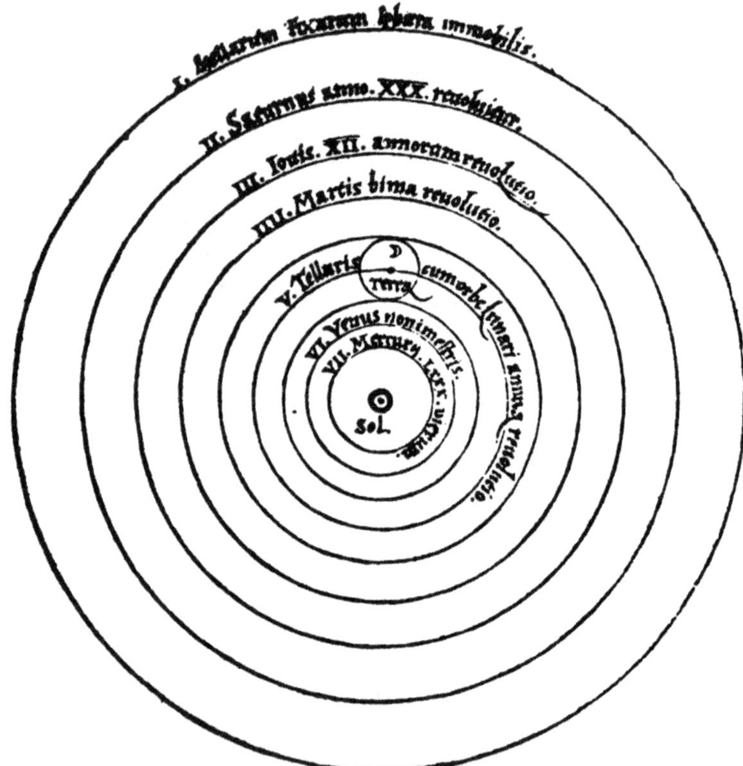

Figure 4. The universe as illustrated by Copernicus in *De revolutionibus orbium coelestium* (1543). I. Sphere of the Fixed Stars. II. Orbit of Saturn. III. Orbit of Jupiter. IV. Orbit of Mars. V. Orbit of the Sun and Moon. VI. Orbit of Venus. VII. Orbit of Mercury: the sun in the center.

hardly a new one, however; various theories involving a moving and rotating earth had been advocated by a number of ancient philosophers, including Aristarchus of Samos, Plato in his later years, the Pythagoreans, Heraclides of Pontus, Seleucus of Seleucia,[19] and Democritus.[20] To this list should be added the still more ancient astronomers of Egypt, according to Macrobius (circa 400 A.D.),[21] Cicero,[22] Tannery (the French historian of science of the late 19th century),[23] and Newton himself, who believed that the most significant astronomical beliefs of the ancient Greeks were derived from the Egyptians.[24] We will have more to say about Newton's views later on in the article.

Copernicus thoroughly studied the works of the ancient astronomers that were available to him, and acknowledged his debt to them.[25-29]

We do not claim here that Copernicus' theory was just a repetition of the ear-

Figure 5. Pen-and-ink drawing of Galileo's legendary experiment at the Leaning Tower of Pisa.

lier heliocentric theories. It represented a distinct advance over the earlier theories, which were lacking in quantitative arguments. After all, Copernicus had the advantage of access to the fruit of centuries of work. He used the *Almagest* itself,[30] which, although it was based on the geocentric theory, still contained a wealth of astronomical data. Copernicus also made extensive use of the data published by the great Muslim astronomers such as al-Battani (d. 929 A.D.),[31] who refined and extended the data of the *Almagest*, as well as making other important and original contributions.

Kepler

The method used by Newton to justify his law of gravitation was to prove that with it he could derive Kepler's three laws of planetary motion. Kepler, a Ger-

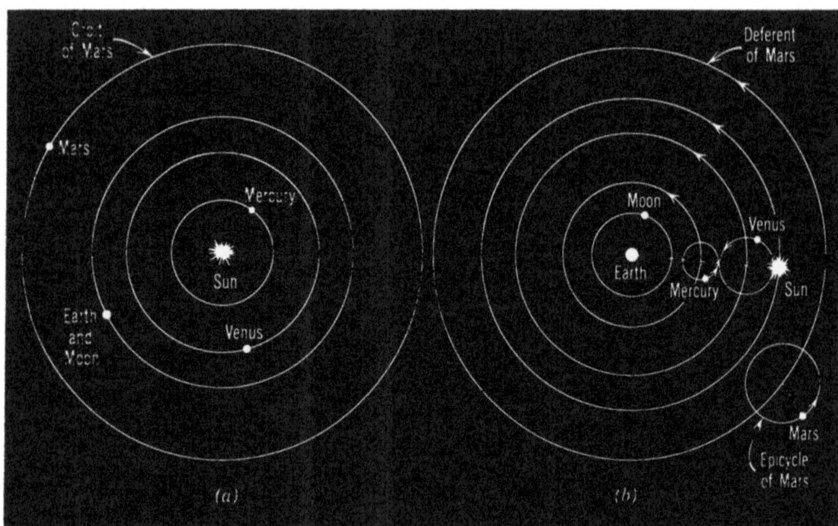

Figure 6. (a) The Copernican view of the solar system. The planets move in concentric orbits with the sun at the center. (b) The Ptolemaic view of the solar system. Each planet undergoes two simultaneous circular motions. For example, Mars travels about an epicycle while the center of the epicycle travels along a deferent. The earth is at the center of the system. Only the moon and sun have no epicycles.

man astronomer, deduced these laws between 1600 and 1620. Thus Kepler's work was vital to the success of Newton's theory of gravitation and motion.

It is well known that Kepler was a Copernican since his student days. Thus having been freed of the intellectual shackles of believing that the earth was the center of the universe, he was in a position to make his own contributions; namely, to eventually show that the planetary orbits are elliptical rather than circular (Law I), that any planet's orbital radius sweeps out equal areas in equal times (Law II), and that the squares of the planets' periods are proportional to the cubes of their mean distances from the sun (Law III). A very good discussion of the background to Kepler's work has been given by Fritz Krafft,[32] who also augments the list given above of ancient opponents of the geocentric hypothesis.

Most accounts of Kepler's life adhere to what Westman[33] has called the "apostolic" or "hagiographic" approach to the history of science. As Westman[33] has put it, "According to this view, the proper subject of historical investigation is the Great Man, for he alone produces the truly revolutionary insights. With some exceptions, the intellectual predecessors of Kepler, excluding Copernicus and Tycho Brahe (the Danish astronomer whose data Kepler used - jp), have not been given sufficient treatment with respect to their influence on him . . .". Westman goes on to cite some recent exceptions to this prevailing view. One of these exceptions is a paper by Fritz Krafft,[34] who has shown the

Figure 7. It is known that Egyptian temples were properly aligned at a ceremony called "The stretching of the cord." Astronomical objects were used to establish the reference lines. Here, the king and goddess grasp mallets and stakes, around which the cord is looped, and lay the foundation stone.

"transmission and modification of Aristotle's aether physics from Sosigenes' (an Egyptian astronomer, circa 45 B.C.-jp) proposals for a non-homocentric physical astronomy (meaning no one center for all celestial circles and spheres), through the mechanical models of Ptolemy's (another Egyptian scientist-jp) *Planetary Hypotheses*, Alhazen's "naturally" self-moving spheres (Alhazen was born in 965 A.D. in Basra and flourished in Egypt-jp), and Copernicus' inheritance of the tradition of Sosigenes in his rejection of the equant . . ."[33] Krafft's work thus gives new insights into Africa's influence on Copernicus, and thus, indirectly, on Kepler and Newton.

Descartes

In 1637 there appeared in print a book destined to have a great influence on the developing Newton. This was René Descartes' *Discourse on Method*, which

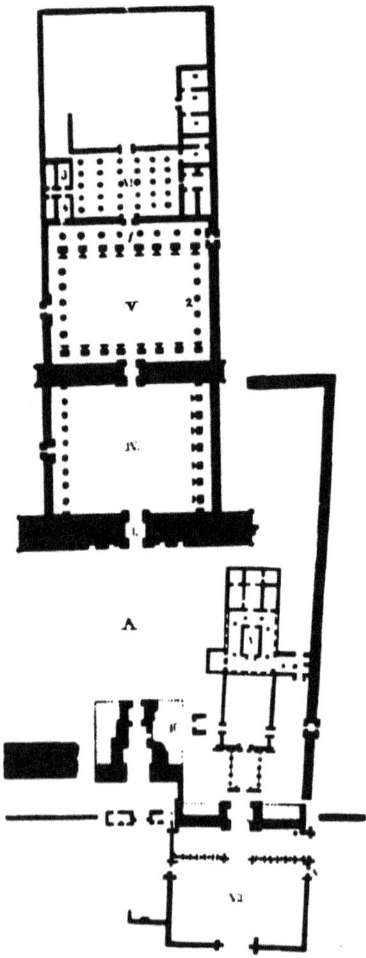

Figure 8. Lockyer interpreted the reorientation of the later buildings (upper) at Medinet-Habu, on the Nile's west bank, across from Luxor, as an Egyptian response to the precession of the equinoxes.

contained an appendix entitled "La Geometrie" (Geometry). As a student in Trinity College, Newton mastered Descartes' so-called analytic geometry,[35] the understanding of which was so important to his own later invention of the calculus. Without in any way belittling the creative genius of Descartes, and in fact to understand the context of his contribution all the better, it must be pointed out that the mathematicians of Alexandria were his primary sources of inspiration.[36] We will mention just three of the most important names: Pappus, Apollonius, and Euclid. More often than not, historians of science regard these as Greek and belonging to the "Greek" mathematical tradition, in utter disregard of the fact that mathematics flourished on Egyptian soil long before the Greek contributors; Egypt continued as the world's leading center of mathematics and astronomy until the death of Hypatia (c. 415 A.D.), and for another six centuries, at least until the death of Alhazen (1039 A.D.), it was one of the leading scientific centers of the world. There is no evidence that the Alexandrians Euclid and Pappus were of Greek origin; Apollonius was born about 262 B.C. in Perga (Asia Minor) but studied in Egypt and spent most of his life in Alexandria.[37] James Gow, the English historian of science, has argued that most of the mathematicians of Alexandria and other contemporary scientific centers such as at Pergamon (Asia Minor) were of Egyptian or Semitic origin.[38] The fact that Descartes drew so heavily on the work of such Alexandrian mathematicians as Apollonius has led some to ascribe credit for the invention of analytic geometry to them, rather than to Descartes.[39]

The Scientific Contributions of Other Non-European Peoples

It should be clear from the above that the work of Newton would have been unthinkable without the prior work in Africa by Egyptian or Egyptian-trained scientists as transmitted and expanded upon by Newton's immediate predecessors Descartes, Galileo, Kepler and Copernicus. We have almost exclusively emphasized the importance of the Nile Valley culture in tracing the genesis of Newtonian mechanics primarily because historians of science have, with few exceptions, allowed the influence of racism to distort their scholarship to such an extent that the importance to science of the Black civilization of the Nile Valley has been neglected and denied. It should not be supposed that the contributions of other non-European peoples (the Arabs, Persians, Jews, Indians, and Chinese, for example) were of no importance in forming the tradition leading to Newton and in general the explosive advance of science in 17th century Europe. Like Africa's contributions, those of other non-European peoples have been belittled, although to a lesser extent.

In our next section, we turn our attention to some writings of Newton himself which bear closely on our subject.

How Newton Himself Recognized That His Work Had Been Anticipated in Ancient Egypt

That Newton drew heavily upon the work of Galileo, Descartes, Kepler, and other Europeans is generally admitted by prevailing historical opinion. However, it is seldom stressed that Newton also was thoroughly familiar with the scientific works of much more ancient writers, especially those of Africa, whose opinions he held in high esteem and from which he drew to support his own arguments. To support this contention, let us let Newton speak for himself. In attributing the first atomic theory to Egypt and Phoenicia, Newton says:[40] "That all matter consists of atoms was a very ancient opinion. This was the teaching of a multitude of philosophers who preceded Aristotle, namely Epicurus, Democritus, Ecphantus, Empedocles, Zenocrates, Heraclides, Asclepiades, Diodorus, Metrodorus of Chios, Pythagoras, and previous to these Moschus the Phoenician, whom Strabo declares to be older than the Trojan War. For I think that the same opinion obtained in that mystic philosophy which flowed down to the Greeks from Egypt and Phoenicia, since atoms are sometimes found to be designated by the mystics as monads." (Newton is not usually thought of in connection with the atomic theory of matter. However, in deriving his results for the gravitational attraction between bodies of macroscopic size, Newton was led to the far-reaching conclusion that the inverse square law governs the force between bodies of atomic size.)

Furthermore, in an early edition of the *Principia*, in justifying his use of the heliocentric theory, Newton says:[41] "It was the most ancient opinion of those who applied themselves to Philosophy, that the fixed stars stood immovable in the highest parts of the world, that under them the planets revolved about the sun, that the earth, as one of the planets, described an annual course about the sun, while by a diurnal motion it turned on its axis, and that the sun remained at rest in the center of the Universe. This was the philosophy taught of old by Philolaus, Aristarchus of Samos, Plato in his riper years, the whole set of Pythagoreans, and that wisest king of the Romans, Numa Pompilius. As a symbol of the round orb with the solar fire in the center, Numa erected a round temple in honor of Vesta, and ordained a perpetual fire to be kept in the middle of it. The Egyptians were the earliest observers of the heavens and from them, probably, this philosophy was spread abroad. For from them it was, and from the nations about them, that the Greeks, a people more addicted to the study of philology than of Nature, derived their first, as well as their soundest, notions of philosophy; and in the Vestal ceremonies we can recognize the spirit of the Egyptians who concealed mysteries that were above the capacity of the common herd under the veil of religious rites and hieroglyphic symbols".

This passage is of extreme importance, because it bears directly on the most central part of Newton's theory of motion and gravitation. For as Westfall notes,[42] "From the observed phenomena of the heliocentric system, Newton argued the necessity of attractive forces to hold bodies in closed orbits, or inverse-square attractive forces to sustain orbits stable in space, and systems that conform to Kepler's Third Laws, and finally of a single inverse-square attractive force that arises 'from the universal nature of matter.'" Newton's firmly held belief that the ancient Egyptians anticipated both the Copernican (heliocentric) theory as well as universal gravitation is corroborated in a memorandum of David Gregory, one of Newton's associates.[43]

Elsewhere, in a set of draft scholia planned for inclusion in a second edition of the *Principia*, Newton makes an effective argument that his own major result—

the law of universal gravitation—had been anticipated two thousand years earlier by the Pythagorean philosophers, and that this was the real meaning of their doctrine of the "harmony of the spheres".[44] (It is of course well-known that Pythagoras spent as much as 22 years in Egypt studying Egyptian science and religion, where it is likely he learned this doctrine. This, in fact, is what Newton believed.)

Some Western authors[44] have attempted, in a sophisticated way, to deny validity to Newton's arguments for an Egyptian anticipation of the heliocentric and gravitational theories by relating his ideas to those of a contemporary philosophical trend in Europe typified by the school known as the "Cambridge Platonists". According to McGuire and Rattansi,[44] this Neo-Platonist trend, and much earlier a number of Alexandrian philosophers such as the early father of the Christian Church, Clement of Alexandria (d. 213 A.D.),[45] established a "cult of Egyptian wisdom," attributing all of pagan (i.e., Greek) philosophy to having been plagiarized from the Egyptians or the Hebrews. But the modern critics of Newton and Clement of Alexandria (such as McGuire and Rattansi[44]) do not adduce an evidence to refute Newton, Clement of Alexandria, and the many others. (From the many we could choose, let us mention just three. Simplicios, the 6th century A.D. commentator on Aristotle, conjectures that Thales (the earliest of the Greek philosophers, who studied in Egypt - jp) derived his ideas from myths current in Egypt. Paul Tannery (the 19th century French historian of science -jp) pointed out the similarity between Thales' view of the origin of the world and that contained in ancient Egyptian papyri.[46] And still more recently, the thesis of Egyptian priority has been masterfully set forth in a book by George G.M. James.)[47] They rely instead on the overwhelmingly prevalent tacit acceptance (in Europe and the U.S. at least) of the "Europeanized" version of the history of science to make Newton and Clement look foolish.

Since the rise of slavery with its offspring the doctrine and practice of racism, the Black civilization of the Nile Valley has had its detractors. As recently as 1975, Otto Neugebauer, the well-known historian of ancient science, had this to say: "Egypt provides us with the exceptional case of a highly sophisticated civilization which flourished for many centuries without making a single contribution to the development of the exact sciences."[48] Although Neugebauer's statement might not be fully accepted by the majority of other historians of science, it is nevertheless true that it is a somewhat extreme reflection of an attitude which prevails among the professional U.S. historians of science. Interestingly enough, in the same book from which the above question was taken, Neugebauer makes the following observation: "(in our study of Babylonian astronomy-jp) . . . we have authentic source materials . . . exactly as they were written. Only for papyri (the writing surface used by the Egyptians-jp) could the same be said, but their number and deplorable state of preservation places them far below the cuneiform tablets. It is particularly fortunate that these Babylonian documents were preserved because they allow us to study a type of mathematical astronomy the existence of which we would never have deduced from our Greek sources.''[49] This statement by Neugebauer himself, which indirectly admits that most Egyptian scientific writings have been lost to us (unlike those of the Babylonians), shows that his belittling of Egyptian astronomy is hardly justified.

A few historians of science have been able to make a fairer assessment; for example, E.C. Krupp states: ''. . . but for all the knowledge we have about ancient Egypt, most Egyptian astronomical lore is lost to us . . . the genuine accomplishments of the Egyptian astronomers, for example, the tropical year and the alignment of the pyramids, are relatively unappreciated by historians of science.''[50] George Sarton also had a high opinion of the astronomical ability of the early Egyptians.[51]

Egyptian Achievements in Astronomy

In order to help counteract such negative views of Egyptian science as those cited above, in this section we will give an admittedly incomplete listing of Egyptian achievements in astronomy. This, as mentioned previously, is one of the three main currents which were eventually synthesized by Newton in his *Principia*, where he set forth his theories of gravitation and dynamics.

Egyptian astronomy has been termed ''primitive'' or ''non-existent'' far too many times: it is appropriate to assemble the actual achievements of Egyptian astronomy and let the facts speak for themselves. The ancients unemcumbered by racism, could take a more honest view of the matter: for example, Aristotle wrote: ''. . . the Egyptians and Babylonians have studied these matters (i.e., planetary and lunar astronomy-jp) thoroughly since time immemorial, and through whom we have many reliable reports about each of the stars.''[52]

The other two currents, mathematics and mechanics, will not be dealt with here, leaving them to others or to a later paper. The elements of the following compendium have all been separately discussed in the literature, but have not received sufficient emphasis nor have they ever been assembled together. They are listed in roughly chronological order.

The invention of the 365-day calendar, based on astronomical observations. Mankind's first scientific measurement of time. This development probably took place at least as far back as 3000 B.C.[53]

The development of instruments for quantitative astronomical measurement. These included the sundial, water clocks, and the merkhet[54] (which, used a straight-edge and a plumb line, enabled measurements of stellar azimuths).

The precise alignment of temples and pyramids from astronomical observations.[50]

Knowledge of stellar constellations. At least 43 constellations were familiar to the Egyptians in the 13th century B.C.[55]

The writing of astronomy texts. Clement of Alexandria gives the titles of four Egyptian astronomy books[56] (which have not survived): a) On the Disposition of Fixed Stars and Stellar Phenomena, b) On the Disposition of the Sun, Moon, and Five Planets, c) On the Syzygies and Phases of the Sun and Moon, d) On Risings. These texts may not have been intended for publication, but were available only to the priesthood. James[57] has stressed that the Egyptian religion forbade the general disclosure of their philosophy. This may help to explain why so little of Egyptian science has come down to us directly from the Egyptians, but rather indirectly from Greeks such as Pythagoras, who was initiated into the Egyptian mysteries.

Tables of star culminations and risings.[51,56]

Knowledge of planetary astronomy. Five planets were known to the Egyptians[55]; the retrograde motion of Mars was known[55]; the revolution of Mercury and Venus around the Sun was known.[55,22]

Prediction of eclipses.[55]

Discovery of the occultations of the stars and planets by the dark side of the half-moon.[58]

Discovery that the earth is spherical. The first measurement of the radius of the earth was made by Eratosthenes (b. 275 B.C.), who was head of the great library of Alexandria.[59] He was born in Cyrene, in what is now Libya. It seems likely that the ancient Egyptians, much before Egypt's conquest by Alexander the Great, had already grasped the idea of a spherical earth,[60,61] and it was from them that this doctrine was adopted by Pythagoras, who, as we know, spent many years of study in Egypt.

Discovery of the obliquity of the ecliptic. Diodorus Siculus (70 B.C.) reports that the Egyptian priests claimed it was from them Oenopides of Chios learned the sun moved in an inclined orbit and oppositely to the motion of the other stars.[62] In this connection, it should be noted that the priority of Oenopides' claim to this discovery is disputed by Pythagoras.[62] In view of the fact that both Pythagoras and Oenopides went to Egypt to study astronomy,[63,64] it would seem only fair to give their Egyptian teachers at least some of the credit.

Discovery of the precession of the equinoxes. The "precession of the equinoxes" refers to the very slow, cyclic changes in the coordinates of the fixed stars that takes place with a period of some 26,000 years. The discovery of this phenomenon can be divided into three stages. The first stage took place in Egypt, where the successive realignment of the axes of symmetry of various temples noted by Lockyer[65] showed that the Egyptians were aware of the change in positions of stars over the course of centuries. (The orientations of Egyptian temples were set with extreme precision by astronomical observations in accordance with their worship of the stars or the sun.) The second stage consisted in the measurement of the rate of rotation of the celestial sphere. Hipparchus (b. circa 190 B.C.; d. 125 B.C.) is generally credited with the first measurement, although some have given priority to the Egyptian astronomers.[66] The third stage consisted in a dynamical explanation of the effect, first given by Isaac Newton in the *Principia*.

First proof that the angular diameters of the sun and moon are unequal. Sosigenes (second century A.D.), the Egyptian astronomer who gave Europe the Julian calendar, showed that the angular diameters are unequal by adverting to the phenomenon of annular eclipses of the sun.[67]

First use of the clepsydra (water-clock) to measure the angular diameter of the sun.[67]

Discovery of the conjunction of the planets with each other as well as with the fixed stars. This is on the testimony of Aristotle in his *Meterology.*[68]

The heliocentric theory of the rotation of the earth and other planets about the sun. Elsewhere we have discussed Newton's belief that the heliocentric hypothesis originated in Egypt. Here we will add the remark that most historians of science credit Aristarchus of Samos with this discovery. About Aristarchus' life, little is known other than that he was born in the Greek island of Samos and lived circa 310-230 B.C.; just where, it is not known. He is also known to have been a pupil of Straton of Lampsacus,[69] an Alexandrian scholar who helped found the Museum there.[70] The principle basis for crediting Aristarchus with this discovery seems to be a passage from archimedes, quoted in full by Heath.[71] But a careful reading of the passage shows that although Aristarchus is charged with backing a heliocentric theory (Archimedes was opposed to this theory), nowhere is he said to be the *first* to advance such a theory. So Heath's argument for Aristarchus' priority seems pretty thin. It is quite possible, in fact probable, since Alexandria was the leading center for astronomy, that Aristarchus worked in Egypt in Alexandria, where his teacher Straton had been, and there heard of, and became convinced of the truth of this Egyptian theory. At any rate, we choose to follow Newton in assigning credit to the Egyptians as the probably originators of the heliocentric theory.

Ptolemy's Almagest. This was the treatise which became the Bible of world astronomy for over a thousand years. Written in Alexandria about 150 A.D. by an Alexandrian, in all probability an Egyptian.

Conclusion

In the preceding sections, we have set forth arguments supporting the thesis that Newton's theories of motion and universal gravitation were not born simply as a result of Newton's Great Intuition, but rather were the fruition of an intellectual tradition whose origins can be traced back to the African science that flourished millenia earlier in dynastic Egypt. To emphasize the extraordinary vitality of that Egyptian science, we have highlighted some of its achievements in astronomy, one of the important components of that tradition leading to the Newtonian Synthesis. As we have seen, each stage in the transmission of this tradition featured the work of scientists (like Aristarchus, Eratosthenes, Alhazen,

Copernicus, and Newton himself) who both inherited the work of the past, and made additional contributions of their own.

In closing, we should note that there is another aspect of the analysis of the origins of scientific advances such as those made by Newton as well as the scientists who paved the way for him. This other aspect, which we will not attempt to explore here, concerns the economic factors which help to propel scientific research forward. A number of authors have discussed the economic and social roots of the *Principia*, starting with the pioneering work of Boris Hessen.[72] Similar studies made for the case of the Nile Valley culture would be of great value in understanding the genesis of Egyptian science.

The author is indebted to Janet Harden and Beatrice Lumpkin in the preparation of this paper.

Notes

1. The New Columbia Encyclopedia. New York: Columbia University Press, 1975, p. 1929.

2. B.L. van der Waerden, *Science Awakening*, Vol. II. New York: Oxford University Press, 1974, p. XV.

3. Louis T. More, *Isaac Newton*, p. 326.

4. Richard S. Westfall, *Never a Rest: A Biography of Isaac Newton*. New York: Cambridge University Press, 1980, p. 151.

5. Wm. A. Wallace (Tr.), *Galileo's Early Notebooks*. Notre Dame, Ind.: University of Notre Dame Press, 1977, pp. 36, 59-60, 71-72, 74 and 76. Also see Stillman Drake, *Galileo Studies*. Ann Arbor, University of Michigan Press, 1970, p. 35.

6. James Weishepl, "Galileo and his Precursors", in: E. McMullin (ed.), *Galileo, Man of Science*. New York: Basic Books, 1968, p. 96.

7. H. Eves, *Introduction to the History of Mathematics* (Rev. Ed.). New York: Holt, Reinhart & Winston, 1964, p. 142.

8. A. Reymond, *History of the Sciences in the Greco-Roman Antiquity*. London: Methuen (1927). Tr. by Ruth G. DeBray, p. 71.

9. J.D. Bernal, *Science in History* (2nd ed.). New York: Cameron, 1956, p. 293.

10. Carl B. Boyer, *A History of Mathematics*. New York: Wiley, 1968, p. 273.

11. G. Sarton, *Introduction to the History of Science*. Vol. I Baltimore: The Williams & Wilkins Co., 1927, p. 422.

12. Stillman Drake, op. cit., p. 22.

13. Stillman Drake, "Velocity and Eudoxian Proportion Theory", Physics, 1973, 15: 49-64.

14. G.J. Allman, *Greek Geometry*. Dublin, 1889, p. 133.

15. Alexander Pogo, "Egyptian Water Clocks," Isis *25*, 403-425, 1936.

16. Silvio Bedini, "The Instruments of Galileo Galilei," in: *Galileo, Man of Science*. (E.A. McMullin, ed.). New York: Basic Books, 1968, p. 258.

17. Sarton, op. cit., p. 721.

18. Thomas Kuhn, *The Copernican Revolution*. Cambridge, Mass.: Harvard University Press, 1957, p. 135.

19. Sir Thomas Heath, *Aristarchus of Samos*. London: Oxford University Press, 1913, pp. 94, 304-306.

20. Gomperz, *Griechische Denker*. Quoted in Heath, op. cit., p. 125.

21. Heath, op. cit., p. 258.

22. Giorgio Abetti, *The History of Astronomy*. New York: Henry Schuman, Inc., 1951, p. 21.

23. Sir Thomas Heath, op. cit., p. 259.

24. Westfall, op. cit., p. 434.

25. Kuhn, op. cit., pp. 136, 141.

26. Francis R. Johnson, *Astronomical Thought in Renaissance England*. Baltimore: The Johns Hopkins Press, 1937, p. 96.

27. E.A. Burtt, *The Metaphysical Foundations of Modern Physical Science*. New York: 1925, pp. 40-44.

28. J.L.E. Dreyer, *History of the Planetary Systems from Thales to Kepler*. Cambridge: 1905, pp. 306-308.

29. John North, "The Medieval Background to Copernicus", in: A. Beer (ed.), *Vistas in Astronomy Vol. 17*. Oxford: Pergamon Press, 1975.

30. Otto Neugebauer, "On the Planetary Theory of Copernicus", in: A. Beer (ed.), *Vistas in Astronomy Vol. 10*. Oxford, Pergamon, Press, 1968, pp. 89-103.

31. Sarton, op. cit., p. 602.

32. Fritz Krafft, "Nicolaus Copernicus and Johannes Kepler: New Astronomy from Old Astronomy", in: A. Beer and P. Beer (eds.), *Vistas in Astronomy Vol. 18*. Oxford: Pergamon, 1975.

33. R.S. Westman, "Continuities in Kepler Scholarship", in *Vistas in Astronomy Vol. 18*. (see Ref. 32).

34. Fritz Krafft, "Keplers Beitrag zur Himmelphysik", in the series "Arbor Scientiarium: Beitrage zur Wissenschaftgeschichte" (Verlag, Dr. H.A. Gerstenberg, Hildesheim, 1973).

35. Westfall, op. city., p. 100.

36. Boyer, op. cit., chap. 17.

37. Eves, op. cit., p. 149.

38. James Gow, *A Short History of Greek Mathematics*. New York: G.E. Stechert & Co., 1884 (1923 reprint), pp. 107-108.

39. Eves, op. cit., p. 151.

40. Quoted by Westfall, op. cit., p. 510.

41. Quoted by Westfall, op. cit., p. 434.

42. Westfall, op. cit., p. 434.

43. J.E. McGuire and P.M. Rattansi, "Newton and the Pipes of Pan", Notes and Records of the Royal Society of London, *21*, (1966), p. 110.

44. McGuire and Rattansi, op. cit., pp. 108-143.

45. William Wilson (tr.), *The Writings of Clement of Alexandria*. 2 vols. Edinburgh: T & T Clark, 1868.

46. Sir Thomas Heath, *Greek Astronomy*, New York: AMS Press, repr. 1932, ed., 1969, p. xx.

47. George G.M. James, *The Stolen Legacy*, New York: *The Philosophical Library*, 1954. Reprinted by Julian Richards Associates, Publishers, San Francisco. 1976.

48. Otto Neugebauer, *A History of Ancient Mathematical Astronomy*, Part 1, Berlin: Springer Verlag, 1975, p. 559.

49. Neugebauer, ibid., p. 3.

50. E.C. Krupp (ed.), *In Search of Ancient Astronomies*. New York: McGraw-Hill, 1978, p. 203.

51. George Sarton, *A History of Science: Ancient Science Through the Golden Age of Greece*. New York: W.W. Norton, 1952, p. 30.

52. Quoted by Van der Waerden, op. cit., p. 37.

53. René Taton (ed.), *History of Science: Ancient and Medieval Science*. New York: Basic Books, p. 35.

54. Taton, ibid., p. 39.

55. Sir Thomas Heath, *Greek Astronomy*. New York: AMS Press (1969) reprint of 1932 ed.), p. xv.

56. Van der Waerden, op. cit., p. 40.

57. James, op. cit., p. 13.
58. Sir Thomas Heath, *Aristarchus of Samos*. Oxford: Oxford University Press, 1913, p. 220.
59. E.A. Parsons, *The Alexandrian Library*. Amsterdam: The Elsevier Press, 1952, p. 145.
60. Heath, *Aristarchus of Samos*, p. 48 (see reference citing the authorities Martin and Berger).
61. Heath, *Greek Astronomy*. New York, 1932, p. xxvi.
62. Quoted by Heath, *Aristarchus of Samos*, p. 131.
63. Gow, op. cit., p. 131.
64. Sarton, *History of Science: Ancient Science through the Golden Age of Greece*, op. cit., p. 200.
65. Heath, *Aristarchus of Samos*, pp. 101-105.
66. Norman Lockyer, *The Dawn of Astronomy*. Cambridge, Mass.: The MIT Press, 1964.
67 Heath, *Aristarchus of Samos*, op. cit., p. 313.
68. Van der Waerden, op. cit., p. 37.
69. Heath, *Aristarchus of Samos*, op. cit., p. 299.
70. George Sarton, *A History of Science: Hellenistic Science and Culture in the Last Three Centuries B.C.*, Cambridge, Mass.: Harvard University Press, 1959, p. 54.
71. Heath, *Aristarchus of Samos*, op. cit., p. 302.
72. B. Hessen, "The Social and Economic Roots of Newton's *Principia*", in: *Science at the Crossroads*, ed. by Gary Wersky, London: Frank Cass, 1978, (reprint of 1931 ed.).

MATHEMATICS AND ENGINEERING IN THE NILE VALLEY

Beatrice Lumpkin

For thousands of years, the Nile Valley was the Main Street of the civilized world. Especially in mathematics and the natural sciences, Egyptian scholars played a major role in building the foundations of our modern science. Yet the full scale of this African contribution is either little known, or attributed to other peoples. This paper will give a brief outline of the 4,000 years of Nile Valley pre-eminence in mathematics, with some reference to the engineering and technology which developed hand-in-hand with mathematics.

Many factors placed the Nile Valley in such an advantageous position. As Bernal points out, productive periods of science are based on a flourishing economy and technology.[1] And in the Nile Valley there was the needed combination of good physical resources and inventive people, people who were the first to grow food, to build brick houses and to develop writing.

Important stages that preceded the modern age in mathematics included the prehistoric, ancient, classical, Middle Ages and the Renaissance. In each of these periods, the mathematics of the Nile Valley played a leading role. In fact, the first task of the European Renaissance concerned the need to bring Europe up to the higher level of African and Asian knowledge, then expressed in the Muslim civilization.

The mathematical and scientific tradition of the Nile Valley was a continuous one. Yet in all the "standard" histories, Egyptian mathematics is dismembered into three parts, with only the first recognized as Egyptian. These texts arbitrarily bring ancient Egyptian mathematics to an abrupt end with the Greek conquest of the Egyptian state. The second part of Egyptian mathematics, from the founding of Alexandria in −332 (i.e., B.C.), up to 500, is not usually recognized as Egyptian, but as "Hellenistic." In this paper, I will use the more accurate term of "classical Egyptian."

The third era of Egyptian learning, also not recognized as Egyptian in the standard histories, is the Muslim period of the Middle Ages. As a whole, contributions of the Muslim culture are slighted in histories permeated by a Eurocentric bias—the belief that no one but Europeans made important contributions to knowledge. Almost completely left out, the work of African mathematicians and scientists of that period remains little known.

Continuity of Egyptian Science

The continuity and pre-eminence of Nile Valley mathematics and science is a concept based on historical fact. The language changed—Greek after Alexander's conquest and Arabic after the Muslim conquest. But the change in language did not represent a change of culture and tradition.[2] Historians have not been consistent in recognizing this continuity, as in Otto Neugebauer's *Exact Sciences in Antiquity:*

> Indeed mathematics of the Hellenistic period, and still more of the later periods, is in part only a link in the unbroken tradition which reaches from the earliest periods of ancient history down to the beginnings of modern times."[3]

Yet in another part of the same book, Neugebauer makes the highly prejudiced statement: "The role of Egyptian mathematics is probably best described as a retarding force upon numerical procedures."[4] Such an unhistoric judgment is much like faulting the inventor of the crystal radio for not inventing solid state television first.

The Beginnings

We must go back to the beginnings of the human race for the beginnings of science, because wherever there are humans, there is, already, the chemistry of fire. Wherever there are humans, there is mathematics, because every language has number words, and the concepts of logic needed for mathematics—the words "and", "or."[5] Since Africa is widely believed to be the birth place of the human race, it follows that Africa was the birthplace of mathematics and science.

Before the beginning of writing, people did record numbers. A fossil bone found near Lake Edwards, Zayre, was carved in year −8000 to make a very early record of numbers that may be a multiplication table,[6] a record of phases of the moon,[7] or even a game score.[8] The tally marks carved in the Ishango bone show numbers 3, 6, a space, 4, 8, then 10, 5, 5, 7 on one side. On the other side are 11, 21, 19, 9, 11, 13, 17, 19.

Although the Ishango bone was found in the Lakes region, the connection to the Nile Valley is immediate. The Ishango people have been traced, through their bone harpoons, down the length of the Nile valley, either by commerce or direct migration.[9]

By the earliest time of recorded Egyptian history, a 360 day calendar (with 5 holidays added) was well established. But there is little agreement on the date of first use. From the astronomical information in the calendar, and based on the Sothic cycle of about 1,460 years (heliacal rising of Sirius) the start-up date of the calendar could be given as −4241 or −2773.[10] Struik argued for the later date, claiming that people, "slowly emerging from neolithic conditions," could not have developed such a calendar.[11] But available evidence argues for earlier dates. Agriculture began much earlier than −4241,[12] giving "Stone Age" man both the incentive and the opportunity to make the astronomical observations necessary for a calendar. Indeed, Diop reminds us that many years of study of the

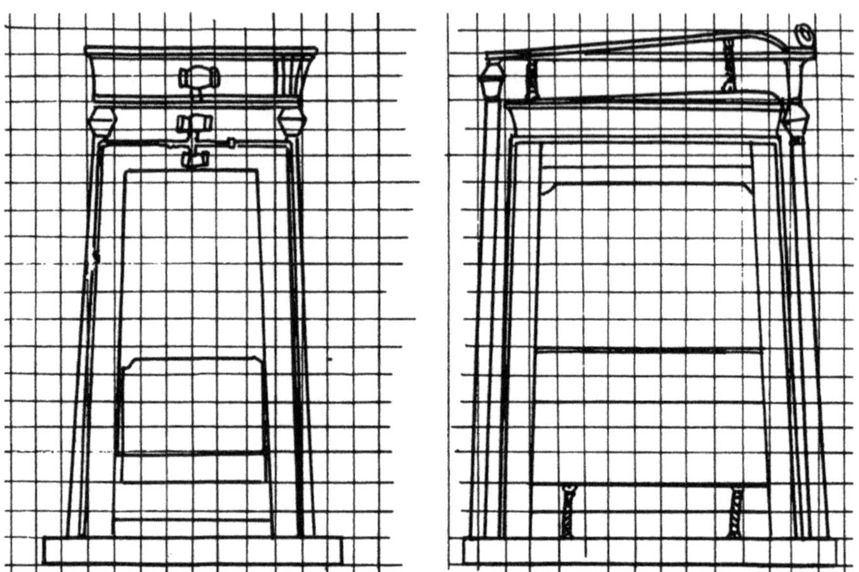

Front and side views of a shrine from Ghorab. (Adapted by Peggy Lipschutz from Clarke and Engelbach, *Ancient Egyptian Masonry*, Fig. 48.) Cited as proof that Egyptians did draw objects from different aspects. Note the square grid used to preserve proportions during construction from the plans.

star cycles were necessary before a calendar could be formalized.[13] Even the date of the origin of Egyptian hieroglyphs and the pharaonic institution has been pushed back in time, and southward in location, by the findings of Bruce Williams and his colleagues.[14]

The Glorious Ancient Egyptians

We may not know the full scope of ancient Egyptian mathematics, but fortunately a few primary sources survived the grave robbers. A few mathematical papyri, limestone chips and leather rolls outline many achievements of ancient Egyptian mathematics. The longest, written by the scribe Ahmose, is known as the "Rhind Mathematical Papyrus", after the Scot who brought it to Europe. We also have books by Greek classical mathematicians in which they fully acknowledged their debt to Egypt.

The first cipherization of numbers took place in Egypt—a huge step forward for human science. Instead of single tally marks to represent numbers, as on the Ishango bone, hieroglyphic numerals used special symbols for powers of 10.

Egyptian arithmetic made use of the commutative, associative and distributive properties of multiplication. Egyptian multiplication needed no memorization of multiplication tables and was well suited to the additive nature of Egyptian numerals. For 32 × 19, they changed to 19 × 32 and proceeded to double:

–1	32	Using just the partial products checked
–2	64	to give 19 in the left column, we add:
4	128	
8	256	
–16	512	

	1	32
	2	64
	16	512
total	19	608

Although problems always involved specific values, they were often followed by a statement of general procedure, a formula.[15] The derogatory claim that Egyptians were limited to solving practical problems and had no interest in the theoretical is refuted by the facts. Certainly, the Egyptian forerunner of the Mother Goose rhyme, "As I was going to St. Ives, I met a man with seven wives . . .", had no narrow, practical purpose. It is problem 79 of the Ahmose papyrus which lists: 7 houses, 49 cats, 343 mice, 2,401 spelt, 16,807 hekat, and the sum of 19,607![16]

Problem 79 seems, "just for fun." Its mathematical significance will be described later. But the path from ancient Egypt to Mother Goose went through Italy where Fibonacci, after study in Egypt, wrote: "Seven old women went to Rome: each woman had seven mules; each mule carried seven sacks; each sack contained seven loaves: and with each loaf were seven knives; each knife was put up in seven sheaths."[17]

Fractions

It is a measure of the advanced Egyptian technology that fractions became necessary very early. The vast construction projects for pyramids, irrigation works, temples and obelisks required accurate measurement of lengths, areas and volumes. Tens of thousands of workers received pay according to fixed rates and provisions had to be divided among members of a work crew.

The concept of fraction was the concept of inverse of integers, or unit fractions of numerator one. Fractions were at the heart of the Egyptian arithmetic, according to Richard J. Gillings, a devoted encyclopedist of ancient Egyptian mathematics.[18] The scribes performed operations that were breathtakingly complex. For example, the proof in problem 33 of the Ahmose papyrus requires the addition of 16 + 1/56 + 1/679 + 1/776 + 10 + 2/3 + 1/84 + 1/1358 + 1/4074 + 1/1164 + 8 + 1/112 + 1/1358 + 1/1552 + 2 + 1/4 + 1/28 + 1/392 + 1/4753 + 1/5432. The sum is 37! The Egyptians used their equivalent of the least common denominator and red helping numbers (new numerators) to find the answer.[19]

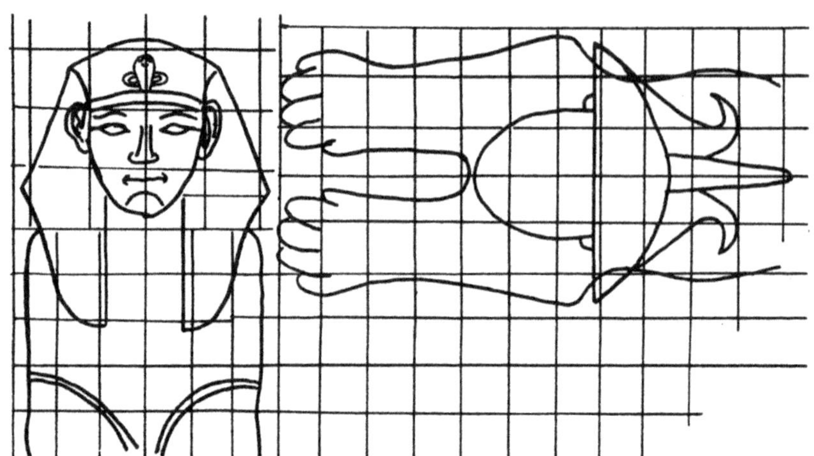

Working drawing for sculpture of a sphinx. (Adapted by Peggy Lipschutz from Heinrich Schafer, *Principles of Egyptian Art*. London: Clarendon, 1974, p. 329.) Common use of grid of squares led to concept of coordinates.

Such complex problems were not easily mastered by some modern translators. Breasted judged that "Fractions, however, caused difficulty."[20] That may be true for some historians. But the virtuosity of the scribes turned their fractions into a very useful tool. These same Egyptian fractions were used by scientists for thousands of years after their invention, right up to the modern period.

Aha Calculus

Aha, or heap, was used as an abstract term for the unknown in an equation, leading historians to call Egyptian algebra, "aha calculus." Equations were solved by a method now called, "false position", which continued in use until the 20th century. A simple example from Ahmose asks for a quantity and its 1/7, whose sum is 19. To find the quantity, Ahmose assumed a false answer of 7. In this case 7 is a convenient choice as the least common denominator. But 7 plus 1/7 of 7 gives 8, not the desired 19. To get 19 from 8, we must multiply 8 by 19/8. Then the correction factor for the assumed false answer is 19/8. Use 19/8 × 7 to get 16 + 5/8, the correct answer. Of course, the Egyptians wrote 5/8 as unit fractions, 1/2 + 1/4.[21]

Until recent times, the rules used by Ahmose to convert common fractions to unit fractions were not seriously investigated. Gillings, the only "Western" historian to write a book-length study of "Mathematics in the Time of the Pharaohs", has proposed some possible formulas. Other scholars are now beginning to join this interesting study.

Problem 61B of Ahmose clearly states the Egyptian rule for finding 2/3 of any odd unit fraction: "The making of 2/3 of a fraction uneven. If it is said to thee, what is 2/3 of 1/5. Make thou times of it 2, times 6 of it; 2/3 of it this is. Behold does one according the like for fraction every uneven which may occur" ($2/3 \times 1/5 = 1/10 + 1/30$).[22] With this statement, the scribe gave a general formula.

Series, Arithmetic and Geometric

Many Ahmose problems involved arithmetic and geometric series arising from wage scales and division-of-bread problems connected with the complex economy and class structure. These problems also shed light on one of the greatest Egyptian achievements, the organization and administration of thousands of people into coherent work forces encompassing many trades and professions.

Just to bring back the stone for a large sarcophagus, King Menthuhotep IV sent 10,000 people to the Hammamat quarry.[23] Then what were the numbers needed to build the huge pyramids? And what were the principles of organization used to coordinate the work teams, to assure a supply of materials and to feed tens of thousands of workers. How many bookkeepers did it take to divide the wages according to scales that went from the lowest to 35 times greater pay at the top?

Ahmose problem 64 asks how to divide 10 hekats of grain among 10 men so that there is a constant difference of 1/8 between portions. Ahmose solves this problem in arithmetic series by a method equivalent to our modern formula. (Arithmetic series have a constant difference between successive terms, for example, 5 + 10 + 15 + 20 + 25 etc.)

Steps	Ahmos	Formula
1. Find the average share	10/10=1	s/n
2. Subtract 1 from 10 to get the number of differences	9	n–1
3. Take half the given difference	½×1/8=1/16	d/2
4. Multiply by the number of differences	9×1/16	d/2(n=1)
5. Add above to average share to find last, highest share, "L"	1+9/16	L=s/n+d/2(n–1)
6. Alternate to steps 5, subtract 9/16 from average share to find lowest term, "a"	1–9/16	2=s/n–d/2(n–1)

Transposing in 6 gives the modern formula, $s = n/2\,(2a + (n-1)d)$. Ahmose's answers in modern terms were: 7/16, 9/16, 11/16, 13/16... up to 1 + 9/16.[24]

Geometric series were also carefully studied. For example. Problem 79, 7 houses with 7 cats each, each got 7 mice, each of whom ate 7 spelts of grain, each of which would have produced 7 hekats of grain, was mentioned earlier. But Ahmose never wasted words. He only listed a second column which shows us further knowledge of geometric series:

1	2801
2	5602
4	11204
7	19607

Here 2,801 = 1 + 7 + 49 + 343 + 2401, according to Gillings.[25]

Long before the Ahmose papyrus was written, Egyptian mathematicians were already guiding the construction of pyramids, measuring the seked (cotangent) to guarantee that the pyramid would be stable. The first example of the use of rectangular coordinates comes from Egypt, a natural step beyond the square grids widely used to transfer art details in correct proportions. Of the thousands of construction plans, only a few have come down to us. One of these gives the height and horizontal spacing for constructing a curved surface, using the same principle of rectangular coordinates found in modern graphs.[26]

Had we not had the luck to find this one remnant, we might not have known that the Egyptians used rectangular coordinates in their building plans. The same is true of the Moscow and Berlin papyruses, known after the museums where they are now housed. Had we not had these papyrus fragments, we would have been unaware of the higher level reached in these problems which include second degree equations, and the formula for the area of a curved surface.

Berlin problem 1 asks for the size of two squares, the sum of whose areas equals a square of 100 square cubits, given that the side of the smaller square is 3/4 the side of the other unknown square.

If the unknown squares are of sides x and y, in modern symbols we have: $x = \frac{3}{4}y$ and $x^2 + y^2 = 100$.

Assuming the false position value of 1 for the side of the larger square, then the smaller would be ¾, and the sum of the two areas would be 1 + 9/16. Since it is the side, not area we are looking for, we need the square root of 1 + 9/16, which the Egyptians found correct to be 1¼. Since the square root of the desired 100 square cubits is 10 cubits, the correction factor is 10 divided by 1¼. We get the correct values for the sides, 8 and 6 cubits, by multiplying first 1, then ¾ by the correction factor. The proof? Areas of squares side 8 and side 6 are 64 + 36 square cubits, and their sum is 100, as required.[27]

Geometry

This problem of the sum of two squares, equal in area to a third square, and sides 6, 8, 10, resembles an application of the "Pythagorean theorem. Another such relationship is built into the Egyptian measurements of length which include cubits, double remens equal to the diagonal of a 1-cubit square, and remens.

Areas can be doubled by changing units from cubits to double remens, or halved by going from cubit to remen measure. These specific examples of Pythagorean triples indicate that Egyptians were conducting investigations that could lead to the formulation of the so-called Pythagorean theorem.[28]

Yet the style in Western historiography is to deny any possibility that ancient Egyptians contributed to the development of this theorem—that the sum of the squares of the sides of a right triangle is equal to the square on the hypotenuse. Some claim that the Babylonians were far superior because their clay tablet, Plimpton 322, contains a long list of Pythagorean triples. Of course, clay tablets of Babylonia proved more durable, although in their day they were less convenient than the Egyptian papyrus. The few, fragile pieces of surviving papyri give us only part of the achievements of ancient Egypt. Disparaging comparisons are not only unwarranted but detract from both the great African and Asian civilizations. And why is this theorem still known after Pythagoras when he came on the scene 1,000 years later?

The Moscow papyrus, although in poor condition, reveals two of the highest achievements of the ancient Egyptian geometers. The volume of a truncated pyramid, cut off at the top, was correctly found. Even more breathtaking, in Moscow problem 10, there is the correct formula for the area of a hemisphere, according to Gillings.[29] A possible method of measuring this area is illustrated in Lumpkin's, *Senefer and Hatshepsut.*[30] Another achievement was the accurate measurement of π as 3.16, compared to the modern 3.14 and the Biblical value of 3.

Classical Period of Egyptian Science

What happened to ancient Egyptian mathematics after the Greek conquest? It is the theme of this paper that ancient Egyptian mathematics did not die but blended into the new mathematics of the classical period, built on the base of the ancients. As Greek city states developed, a few Greeks had traveled to Egypt to study. Thales (c. −600) is credited with being the first to bring the study of geometry from Egypt to Greece. In all arrogance, some historians call Thales the first mathematician, as the first to give a deductive proof. Half a century later, Pythagoras spent 20 years in Egypt and also visited Mesopotamia before founding a school in Crotona, Southern Italy.[31] Democritus of Abdera (c. −400) also spent time in Egypt and boasted that not even the rope stretchers of Egypt surpassed him.

The Egyptian city of Alexandria, founded in −332, became the greatest center of classical mathematics. Most Egyptian mathematicians of the classical period wrote in the Greek language. But that did not make them Greek, any more than the current use of English by Japanese scientists makes them English or North American.

Alexandria, itself, was peopled by Egyptians and a few people from

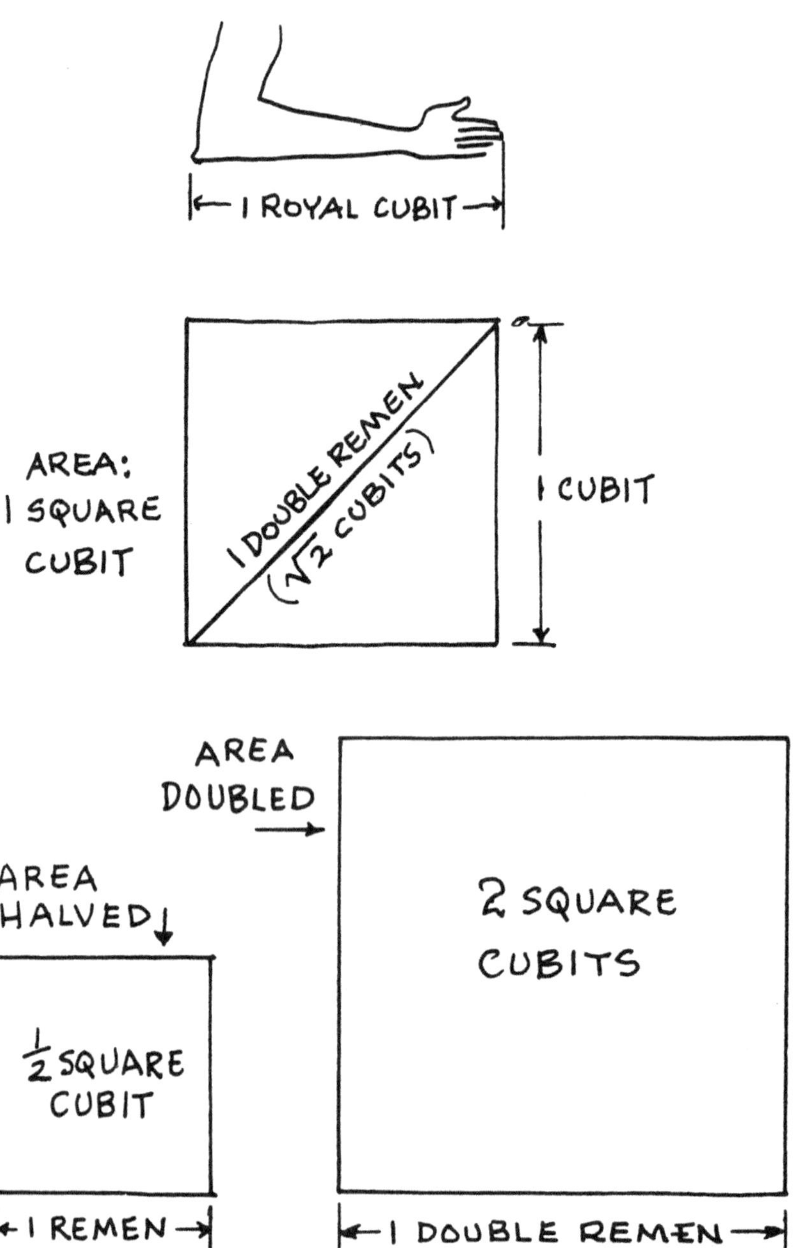

Egyptian Measurements. Relationships between cubit, double remen, and remen give an example of so-called Pythagorean theorem that $1^2 + 1^2 = (\sqrt{2}\,)^2$. (From Lumpkin, *Senefer and Hatshepsut*, p. 55)

neighboring countries. George Sarton, the respected encyclopedist of the history of science, reminds us that, "Greek emigrants were too few in pre-Christian times and too little interested in science and scholarship to affect and change Eastern minds."[32] Then why, we must ask, is this period of Alexandrian science not credited to the African people of Alexandria, the people of the Nile Valley?

Euclid of Alexandria, one of the greatest mathematicians of this era, lived and died in Egypt. There is no suggesion that he ever left Africa. Yet he is pictured in textbooks as a fair, European Greek, not as an Egyptian. We have no pictures of these ancients, but we could at least visualize them honestly, in costumes, complexions and features true to their peoples and their times. George Sarton decried the historical forgery of fabricating pictures of mathematicians, but the racist aspect, representing Egyptians as Europeans, is even more serious.

Euclid's fame rests above all on his *Elements*, containing 13 books and 465 propositions.[34] The logical arrangement of this work is so masterful, that the *Elements* has dominated the teaching of geometry for 2,000 years. The deductive method of proof did more than add rigor to the largely experimental geometry of earlier Egyptians. With the deductive method, new theorems could be proved, allowing mathematics to progress beyond the immediate needs of the economy of that time. The practical side of mathematics continued, side by side with the theoretical.

The first person to measure the circumference of the earth accurately, Eratosthenes of Cyrene, Libya, was also African born.[35] He measured the shadow cast by the sun in Alexandria the same day that the sun shone down a deep well in Syene, 500 miles south. The shadow showed an angle of 1/50 of a circle from zenith, directly overhead. Multiplying the 500 miles by 50 gave 25,000 compared to the modern 24,830 miles, an error of only .6 of 1%. Eratosthenes is also known for his "sieve" for prime numbers.

In trigonometry, Egyptians had always been pre-eminent, up to and including the Middle Ages. The ancients had used the concept of the seked or cotangent as a guide in building the pyramids. Menelaus of Alexandria (c. 100) laid the foundations for spherical trigonometry and its application to astronomy. He was followed by another great Egyptian, half a century later, Ptolemy of Alexandria, author of the *Almagest*. Known as an astronomer, his work in trigonometry alone would have assured his fame. To aid him in the extensive calculations needed for his astronomical tables, Ptolemy developed formulas for the sines and cosines of the sum and differences of two angles and half angles. His tables remained in use for 1,000 years. Ptolemy also improved on the excellent ancient Egyptian approximation of π with his value of 377/120, $\approx$ 3.14167.[36]

In this same period, the mathematician and engineering genius, Heron of Alexandria, invented 100 machines and wrote extensive mathematical works. He is one Alexandrian often acknowledged as Egyptian, but for the wrong reasons. Eves follows other historians in describing Heron as Egyptian: "At any rate, his

Area of a hemisphere. The Moscow Papyrus correctly gives the area of a hemisphere as the area of two great circles of the sphere, or twice the area of the base of the hemisphere. This formula could have been checked approximately by counting the number of squares drawn on a large hemisphere and comparing with the number of squares of the same size, drawn on the base (From *Senefer and Hatshepsut*, p. 126)

writings, which so often aim at practical utility rather than theoretical completeness, show a curious blend of the Greek and Oriental.''[37] Indeed, isn't it strange that nationality or race should be deduced from the nature of a person's writings, rather than place of birth and homeland?

On the same grounds, Diophantus of Alexandria is judged to have been Egyptian, because his mathematical work had a practical orientation. Often considered "the father of algebra", Diophantus introduced efficient, algebraic abbreviations and proposed problems which inspired Fermat, the great 17th century mathematician.

Longer than any other city, Alexandria endured as a scientific center. Its last days of the classical period were highlighted by the short, brilliant career of Hypatia, a woman algebraist who held the chair of the department of philosophy at the University of Alexandria. In 415, a fanatical Christian mob brutally murdered Hypatia, literally tearing her apart. Some textbooks "picture" Hypatia as a white European, although she was born in Egypt, the daughter of Theon, also an Egyptian. Her prominence as a department chair was certainly in the Egyptian tradition of greater rights for women as compared to the near slave status of Greek women.

The Alexandria of Euclid, Ptolemy, Heron, Diophantus, Hypatia, Pappus, Menelaus, Theon, Proclus and many more, was Egyptian in every sense. Its economy was nourished by the productive agriculture of the Nile as well as the commerce between the Nile and the Mediterranean. Its population was Egyptian, and the number of immigrants, as Sarton said above, was small. As for all the Egyptians named Ptolemy in the first century, if they were descended at all from Alexander's general, after 15 generations they were Egyptians, in every sense of the word.

Egyptian Mathematics in the Middle Ages

With Hypatia murdered in 415, and the death of Proclus of Alexandria in 485, any possible later works of the Alexandrians have not survived. But by the year 750, Islam began to revive centers of learning and Euclid's *Elements*, Ptolemy's *Almagest* etc. appeared in Arabic. In the Nile Valley, a new center of learning arose in the city we call Cairo. But in Europe, little if anything was left of the mathematical schools. For lack of anyone to read and understand the great classics, even the books were lost.

In the 9th century, a textbook on Muslim arithmetic and algebra was brought into Europe from North Africa. It introduced the Europeans to Arabic numerals. Laws were passed forbidding their use, but the spread of Arabic numerals could not be stopped. The Arabic-Hindu numerals were vastly superior to the Roman numerals then used in Europe. Our word for algebra was taken from the name of this famous text, *Al-jabr wa'l muqabalah*. From the author's name, al-Khwarizmi, came our word for "algorithm", a mathematical procedure.

Al Khwarizmi stated that his purpose in writing his book was to serve the practical needs of the people concerning matters of inheritance, legacies, partition, lawsuits and commerce.[38]

Just a few years after Khwarizmi, a more advanced algebra was written by a

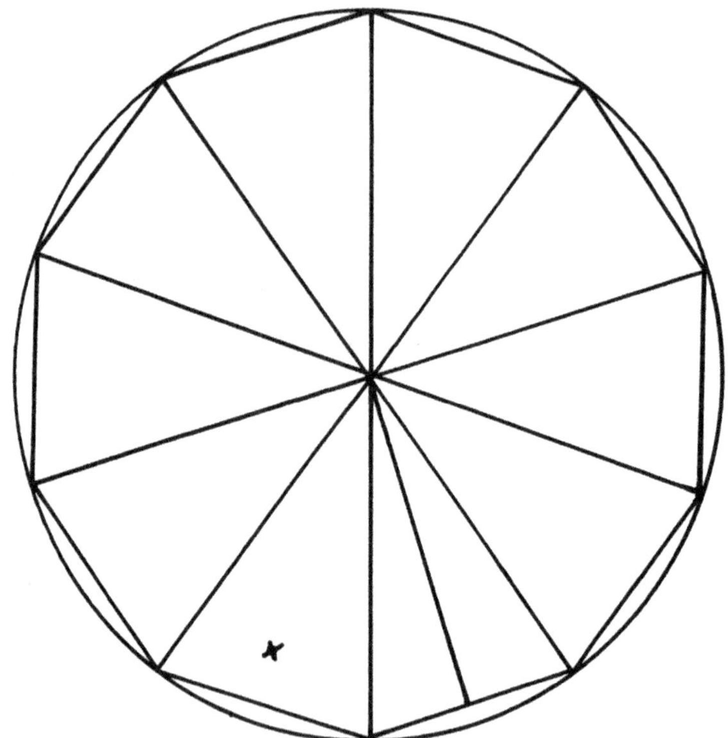

Abu Kamil's decagon (with construction line added). Area, 100; unknown side $x\ ^{7}$ 3.6

man called, "the Egyptian calculator", al-Hasib Abu-Kamil Shiya ibn Aslam ibn Muhammad al-Hasib al-Misri (850-930). His work influenced mathematicians for centuries and was copied wholesale by Leonardo of Pisa (Fibonacci), 300 years later. Yet few today know the name of this great African mathematician, Abu Kamil.

New features of Kamil's work included use of several variables—Khwarizmi was restricted to one—a study of equal roots of quadratic equations, and especially the use of irrational numbers as terms of proportions, roots and coefficients of equations. For example, to solve the system:

$$x + y + z = 10$$
$$xz = y^2$$
$$x^2 + y^2 = z^2$$

Kamil used the false position value of $x = 1$. This lead to

$$x + y + z = 1\tfrac{1}{2} + \sqrt{1\tfrac{1}{4}} + \sqrt{1\tfrac{1}{2}} + \sqrt{1\tfrac{1}{4}}$$

Since the right side should have been 10, Kamil set up a proportion to find the correction factor needed.[39] And all of this was done with words, without the advantage of modern symbols, square root signs, etc. Diophantus, an earlier Egyptian, had introduced symbols for squares, cubes, etc. but his lead was not followed until much later. Kamil called the unknown, "the thing", and its square, "mal". Than x^4 he called mal mal, x^6, mal mal mal, etc.[40] Diophantus' work in indeterminate equations was the subject of other work by Kamil, his *Book of Rare Things in Arithmetic*.[41]

Kamil presented 20 geometric problems in *The Decagon and Pentagon*, a work copied extensively by Fibonacci, 300 years later.[42] In one problem Kamil asks for the side of a regular decagon whose area is 100—a specific value. Yet his method is general and his approach is almost entirely algebraic. Step by Step, Kamil finds the unknown side X from $x^{5/8}4 = 1600 - \sqrt{2,048,000}$, (approximately 3.6).[43]

Just a few years after Abu Kamil, Egypt came under the rule of the Fatimids (969-1171). The power of Egypt extended from North Africa to Syria and Western Arabia. There was a general surge of rapid development, economic as well as cultural. Windmills were built in Egypt and other new devices came into use. All of the sciences flourished; "Chemistry, medicine, pharmacology, zoology, botany and mineralogy knew an extraordinary development," wrote Yushkevitch, the Soviet historian of mathematics.[44] Cairo, founded in 969, became the capital and the site of a Science Academy, the Dar el Hikma, or House of Wisdom.

A very well equipped observatory was built on the Mukattam heights. There Ibn Yunus, probably the greatest Muslim astronomer, according to al-Battani and Abu'l Wafa, worked on his famous Hakimi Tables which included observations of eclipses and conjunctions of planets.

Yunus improved on the work of Ptolemy, the Egyptian astronomer of 900 years earlier. In trigonometry, Yunus was the first to use the prosthapherical formula: $\cos A \cos B = \frac{1}{2}(\cos(A+B) + \cos(A-B))$.[45]

For those who doubt that something called prosthapherisis could really simplify anything, Yunus' formula converts multiplication to addition, a simpler operation.[46] Indeed Yunus' method was used by the famous Danish astronomer, Tycho Brahe (1546-1601) and became known to Napier in Scotland. Then Napier used this principle to invent logarithms.[47] Yunus was able to calculate the sine of 1° accurately to 5 decimal places. So accurate were Yunus' calculations, that he succeeded in developing a table of sines for angles differing by just one second.[48]

At the same Cairo Science Academy where Ibn Yunus worked, the Iraqui-born ibn al-Haytham (died c. 1039) did the crowning work of his career. Haytham was famous for his work in optics. Less well known, but of the greatest importance, were Haytham's contributions to mathematics.[49] He developed a formula for the sum of a series of 4th powers which enabled him to evaluate the equivalent of $\int_0^a t^4\, dt$. His original work in geometry was developed by other famous Muslim mathematicians, especially Omar Khayyam and Nasir Eddin. They laid the basis for modern non-Euclidean geometry which describes the curvature of space. It is a fact that Saccheri, the European pioneer in this field in the 18th century, used the work of Muslim mathematicians. The "Saccheri quadrilateral" closely resembled ibn Haytham's quadrilateral of 700 years earlier.[50]

Important discoveries were still made by Muslim mathematicians (the term "Muslim" here is cultural, not religious) as late as the 15th century. Al Kashi in central Asia, developed decimal fractions although Stevin is given credit for their popularization.[51] Al Qasadi of Granada, who died in Africa in 1486, did remarkable work in bringing symbols into algebra, before this development began in Europe. He used the first letters of the Arabic words to show unknown, square, or cube and a symbolic equal sign. The symbolization was so advanced, that Yushkevitch believes there were other Muslim mathematicians, before Qasadi, who began this development.[52] Yet this outstanding work has remained practically unknown here and is still available only to the Arabic speaking world.

In summarizing the contributions of the African Muslim mathematicians, especially those of the Nile Valley, an author is overwhelmed by an embarrassment of riches. These facts have led some historians to revise the standard Euro-centric evaluation—that the Muslim mathematicians added nothing new, and served only to preserve the classics of the Greek mathematicians. Such bias is expressed by Morris Kline, that mathematics, "finally secured a firm grip on life in the highly congenial soil of Greece and waxed strong for a brief period . . . With the decline of Greek civilization, the plant remained dormant for a thousand years . . . when the plant was transported to Europe proper and once more imbedded in fertile soil."[53]

Other writers, for example, J.F. Scott, admit that Muslim mathematicians "did more than preserve; they made some significant contributions of their own."[54] But two pages later, the same writer, in the same book declares that, "The debt which the west owes to the Arabs for their part in preserving and transmitting Greek science is very great. It must not be forgotten, however, that preservation is one thing; creation is something different. Mathematics for its development requires the creative faculty, and there is little evidence of this in the many centuries which separate the decline of Alexandrian science and its revival in the West."[55]

Such unhistoric views are refuted by the same Europeans who borrowed so heavily from the culture of Egypt in the Middle Ages. For example, Leonardo Fibonacci of Pisa wrote:

> All that was studied in Egypt, in Syria, in Greece, in Sicily, and in Provence . . . I investigated very carefully . . . I wanted to write a work of 15 chapters, with nothing capital left without a demonstration and this I did so that the science might be easily understood, and *the Latin people should no longer be deprived of it*.[56]

Conclusion

When Fibonacci wrote these words, Egypt, compared to Italy, was more advanced in science and culture. But unfavorable changes during the rule of the Turkic Mamelukes and the Ottomans slowed down Egyptian development.[57] With the strengthening of feudal structures, the economy of the prosperous Muslim states retrogressed and scientific output declined. While the growth of capitalism and industry was being stifled in Egypt, the merchant capitalists in the city states of Europe were gaining power. Western Europe was also spared the damaging invasions suffered by North Africa and Western and Central Asia.

Still there was a rough parity between Western Europe and many African states in the 15th century. This equality was destroyed, and the economies of African countries were devastated, by the slavery and colonialism that followed. Not only did mathematic and scientific output come to a halt with the disruption of the Nile Valley economy, but even the memory of these achievements was almost destroyed by a flood of misinformation and racism, let loose to justify slavery and imperialism.

This historical account reveals just a part of the mathematic and scientific genius of the people of the Nile Valley. Now suppressed, this genius will be free to produce again when there will be peace and freedom from imperialist oppression. Here, the true history of the achievements of the Nile Valley civilization can play a liberating role by restoring the sense of continuity and identity with a great past, pointing to a great future. In particular, knowledge of the mathematical achievements can help allay "math anxiety" among the descendants of the Nile Valley peoples in Africa and in the Americas.

Notes

1. J.D. Bernal, *Science in History*, Vol. 1, (N.Y.: Cameron, 1954), p. 23.
2. Dirk Struik, *A Concise History of Mathematics*, (N.Y.: Dover, 1967), p. 69.
3. Otto Neugebauer, *Exact Sciences In Antiquity*, (N.Y.: Dover, 1957), p. 146.
4. ibid., p. 80.
5. Karl Menger, lecture on History of Mathematics, I.I.T., 1970.
6. Claudia Zaslavsky, Africa Counts, (N.Y.: Prindle, Weber and Schmidt, 1973), p. 18.
7. Alexander Marshack, *The Roots of Civilization*, (N.Y.: McGraw Hill, 1972), p. 364
8. Ruth Helen Washington, "The Game Hypothesis of Notations on the Ishango Bone", *Journal of African Civilizations*, Vol. 4, No. 1, pp. 102-6
9. Sonia Cole, *The Prehistory of East Africa*, (N.Y.: Macmillan, 1963), p. 251.
10. Carl Boyer, History of Mathematics, (N.Y.: Wiley, 1968), p. 683.
11. Struik, op. cit., pp. 24-5.
12. Fred Wendorf and Rushdi Said, "Palaeolithic Remains in Upper Egypt", *Nature*, Vol. 215, July 15, 1967, pp. 244-247.
13. Cheikh Anta Diop, *The African Origin of Civilization*, (Westport: Lawrence Hill, 1974), p. 22.

14. Bruce Williams, "The Lost Pharaohs of Nubia", *Journal of African Civilizations*, Vol. 4, No. 2, pp. 38-42.

15. Richard J. Gillings, *Mathematics in the Time of the Pharaohs*, (Cambridge: M.I.T., 1973) p. 232.

16. Arnold Buffum Chace, *The Rhind Mathematical Papyrus*, (Reston: NCTM, 1979), pp. 136-7.

17. Quoted by Boyer, op. cit., p. 281.

18. Gillings, op. cit., p. 3

19. Chace, op. cit., p. 75.

20. James Breasted, *History of Egypt*, (N.Y.: Bantam, 1967 edition), p. 85.

21. Chace, op. cit., p. 67.

22. Ibid., p. 124.

23. Somers Clarke and Engelbach, *Ancient Egyptian Masonry*, (London: Oxford), pp. 32-3.

24. Gillings, op. cit., pp. 173-5.

25. Ibid., pp. 167-9.

26. Clarke and Engelbach, op. cit., pp. 52-3.

27. Gillings, op. cit., p. 161.

28. Beatrice Lumpkin, "The Egyptians and Pythagorean Triples", *Historia Mathematica*, Vol. 7, No. 2, p. 186-7.

29. Gillings, op. cit., pp. 198-9.

30. Beatrice Lumpkin, *Senefer and Hatshepsut*, (Chicago: DuSable, 1983), p. 126.

31. Howard Eves, *An Introduction to the History of Mathematics*, (N.Y.: Holt, Rinehart and Winston, 1969), p. 52.

32. George Sarton, *A History of Science*, (Cambridge: Harvard, 1959), p. IX.

33. George Sarton, "Iconographic Honesty", *Isis*, Vol. 30(1939), p. 226.

34. Eves, op. cit., pp. 114-5.

35. Boyer, op. cit., p. 176.

36. Ibid., p. 187.

37. Eves, op. cit., p. 157.

38. Ali Abdullah Al-Daffa, *The Muslim Contribution to Mathematics*, (Atlantic Highlands: Humanities Press, 1977), p. 53.

39. Adolf P. Youschkevich (Yushkevitch), *Les Mathematiques Arabes*, (8th-15th centuries), translated from Russian to French, Vrin, Paris, 1976, p. 59 Translations quoted are my translation from the French. B. Lumpkin.

40. Mohammad Yadegari and Martin Levey, Abu Kamil's " *On the Pentagon and Decagon*", (Tokyo: History of Science Society of Japan, Supplement 2, 1971), p. 3.

41. Yushkevitch, op. cit., p. 66.

42. Yadegari and Levey, op. cit., p. 1.

43. Ibid., p. 31.

44. Yushkevitch, op. cit., p. 5.

45. George Sarton, *Introduction to the History of Science*, Vol. 1, (Baltimore: Carnegie, 1927), p. 717.

46. *Encylcopedia of Islam*.

47. Boyer, op. cit., pp. 340-3.

48. Yushkevitch, op. cit. p. 148.

49. Gordon and Jeff Deboo, "Ibn al-Haytham, Pioneer Physicist of the Middle Ages", *Arab Perspectives*, Vol. 2, Nov. 1981, p. 13.

50. Dirk Struik, "Omar Khayyam as Mathematician", *The Mathematics Teacher* Vol. 51(1958), pp. 280-5.

51. Boyer, op. cit., p. 268.

52. Yushkevitch, op. cit., p. 104.

53. Morris Kline, Mathematics in Western Culture, (N.Y.: Oxford, 1953), pp. 9-10.
54. J.F. Scott, History of Mathematics (London: Taylor and Francis, 1960), p. 61.
55. Ibid., p. 63.
56. Ettore Caruccio, *Mathematics and Logic in History and Contemporary Thought*, translated by Isabel Quigley, (Chicago: Aldine, 1964), p. 159.
57. Paulus Gerdes, *A Matematica Nos Paises Islamicos*, (Maputo: Tlanu, 1984), p. 13.

NILE VALLEY ORIGINS OF THE SCIENCE OF THE MIND

Na'im Akbar

Despite the impressive technological advancement of modern Western man relative to his own history, he ranks far behind the Ancient African people of KMT (Egypt) both technologically and spiritually. Part of the reason for this mental devolution is the limited conception of human potential that one finds in Western science. Western man's limitation is a disaster for his captives, who are the descendants of the people of Ancient Kemit. The possible advancement of Western man and the redemption or "renaissance" of African man is contingent upon rediscovering those concepts of human development which inspired the ascension of the people of Ancient Africa.

The originators of modern thought, as it emerged from its genesis in the Nile Valley, were the early and indigenous people of Northern Africa: Black people! It is important to be explicit about the race of these fathers of civilization, not because the fathers emphasized race as the basis of their greatness, but because the subsequent thieves of Kemitic civilization intentionally concealed the racial identity of their teachers in order to take credit for Africa's accomplishments and to deny her (Africa's) heirs the dignity of knowing their true ancestral legacy. So, we affirm the Blackness of those Ancient Masters in order to redeem the orphans of these authors of civilization. The certainty of the origin of those authors of civilization has been well-documented by Diop (1967), Garvey (1923), James (1976), Ben Jochannan (1971), Muhammad (1965), Rogers (1961) and Williams (1976). Beginning to assert the source of this higher knowledge of humanity and of the universe becomes for African people what James (1976) referred to as a "philosophy of redemption." Just an awareness of the source is redemptive, not to mention the knowledge itself which is transformative. James (1976) observed:

> This proposition (Greeks were not the authors of Greek philosophy, but the Black people of North Africa, the Egyptians) will become a philosophy of redemption to all Black people, when they accept it as a belief and live up to it. . . . Our philosophy of redemption is a psychological process involving a change in behaviors. It really signifies a mental emancipation in which the Black people will be liberated from the chain of traditional falsehood, which for centuries has incarcerated them in the prison of inferiority complex and world humiliation and insult.

Western Psychology

Psychology is a Greek word revealing its most recent origins among the Greek students of the Ancient African masters. "Psyche", frequently identified with a

Greek goddess of the same name actually means "soul". According to Massey (1974) the word *Psyche* is actually derived from the Egyptian in which *Khe* is the soul and *Su* is she; hence the feminine nature of the Greek *Psu-khe*. Without the article "P", *Sakhu* means the "understanding, the illuminator, the eye and soul of being, that which inspires." Not only is the study of the mind derived from ancient Egypt, but even the word used to characterize that study.

The serious handicap of this Western development is the devastation wrought by the distortions of the Divine Sciences as they were taken from their original teachers and forms. We will not review the steps in the devolution of Western conceptions of Ancient African science as this has been well-documented by Diop (1967), James (1976), Ben Jochannan (1971) and Williams (1976). A recent review by Wade Nobles (1982) is particularly relevant to understanding how psychology has suffered from this distortion by the Western mind.

For purposes of contrast, let us briefly review some of the Western assumptions about the study of man as he is currently defined in the Judeo-Christian, Euro-American psychology. We are aware of wide diversity among the various "schools" of Western psychology and our description merely summarizes the pervading ethos. We are aware that increasing numbers of Western-trained scientists are raising similar concerns about the limitations of Western mental science. Euro-American psychology approaches its study of man in the following ways:

1. Man is viewed as an object and the emphasis is upon objective methods for studying him.
2. Quantification is the only acceptable measure of reality.
3. The material world is viewed as essential and the essence of man is material.
4. There is no superior power or purpose beyond man.
5. The observable activities of a person are the critical dimensions of his being.
6. Concepts such as soul, spirits, revelations or any non-observable phenomena is viewed as superstition or delusion and has no relevance to understanding man.
7. Life and consciousness are identical with physical processes.
8. Man's individuality is paramount and there is no transpersonal awareness.
9. Man is a product of biological determinants, personal experiences and chance.
10. There is no "correct" order for man's development, he survives against odds by adaptation to his environment.
11. Morality and values have no meaning outside of personal experience.
12. Death of the body is death of the mind and one need not attend to life before or after the body.

Such an orientation to the study of the human being results in what Schwaller de Lubicz (1978) calls "a research without illumination." He observes that "this indecision colors everything, art as well as social organization, and even, in many cases, faith.''

In addition to these characteristics which, as we shall see, stand in stark contrast to the Ancient conception of man, there is another problem which has served to distort the Western study of mind (man). This problem is rooted in the need of Western scholars to dichotomize reality and assert their superiority and to discredit the source of their knowledge. This distortion resulted in two rather serious problems for the Western scholar. One problem was his fear of the matriarchy and the need to inferiorize women. This is a problem with deep and ancient roots in Western culture, but this fear of women and feminine power resulted in the need to sharply delineate themselves from characteristics identified as feminine. The further need to control those forces led to a derogation of femininity and feminine characteristics which resulted in a limited view of the whole human form that was always present in the masculine and feminine *neters* or principles constantly interacting in the Kemitic Cosmos.

The other problem affecting the European distortion of mental science was a pervasive racism which has permeated the interaction of Europeans with African people and African knowledge. As Diop (1967) has pointed out: ''the common denominator which characterizes the mindset of Egyptologists (as repeated in their various theses about ancient Africa) is their seeming desperate necessity and unrelentless attempt to refute ancient Africa's Blackness.'' Egypt has been summarily lifted from the African continent in the intellectual view of most scholars. Egypt in modern parlance is identified as the ''Middle East'' and rarely as Africa. What's even worse, the effort to displace the origin of Egypt's genius outside of Egypt altogether, has served to further the conspiracy of exclusion. Diop (1967) observes:

> As Egypt is a Negro Country, with a civilization created by Blacks, any thesis tended to prove the contrary would have no future. The protagonists of such theories are not unaware of this. So it is wiser and safer to strip Egypt, simply and most discretely of all its creations in favor of a really White nation (Greece).

Such racist intention by Aryan scholars led to the need to dissociate themselves from any qualities which were undeniably Black. The fundamental error of dichotomizing man's make-up into mind and body and eliminating the spirit altogether was done in glory of the material or the physical. Therefore, the spiritual or non-material world was relegated to the practitioners of the ''Dark Sciences'' and essentially given to the dark races, but not without degrading such involvements as superstitious, primitive (in the sense of uncivilized) and unscientific (i.e. ignorant). On the other hand, the physical and material was the source of thought, action, intellect and science. Therefore, the material was superior and its practitioners (The Aryan races) were a superior people. (Again, a lengthy review of this development in a 1983 paper by Wade Nobles entitled "Standing in the River, Transformed and transforming: (The (Re) Ascension of Black Psychology" is recommended for more detail on this issue.) Suffice it to say that the racist motive to distinguish themselves from the African teachers and to place themselves above their conquered mentors was fundamental in fueling the distortions which came to characterize Western Psychology. Many reviews of the distinctions between Western and African Psychology over the last two decades are recommended as an extension of this discussion which space will not currently accommodate. See: Akbar (1981, 1984), Asante (1980), Baldwin (1976), Clark (1972), Jackson (1979), King (1976), and Nobles (1980).

The Psychology of Ancient Kemit

The wisdom of Ancient Kemit is like a vast tapestry of amazing complexity. Each thread of the tapestry has been carefully woven such that every thread is defined by every other and the tapestry holds together in its wholeness only because every thread is present. No thread can be unravelled meaningfully without destroying the tapestry. Such is the task which faces anyone who seeks to explore any "thread" of the knowledge of Ancient Egypt. As Schwaller de Lubicz (1977) observes:

> Excavations and philological studies supply the Egyptologists with abundant material for a knowledge of the life, beliefs and theology of Ancient Egypt. An encyclopedic amount of work is available to the researcher. Nevertheless, Pharaonic Egypt remains unknown in terms of its true science, its contingent psychospiritual knowledge and its philosophical mentality.

In short, the task that we have set for ourselves is an impossible one for even the Egyptologist of advanced knowledge. The other confounding factor is that our approach to knowledge within the Western context, is fragmentary and rational which automatically eliminates the holistic, suprarational and symbolic knowledge which typifies Egyptian thought. The most that we can hope to accomplish is to focus on a small design in this massive tapestry and hope that by analogy and induction we may come to appreciate something of the comprehensiveness of the Egyptian understanding of the mind.

Let us be clear, though a psychology of Ancient Egypt does not exist in any explicitly identifiable sense, it is important to realize that man was viewed as the fundamental metaphor for all higher Truth. The gods (*neters*) and most importantly the Pharoah, all stood as symbols of profound truth. So, clearly the understanding of man (mind) was viewed as paramount in the science, the wisdom and the theology of Ancient Egypt. The study of religion, science (principles of nature), mathematics, psychology and government was the study of man. Contrariwise, the study of man (mind) was the study of religion, etc. The threads of the tapestry are inseparable. Schwaller de Lubicz (1967) describes the Egyptian view of the man as microcosm:

> Man is a microcosm in the sense of a tree in relation to the seed potentially containing it; the potentiality is its macrocosm, since the seed includes all the possibilities of the tree . . . The seed will develop these possibilities, however, only if it receives corresponding energies from the earth and sky. Even more so, man—who bears within him the total seed of the universe, including the seed of spiritual states—can identify with the totality and gain nourishment from it. The relationship of this microcosm with the macrocosm is . . . a unity depending only upon his degree of perfection as a human being relative to man as the final achievement foreseen by the cause.

The dictum (now correctly identified with its source) of "man know thyself," is the fundamental principle of the psychology of Kemit. James (1976) observes:

> The doctrine of self-knowledge, for centuries attributed to Socrates is now definitely known to have originated from Egyptian Temples, on the outside of which the words "man know thyself," were written.

James goes on to describe the Ancient Egyptian doctrine of self-knowledge by observing:

> Self-knowledge is the basis of all true knowledge. The mysteries required as a first step, the mastery of the passions, which made room for the occupation of unlimited powers. Hence as a second step, the neophyte was required to search within himself for the new powers which had taken possession of him.

Essentially, we find in this doctrine of self-knowledge, a simplified description of the initial psychology of consciousness. Man's capacity to know himself was established as a fundamental human characteristic and in pursuit of that knowledge of oneself one was in pursuit of knowledge of all things. Again, in her description of Kemitic thought, Schwaller de Lubicz (1967) observes:

> . . . the universe is only consciousness and presents only an evolution of consciousness from beginning to the end—the end being a return to its cause. This implies evolution of an innate consciousness toward the psychological consciousness that is consciousness of the innate consciousness, the first step towards the liberated consciousness of physical contingencies.

The question of consciousness is fundamental for understanding the Ancient Egyptian conception of human psychology. Initiation into the mysteries was not only a system of education but a metaphor for the total development of the human soul throughout life and death. This system of education (or more appropriately, "initiation"), was a formalized system of evolving consciousness of the person which was the nation (symbolized in the Pharoah) which was the entire cosmos.

What was to be known in this pursuit of consciousness? The initiate was instructed that he must know ''self'' and self in the conception of the Ancients (as well as modern) Africans meant ''soul.'' The kind of consciousness which had to be developed was, therefore, of much greater depth than the ''brain consciousness'' which most Westerners have reference to when they speak of ''consciousness of self.'' Such consciousness, Schwaller de Lubicz (1981) describes as no more than a ''a mental projection of what a man believes himself to want and do.'' The soul in its various dimensions as conceived by the Ancients is the most explicit description of the Egyptian conceptualization of human psychology. Therefore, a description of these components of the psyche (soul) will constitute the core of this discussion with its implications for the ''natural'' form of the human being.

Ancient Kemitic Dimensions of Self (Soul)

The soul is the fundamental subject of study for these wise men of Ancient Kemit. As Schwaller de Lubicz (1978) observes:

> The tombs of the leaders of this people (from Ancient Egypt) are consecrated to their profession of faith in the survival of the soul . . . The West labels this attitude of wisdom a state of science that is 'still mystical.' But the Egyptian technique and their symbolic attest to a realistic sense and to faculties of reasoning, contradicting the view held that this epoch is a ''primitive, mystical'' age.

Unfortunately, any science which delves into understanding the real ''psyche'' (soul) has come to be seen as ''mystical'' in Western scholarship. It was precisely these components of the person which have been discredited and excluded from the Western study of the mind which has resulted in its limitations. It is the inclusion of these elements in the studies of the Ancients which has given that science its power and permanence.

There is some inconsistency in the translation and identification of the components of the soul among various Egyptologists. Table 1 presents a comparison of how various writers have described the way that the world's earliest psychologists characterized the dimensions of man. Generally the dimensions which are identified are all similar to Massey's (1974) list: (1) *Ka (Kha)*, (2) *Ba*, (3) *Khaba*, (4) *Akhu*, (5) *Seb*, (6) *Putah*, (7) Atmu. These seven souls constituted the natural form of the human being's psychology as well as his evolution. The challenge to man was to become knowledgeable of these souls and achieve a crystallization of them into an Eighth or Divinely permanent form.

The *Ka* is described by Massey (1974) as ''the soul of Blood.'' This psychic dimension is the formal element of the person which gives form to substance and

TABLE 1
A Comparison of the Ancient Kemitic Conception of the Dimensions of the Soul (Self) as Identified by Four Prominent Egyptologists

Massey (1974)	James (1954, 1971)	Budge (1960)	Schwaller de Lubicz (1981)
Ka—formal structure that would return to the elements; soul of blood	*Ka*—abstract personality of the man to whom it belongs possessing the form and attributes of a man with power of locomotion.	*Ka*—double or inner self which comes into being with each person and follows him throughout life. It is the thread of connection between man's tangible and intangible being.	*Ka*—Formal element which gives form to substance and creates matter. 1. original Ka—Creator of all the others. Divine Ka. 2. Kas of nature, mineral, vegetable and animal. Intermediate Ka—personal consciousness. 3. Individualized Ka, Inherited characteristics of psychological consciousness; Inferior Ka
Ba—Breath of life; Eternal, invisible energy that runs through all visible functions. Essence of all things.	*Ba*—heart-soul dwells in the *Ka*. It has the power of metamorphosis and changes its form at will.	*Ba*—a combination of intelligence and spirit which leaves the body at death.	*Ba*—most spiritual element in man; it is his link with the Creator. It is free, unfixed and unaffected by the human being whose only link with it is a link of consciousness. 1. *Ba* is the cosmic soul in all constituents of the world (*Universal soul*) 2. Ba—the *natural soul* stabilized in the bodily form; 3. Ba—represented by bird with human head is symbol of *human soul* which comes and goes between heaven and earth.
Khaba—veil of the vital principle produced emotion and motion; sustains the sensory perceptions, total harmony and circulation of the blood shade soul.	*Kaibit*—Shadow. Associated with Ba. It has the power of locomotion and omnipresence.	*Khabit*—the shadow or soul of the blood	*Khabit*—astral or etheric body, ghost or shadow. Holds the records of all pictures or imaginings in our universe.

TABLE 1 (cont.)

Massey (1974)	James (1954, 1971)	Budge (1960)	Schwaller de Lubicz (1981)
Akhu—Seat of intelligence and "mental perception." Attributes of judgment, analysis, and mental reflection all of which could be dedicated to service of higher being.	*Ab*—The heart, the animal life in man that is rational, spiritual and ethical. Associated with the Ba and undergoes examination in the Judgment.	*Hati*—represents the heart or conscience and understanding	*Inferior Ka* (see above)
Seb—manifested at puberty; self-creative power of the human being. Ancestral soul. Procreational soul.	*Khat*—the concrete personality, the physical body which is mortal.		*Inferior Ka*
Putah—"first intellectual father," marked the union of the brain with the mind. From its attainment the intellect governs conduct, Intellectual soul.	*Sahu*—body in which the Khu or spiritual self dwells. All mental and spiritual attributes of the natural body are united to the new powers of its own nature	*Sahu*—the spiritual body	*Ba*—natural soul
Atmu—the Divine or eternal soul. Represented as parenthood which symbolized the full creative power and perpetual continuation.	*Khu*—spiritual soul which is immortal. It is immortal. It is closely associated with the Ba (heart-soul) which is immortal.	*Khu*—the pure spirit or Horus—the highest expression of the personality, the perfect spirit or Christ consciousness	*Divine Ka*—"Father of the father of the *Neters*" (Spiritual Witness)

creates matter. It is formative or the foundation of the abstract personality structure which has a formal structure capable of ultimate disintegration and return to the elements from which it came unless it is Osirified or mummified. The structure would have to become Divinely or permanently set (which is the symbol of the Mummy) as an eternally preserved form of the person. The body is usually identified as the symbol of the *Ka* though the *Ka* soul was certainly transcendant. Budge (1960) describes the *Ka* as "the thread of connection between man's tangible and intangible being."

The *Ka* is refined through the other dimensions of the soul, but it has a multiple expression of its own. Schwaller de Lubicz (1981) identifies these three manifestations of the *Ka* as:

1. *Divine Ka*—the original *Ka* which is the creator of all the others.
2. *Intermediate Ka*—Kas of nature, mineral, vegetable and animal.

3. *Inferior Ka*—individualized Ka; inherited characteristics of psychological consciousness. Consciousness of the *Ka* evolved from the Inferior to the Divine Ka.

Schwaller de Lubicz (1981) observes:

> A man ignorant of his own spiritual world has little or no contact with his Divine *Ka*. His personal *Ka* is brought down to the whole of his lower *Kas*; therefore after death, he will become his own shade or ghost . . . the quest for spiritual springs of action and the enlargement of consciousness, can modify the character of his "personal" *Ka* until the spiritual faculties are awakened and it makes contact with the Divine Ka.

The *Ba* called the "Soul of breath" by Massey (1974) is the second division of the psychic nature. It represented the transmission of the invisible energy source (like electricity) which runs through all visible functions. The Ancients believed that there was only one power, which was symbolically represented as "the breath," and, that this power or breath was transmitted from the ancestors to the descendants. They believed that this power or energy has always existed and will always exist. The *Ba* was in effect the vital principle which represented the essence of all things.

The *Ba* as represented by a bird with a human head is the symbol of the "human soul" which comes and goes between heaven and earth. It is the most spiritual element in man for by its divine nature it is linked with the Creator. It is incommensurable, and indivisible, free, unfixed and unaffected by the Vicissitudes of the human being whose only link with it is a link of consciousness. Schwaller de Lubicz (1981) also, divides the *Ba* into three aspects:

1. *Ba* (universal soul) the spirit of fire which gives life to the world in all its parts. The spirit of *Ba* is in all constituents of the world and in its final perfection.
2. *Ba* (natural soul) stabilized the bodily form (Ka), and its character is Osirian, that is, it is subject to cyclic renewal.
3. *Ba* as the human soul described above as represented by the bird.

The *Ka* by assimilating the universal *Ba* generates a new being which is the individualized soul which remains divine, incorruptible and therefore immortal. In fact the definitions of *Ba* and *Ka* must always be relative to each other, since they can only refer to one aspect in its relation to the other.

The *Khaba* is the shade or covering soul, corresponding to the popular notion of the ghost. It is the astral or "etheric" body. It is related to the Akasha, the world or state which holds the records of all the pictures or imaginings in our universe. The *Khaba* (call *Khabit* or *Kaibit* by some writers) produced emotion and motion. It was further thought to be responsible for sustaining the sensory perceptions and the phenomena of color, total harmony and the circulation of blood.

The *Akhu* is the fourth division of the psychic nature and is described as the seat of intelligence and mental perception. It was in the area of the *Akhu*, the Ancients believed, that the whole mystery of the human mind was to be comprehended. The mind was in fact, an entity in and of itself and only during physical life was the mind the instrument of the human spirit. The concerns of the mind were primarily the survival of its own thinking processes. The *Akhu* was characterized by attributes like judgment, analysis and mental reflection, all of which could be trained and disciplined so as to be dedicated to the service of the higher being. The intelligence was considered to be located in the heart and it was considered to be not only rational but also spiritual and ethical. In the Ancient Kemitic Judgment drama it undergoes examination and is weighed on the scale of justice against a feather in the presence of Osiris, the great judge of the unseen world.

The *Seb* is the soul of pubescence in that it doesn't manifest itself in humans until puberty or adolescence. The evidence of the presence of the *Seb* was the power of the human being to generate his own kind. The *Seb* is in effect the self-creative power of Being.

The *Putah* was the intellectual soul or the "first intellectual father." Unlike the *Akhu*, the *Putah* was associated with the mental maturity of the individual and marked the union of the brain with the mind. It was the *Putah* which established the fact of the person and from the moment of its manifestation or attainment it was believed that intellect (i.e., will and intent) alone governed conduct. The maturity of the *Putah* represents the person's ability to reproduce intellectually.

The *Atmu* as the seventh division of the psyche was considered the divine or eternal soul. In some texts it is identified with the seventh creation, the god *Atmu* who inspired the breath of life everlasting. In ritual this division of the soul is represented as parenthood which symbolically stood for the presence of full creative powers and perpetual continuation.

Some writers, such as Massey, identify an eighth form of the soul which represents a synthesis or crystallization of the other seven. Massey (1974) refers to it as "Horus" or the Christ." It is the same as the "Divine Ka," described above by Schwaller de Lubicz (1981) and by Frankfort (1946). This component is described as enwrapping and serving as the essence of all the divisions of the soul and was the *Ka* of God. The Ka was the divine spirit which endowed all things and which survived past the physical life of the individual. The *Ka*, it was thought, had magical powers and could cause the dead to live again (the resurrected Christ) and could even enter a mummified being, animate it internally and cause it to have a continued inner life or existence.

Conclusion

This discussion has focused on just one aspect of a multi-faceted and complex system which describes the human psyche according to Ancient Kemitic tradition. As we cautioned from the outset, the entirety of the Kemitic cosmology is actually a comprehensive description of the Psyche of man. The amazingly complex theology of Ancient Kemit represents a series of allegories which define the workings of nature and most importantly the genesis and implied potentialities of man. These myths and symbols actually transcend the empirical conclusions of Western Science and describe man, not only on the basis of what he does but what he is.

We chose to look at the psychic dimensions as the Ancients described it because in that system we find a summary of what the human being is. By implication we can more effectively describe the properly functioning human being and can actually see the distinctions from the African perspective. Each of the components of the septenary soul which we have described has implications for understanding the "nature" of the human being.

The fundamental conclusion about human nature as implied by the description of the *Ba* and the *Atmu,* as well as the Divine *Ka* is that the human being is essentially connected with the Divine and with everything else in nature. There is continuity in all that is, having its origin in the Creator. This is consistent with the African psychologists (Akbar 1976; Baldwin, 1976; Jackson, 1979; Nobles, 1980 and X, et als, 1976) who have suggested the principle of consubstantiation as expressed in the idea "I am because we are and because we are, therefore I am," (Mbiti, 1970) as fundamental to understanding the African psyche. We have identified that this same concept called *Ba* in Ancient Africa is called *dya* by the Bambara people and the *Okra* by the Akan people of Ghana and more generally "soul" by African-American people, showing a continuity in this Ancient Kemitic conception of the human being among African people. This is in contrast with the dualistic and materialistic conception of the Euro-American psychologists who would be appalled at even admitting that "psyche" once meant soul even to them.

The *Ka* on the other hand brings balance to the picture of the human being and shows that the human being is not only of "heavenly" material but also of "earthly" material. There is implicit in this system, a recognition that the human being has a connection and an involvement in the earthly sphere. He has a physical component that is tangible, but this is a dimension and not an exclusive view of the person. The Ancients were able to construct impressive physical structures, feed their citizenry with advanced technology, master physics and physical medicine while understanding that all of those structures were transient in comparison with the higher being.

The *Kaibit* suggests that man has access to Universal knowledge from the so-called "Akashic records." Man can reach into the recesses of his own consciousness and retrieve the world's most valuable knowledge. This eliminates the apparent inequity in knowledge when it is assumed to emanate from outside.

Intelligence is multiple in its dimensions: rational, spiritual and ethical. The intelligent person is not simply one who has mastered a technique but is prudent enough to know when and how to apply that technique. The intelligent one is not one who is capable of performing independent of his moral and spiritual obligation to the rest of humanity. The *Akhu* and *Putah* give a conception of intelligence which requires self-mastery, and service to ones higher being in order to be considered intelligent.

Seb reminds the person that his nature is not only one which permits reproduction, but is procreative and self-creative. The human being is equipped not just to reproduce himself, but to re-create and then perpetuate his creation.

Ultimately, the human being becomes the fullness of what he is from his inception and that is a Divine form reunited with his Divine genesis. Through realization of one of Ancient Kemit's most consistent motifs (that is) transformation. The person transforms the raw material of his transient form and self-consciously forms and is transformed to the higher being from which he sprang.

> The deceased cries, "Do not take my soul!" (*Ba*) "Do not detain my shade!" (Khaba) "Open the path to my shade, and my soul, and my intelligence (Akhu) to see the great God on the day of reckoning souls."
>
> —From the Coffin Text

References

Akbar, N. Africentric social sciences for human liberation. *J. of Black Studies*, 14(4), 1984, 395-414.

Akbar, N. Our destiny: Authors of a scientific revolution. *The Fifth Conference on Empirical Research in Black Psychology*. Washington, D.C.: Howard University Institute for Urban Affairs, 1981.

Asante, M. & Vandi, A. (eds.) *Contemporary Black Thought*. Beverly Hills: Sage, 1980.

Baldwin, J. Black psychology and black personality. *Black Books Bulletin*, 4(3), 19.

Budge, E.A.W. *The Book of the Dead:* An English translation of the *Papyrus of Ani*. New Hyde Park, New York: University Books, 1960.

Ben-Jochannan, Y. *Africa: Mother of Western Civilization*. New York: Alkebu-lan Books Assoc., 1971.

Clark, C. Black Studies or the study of black people in Jones, R. (ed.) *Black Psychology* (1st edition). New York: Harper & Row, 1972.

Diop, C.A. *The African Origin of Civilization: Myth or Reality*. Westport: Lawrence Hill & Co., 1967.

Frankfort, H., et al. *The Intellectual Adventure of Ancient Man*, Chicago: University of Chicago Press, 1946.

Garvey, A.J. (ed.) *Philosophy and Opinions of Marcus Garvey*. New York: Universal Publishing House, 1923,

Jackson, G. The origins and development of Black Psychology: implications for Black Studies and human behavior. *Studia Africana*, 1(3), 1979, 270-293.

James, G.G.M. *Stolen Legacy*. San Francisco: Julian Richardson Assoc., 1976 (1954).

King, L. et al. *African Philosophy: Assumptions and Paradigms for Research on Black Persons*. Los Angeles: Fanon Center Publication, 1976.

Massey, G. *A Book of the Beginnings*, Vol. 1. Secaucus, N.J.: University Books, Inc., 1974.

Massey, G. *Gerald Massey's Lectures*. New York: Samuel Weiser, Inc., 1974.

Mbiti, J. *African Religion and Philosophy*. Garden City: Doubleday and Co., 1970.

Muhammad, E. *Message to the Black Man*. Chicago: Muhammad Mosque of Islam, No. 2, 1965.

Nobles, W.W. African Philosophy: Foundations for Black Psychology in Jones, R. (ed.) *Black Psychology* (2nd ed.) New York: Harper and Row, 1980.

Nobles, W.W. Ancient Egyptian thought and the development of Afrikan (Black) psychology. Presented to "The First Annual Ancient Egyptian Studies Conference: The Social Life Area." Los Angeles, February 24-26, 1984.

Nobles, W.W. Standing in the river, transformed and transforming: The re(ascension) of Black psychology, Unpublished manuscript, 1982.

Rogers, J.A. *Africa's Gift to America*. New York: Helga M. Rogers, 1961.

Schwaller de Lubicz, I. *Her-Bak: Egyptian Initiate*. New York: Inner Traditions International, 1978.

Schwaller de Lubicz, I. *The Opening of the Way:* New York: Inner Traditions International, 1981.

Schwaller de Lubicz, R.A. *The Temple in Man*. New York: Inner Traditions International, 1977.

Schwaller de Lubicz, R.A. *Symbol and the Symbolic*. New York: Inner Traditional International, 1978.

Williams, C. *The Destruction of Black Civilization*. Chicago: Third World Press, 1976.

THE SYMBOLISM OF THE CROWN IN ANCIENT EGYPT

Richard D. King

The historical origin of the twin pillars of modern European-African psychiatry, biological psychiatry and psychoanalytic depth psychiatry, can be directly linked to a common historical parent, The Science Of The Mind or The Way Of The Heart of ancient Egypt.[1] This premise arose from the observation of the crown, jewels, and tableaux found in the tomb of the 18th dynasty pharaoh Tut-ankh-amun (?-1349 B.C.E.).[2-10] These items of material evidence are excellent examples of symbolic references to a historical stream of ancient African philosophical thought that runs from the predynastic Egyptian period, Memphite cosmology, through dynastic Egypt and later postdynastic heirs of Egypt, Dogon cosmology. The evidence cited is not new, having been in the hands of investigators for over fifty years. Rather, it is the order in which the facts are arranged that is both new and very old, the meaning given to the evidence, an acknowledgement of a greater whole from which these ideas are abstracted. For it is an Afrocentric corpus of thought, an Afrocentric world view on the part of the investigator that appears to be an absolutely critical focus and tool of analysis in an examination of the crown, jewels, and tableaus of the pharaoh Tut-ankh-amun. From such an analysis there may come an appreciation of more subtle issues relating to the pineal gland, melanin, light and depth psychology issues of the unconscious, dreams, and levels of consciousness.

The largely intact tomb of the Pharaoh Tut-ankh-amun was discovered in 1922 by Howard Carter and excavated over a six year period.[2, 3, 8, 12] A diadem crown was found atop the pharaoh's head which was covered in linen wrappings that extended over the entire mummy. Upon the mummy was a golden mask that was placed within one coffin and this was enclosed inside of two successive coffins. The three coffins were found inside of a quartzite sarcophagus. These four coffins were enclosed within four successive shrines. The surface of each of the four were covered with elaborate tableaus.

The right side of the second tableau of the second shrine contains a scene of a serpent passing rays of light into the forehead of the first of six human figures of Pharaoh Tut-ankh-amun. The next two human figures have rays of light entering their foreheads from a star anterior and above the head. The last three human figures have stars passing rays of light from star to star, each star in all cases being directly over the head of each human figure. In front of each of the six human figures are two columns with a human headed hawk-like bird standing atop the two columns. The bird stands in such a manner that its left foot rests atop the left column, right foot rests atop the right column and the body and human head of the bird is situated between the two columns (see Fig. 1).[9, 14]

Two of the jewels taken from the tomb of Tut-ankh-amun are symbolic replicas of the ancient Egyptian concept of the left eye and right eye.[4] The replica of the left eye (Fig. 2a) is framed by a serpent wearing the crown of Lower Egypt at the left corner and a vulture wearing the crown of Upper Egypt at right corner of the eye, whereas the replica of the right eye (Fig. 2b) depicts a scarab body of a hawk whose outstretched wings and front legs uphold a boat. Within the boat is an eye framed on each side by cobras with sun disks above each serpent's head. Above the eye there is a crescent shaped moon containing a moon disc with the figures of the ibis-headed moon god Thoth wearing the moon disc, the king wearing the moon disc, sun god Ra wearing the sun with a serpent uraeus. Importantly, the god Thoth is on the left, the king in the center and the god Ra on the right.

There were at least five crowns found over the head of the Pharaoh Tut-ankamun in his tomb—diadem, mask, and three whole-body coffins. In all cases there is the same representation over the forehead of the king, the head of a serpent on the left and the head of bird, vulture, on the right (Fig. 3).[15] Both of these objects were placed in the mid forehead location above the level of the eye

Figure 2A. From *Egyptian Mysteries: New Light on Ancient Spiritual Knowledge* by Lucie Lamay (Crossword, N.Y., 1981, p. 44).

Figures 1, 10, 11, and 13 have been omitted due to the uneven quality of the submitted photographs—*Ed.*

Figure 2B. From *Egyptian Mysteries* (1981, p. 45).

brows. The crown closest to the head, the diadem (Fig. 4), which was actually enclosed inside of the mummy's linen wrappings not only displays the mid-forehead serpent and bird but also the wave-form body of the serpent across the midline of the crown of the skull from front to back. Futhermore, the diadem crown has the head and body of two serpents attached at the back of the head with the head of the serpent positioned at about the site of the temple on each side.

Figure 3. Private photo by author. Cairo Museum.

Figure 4. John West, *Serpent in the Sky: The High Wisdom of Ancient Egypt* (Harper & Row, N.Y., 1979, p. 47).

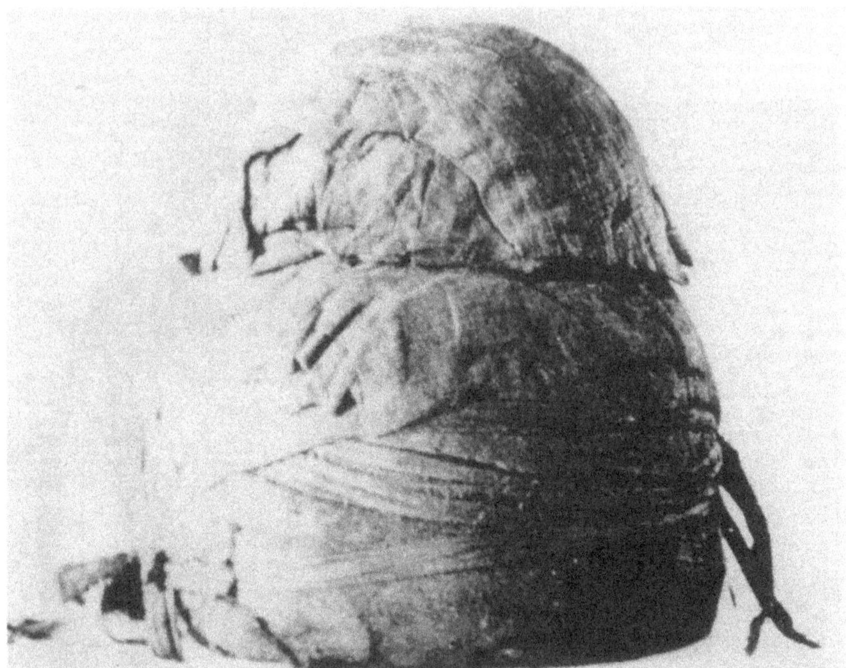

Figure 5. F. Leek, "The Human Remains from the Tomb of Tut'ankhamun" *Tut'ankhamun Tomb Series*, V (Griffith Institute, Oxford University Press, 1972, plate X).

Upon unwrapping the successive line wrappings of the head of the Pharaoh Tut-ankh-amun, after the diadem crown was removed there was found a golden serpent and bird crowning the mid-forehead brow location (Fig. 9).[16] The wings of the golden bird were outstretched and covered the frontal portion of the crown of the head. The body of the golden bird rest atop the center line of the crown of the head from front to back. Yet, even before the head of the pharaoh was unwrapped, the symbolic importance of the crown of the head was clearly defined by the ancient Egyptian priests by their placing an extra pad of linen upon the top of the head. (Fig. 5.)[17] Last, directly on top of the pharaoh's head there was a skull-cap with golden beads arranged in the form of four serpents, (Fig. 6) two serpents with heads at about the middle of the crown of the skull and two serpents with heads over the temple regions on each side respectively. (Fig. 6).

It is well known and reported in European-African archaelogical literature that the serpent was used throughout Lower or Northern Egypt as a symbol of the Goddess Uatchet. This was so most particularly in the city of Per-uatchet, the capital of the seventh nome. This city of Uraeus worship as well as the other sites of its worship were collectively known as Pe-tep, within which were two distinct

Figure 6. F. Leek, "The Human Remains from the Tomb of Tut'ankhamun," plate XI.

divisions. The first group *Tep* was identified with Isis and Uatchet. Isis was the worshipped divinity. The other, *Pe* was identified with Horus and Uatchet. Horus was the primary deity. Uatchet was regarded as the goddess of the elements and months of the Egyptian year, Epiphi, and during later dynastic times, was given the name Ap-tavi. Thus, in time the serpent and crown with a projecting coiled serpent-like body became a political symbol for royal rulership of Lower Egypt.

In a similar fashion the bird as a vulture became a symbol for royal rulership of Southern or Upper Egypt.[19] Nekhebet was the vulture Goddess of the South. She was worshipped throughout Upper Egypt in the city named Nekhebet by the Egyptians, which was, moreover, the capital of the third nome. This same city was called Eilethyiaspolis and "Civitas Lucinae", by the Greeks and Romans respectively. The shrine of the Goddess Nekhebet, is presently located in the current Arab village of El-Kab. Nekhebet was also believed to be the daughter of Sun God Ra, the divine wife of Khent-Amenti, the holy vulture, and Hathor.

Figure 7. William J. Murname, *The Penguin Guide to Ancient Egypt* (Penguin Books, England, 1983, p. 47).

Following the unification of Upper and Lower Egypt by the Lower or Southern Egyptian Pharaoh Aha or Narmer (4000?, 3200 B.C.E.) all rulers of unified Egypt wore the composite crown of Egypt (Fig. 7).[17] The crown contained the bulbous top of Upper Egypt and the coil of the crown of Lower Egypt. Certainly this was a great political event and an even greater psychological achievement to develop a real unified sense of shared commonality, purpose, and philosophical base between two previously antagonistic groups of Africans. Clearly, there is a strong suggestion of a similar process having taken place earlier in Upper Egypt with the collective name of Pe-Tep being derived from the unification of the two distinct divisions of *Pe* and *Tep*. Likewise, in Southern or Upper Egypt in pre dynastic times there had been a unification of at least three distinct divisions that worshipped the Gods Nekhebet, Sun God Ra, and the Goddess Hathor. It is of the utmost importance, with regard to the political unity of Africans in the past and present, to appreciate not only the political and military issues of such unification events but even more to consider the psychological basis that allowed mutual respect, synthesis, and flourishing of all parties involved in such a union. With this in mind, one may consider the symbolism of the crown of ancient Egypt. For, in reviewing the crown, shrine tableau, and jewels it is readily apparent that the serpent of Lower Egypt and the vulture of Upper Egypt were found to have other symbolic meanings than just political rulership over the two-geo-political units of Southern and Northern Egypt.

From a psychoanalytic perspective a symbol has been defined as an act or object that represents an unconscious desire which has been repressed or automatically forgotten without ever having become conscious to the observer.[20] Symbols are inherently linked to deep spontaneous unconscious psychological processes. In contrast, signs are linked to largely conscious processes in which the observer consciously and arbitrarily allows one thing to stand for another. For example, in the case of a sign, ten different observers may use ten different signs to represent the same item. In the case of a symbol, different observers may use the same symbol to represent a wide variety of different classes of objects because it

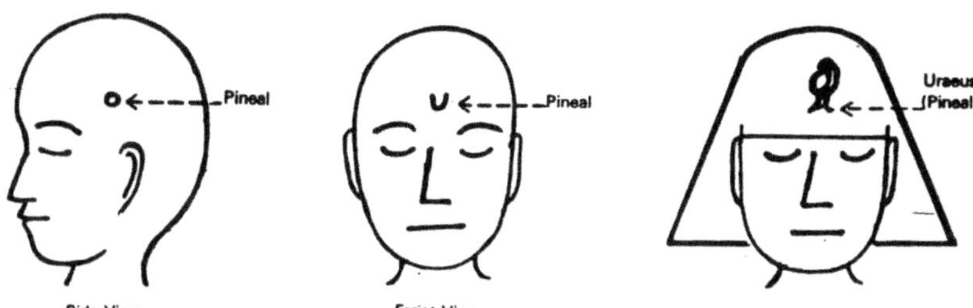

Figure 8. Richard King, "Uraeus: From Mental Slavery to Mastership," Part III, *Uraeus* (vol. 1, no. 3, 1978, p. 26).

somehow spontaneously occurred to them to use the same symbol. The serpent and vulture found in the central mid forehead position of the crown of Tut-ankh-amun is a symbol in that it is linked to deep unconscious psychological processes that tie together seemingly unrelated items from a purely conscious perspective such as religion, political unification, rulership, sun, moon, psychology and brain anatomy.

To appreciate the psychological concept of symbolism it may be helpful to consider the issues of projection, collective unconscious, and the ancient Egyptian concepts of body, mind, soul, and spirit. First, the word symbol is partially derived from the word *ballein,* to throw. The process, to throw, speaks of a psychological state "projection," the unconscious act of ascribing to or throwing upon external things one's own ideas or impulses. What one sees externally as a good symbol to link together several seemingly unrelated items comes from a preexisting unconscious memory of an idea. There exists many different levels of the unconscious, one of which is the collective unconscious which contains the genetic memory of all that was ever known or experienced by one's ancestors. The collective unconscious is the living library, eternal memory bank that is hidden by ignorance or mental slavery but, unlike the physical libraries, was never destroyed. This concept was reintroduced by European-African psychiatrist C.G. Jung. Another concept, closely allied to the collective unconscious is the word archetype, the original pattern, or model, from which all other things of the same kind are made. C.G. Jung took the term "Archetype" from the Corpus Hermeticum (Scott Hermetica, vol. I, 140, 12b) and from Chap. 2, Par. 6, of the *De Divinis nominibus* of Dionysius the pseudo-Aeropagite, which reads: "But someone may say that the seal is not the same and entire in all its impressions. The seal, however, is not the cause of this, for it imparts itself wholly and alike in each case, but the difference in the participants make the impressions unlike, although the archetype is one, whole and the same."[4] However, Jung was drawn to the term archetype most of all by the writings of the African scholar St. Augus-

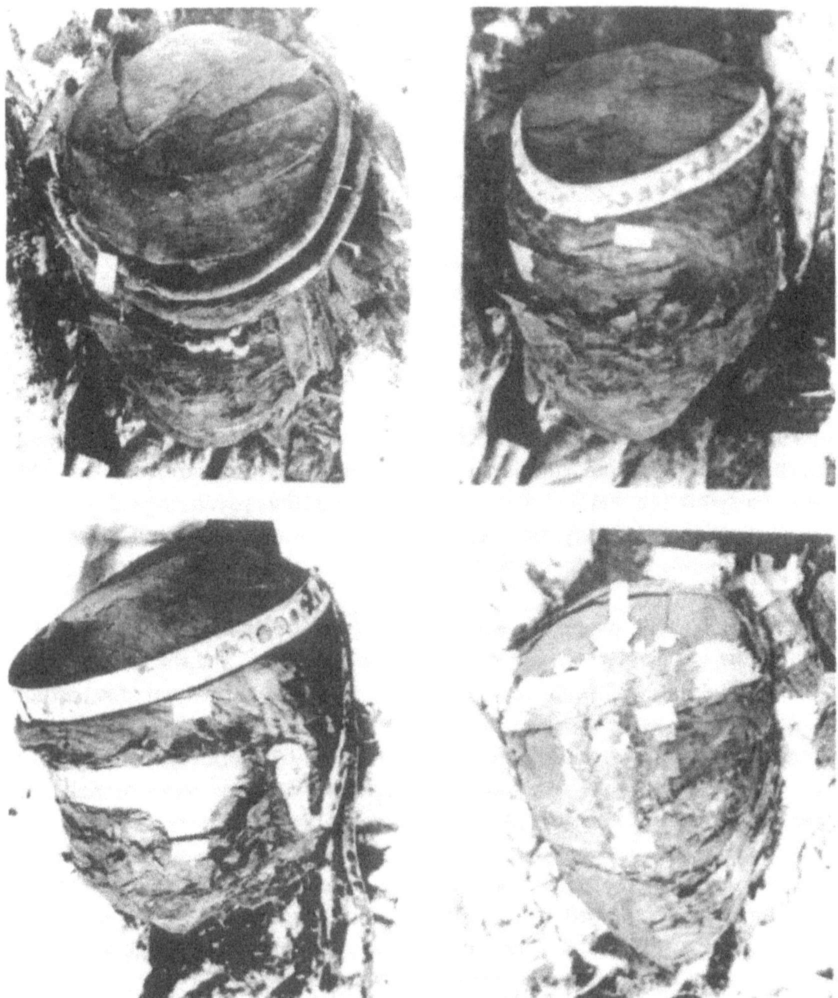

Figure 9. F. Leek, "The Human Remains from the Tomb of Tut'ankhamun," plate V.

tine, in particular St. Augustine's idea *Principales*, "For the principal ideas are certain forms, or stable and unchangeable reasons of things, themselves not formed, and so continuing eternal and always after the same manner, which are contained in the divine understanding. And though they themselves do not perish, yet after their pattern everything is said to formed that is able to come into being and to perish, and everything that does come into being and perish. But it is affirmed that the soul is not able to behold them, save it be the rational soul." Thus, symbols may be used to tie together a number of seemingly unrelated items because there exists in the collective unconscious of the observer the memories of one's ancestors, their experiences and discoveries, as well as analyses and philosophical interpretations of all these things.

Ancient Egyptian priests or scientists defined not only the body and mind but also the soul and spirit. Additionally, the concepts of mind, soul and spirit were so important that this triune or trinity concept was a constant theme throughout many layers of their philosophical thought and scientific disciplines. There was a division of many things into three. There were three grades of students (neophyte, intelligence, sons of light).[23] Temple architecture comprised an outer court for public congregations, a middle hall for priests and nobles, and an inner middle chamber, adytum, Holy of Holies, solely used by the high priest.[24] There was the Goddess Isis (female), God Osiris (male), and God Horus (child, union of opposites).[25] An entrance to the temple was formed by a doorway in which the left pillar represented the masculine energy of creation, right pillar the feminine energy of creation, and the arch way that joined or united the two pillars or opposites represented the soul or self with the words written upon it, "Man Know Thy Self."[11] Thus, it is likely that Pharaoh Tut-ankh-amun's tomb with three successive coffins enclosed within a quartzite sarcophagus are symbolic replicas of the soul, spirit, mind, and body (the last being the quartzite sarcophagus). The three shrines which successively enclose the coffins and sarcophagus may represent the freedom of the spirit, soul, and mind of humans following the death of the physical body. "The Egyptian Mystery System" as George James in his book *Stolen Legacy* points out "had as its most important object, the deification of man, and taught that the soul of man, if liberated from its bodily fetters, could enable him to become godlike and see the Gods in this life and attain the beatific vision and hold communion with the Immortals." It sought "the liberation of the mind from its finite consciousness, when it becomes one and is identified with the Infinite. This liberation was not only freedom of the soul from bodily impediments, but also from the wheel of reincarnation or rebirth. It involved a process of disciplines (several liberal arts) or purification (ten virtues, negative confessions, Book of the Coming Forth by Day) both for the body and soul."[23] James further cited nine aspects of the soul as defined by the ancient Egyptians, of which four are central to the concept of spirit (Khu), soul (Ba), mind (Ka), and body (Khat). "The *Ka* is the abstract personality of the man to whom it belongs, possessing the form and attributes of a man with power of locomotion, omnipresence and ability to receive nourishment like a man. It is equivalent to (Eidolon), i.e., image; the *Khat*, i.e., the concrete personality, is the physical body, which is mortal; the *Ba*, i.e., the heart-soul, dwells in the *Ka* and sometimes alongside it, in order to supply it with air and food. It has the power of metamorphosis and changes its form at will; and the *Khu*, i.e., spiritual soul, is immortal. It is also closely associated with the *Ba* (heart-soul), and is an Ethereal Being."[26] From these considerations it is possible that symbols not only arise from the deep unconscious of one's own present historical life, shared experience of one's genetic ancestors (Ba), but also the past reincarnations of one's *Khu* (spirit). The Ba and Khu are well known to have been symbolized by ancient Egyptians as birds[27] and indeed it was the Ba as a human-headed bird that was depicted atop the two columns in front of each of the six human figures of pharaoh Tut-ankh-amun in the second shrine tableau scene we referred to earlier.

Further, it is interesting to observe in the tomb of Tut-ankh-amun the jewels of the lateral eyes, for the moon rose on the side of the left eye as the sun descended on the side of the right eye, a position that can only occur if one is facing south, towards the Great Lakes ancestral homelands of the ancient Egyptians, Khui Land, and place of origin of those who later unified Egypt through military might, politics, but most of all knowledge.

One should consider even deeper questions by examining the crown, jewels, and tableau from the tomb of pharaoh Tut-ankh-amun. May it not be that these African people gave great thought to the symbolism of the color of their own skin and the physiological operations involved in maintaining such Black skin color in response to the radiation of the sun and the moon? What were the discoveries of these worshippers of the sun and moon on the relationship of the human form to light? The scene of the tableau clearly poses such questions, serpent passing rays of light into a midforehead site of the human figure, and stars passing rays of light into a midforehead site of two successive human figures. This is a crucial item of physical evidence of the African knowledge of biological psychiatry and depth psychiatry thousands of years before the rediscovery of the same bodies of knowledge by Europeans. This scene was probably already ancient and well known by the Africans when placed inside of Pharaoh Tut-ankh-amun's tomb in the year 1349 B.C.E., three thousand three hundred years before the European scientists Axelrod and Lerner rediscovered in the 1950's that the pineal was not a nonfunctional vestigial organ but an active brain endocrine gland that released the hormones melatonin and serotonin.[28-35] It was later found that the pineal gland, an organ long known to be located in the interior of the brain at a level above the eye brows and in the exact midline of the forehead, released the hormone melatonin into the blood during the hours of darkness, night, time of the moon (Fig. 8.). On the other hand, the hormone serotonin was released into the blood during the hours of sunlight, day, time of the sun. Furthermore, it has since been discovered that melatonin is actively involved in shifting levels of consciousness and access to the unconcious, such as dream states, rapid eye movement (or REM) sleep. Melatonin is now known to increase the flow of unconscious memories from the deeper levels of the mind-brain up to the cortex for conscious expression, whereas serotonin increases the flow of memories from the cortex down to the deeper levels of the mind-brain, memory storage.

Further evidence of the ancient Egyptian's earlier knowledge of site and function of the pineal gland is suggested by following the origin of the knowledge of the pineal in the early scientific literature of Greece, the first major European nation and one profoundly influenced by Africa. Herophilos (325-280 B.C.), deemed by Europeans as the "father of anatomy," has been held to be the first to discover the pineal. He was an anatomist at the University of Alexandria. However, it was the ancient Egyptians (Africans) who were the true discovers of the pineal and the mothers and fathers of anatomy. According to George James, "owing to the practice of piracy, in which the Ionians and Carians were active, the Egyptians were forced to make immigration laws restricting the immigration of the Greeks and punishing their infringement by capital punishment, i.e., the sacrifice of the victim. Before the time of Psammitichus, the Greeks were not allowed to go beyond the coast of Lower Egypt but during his reign and that of Amasis (670 B.C.E.), those conditions were modified. For the first time in Egyptian history Ionians and Carians were employed as Mercenaries in the Egyptian Army. . . . In addition to these changes, King Amasis removed the restrictions against the Greeks and permitted them to enter Egypt and settle in Naucratis. About this same time (i.e., the reign of Amasis) the Persians, through Cambyses, invaded Egypt, and the whole country was thrown open to the researches of the Greeks. . . . The immigration of Greeks to Egypt for the purpose of their education, began as a result of the Persian invasion (525 B.C.E.), and continued until the Greeks gained possession of that land and access to the Royal Library, through the conquest of Alexander the Great (332 B.C.E.). Alexandria was converted into a Greek city, a centre of research (University and Library of Alexandria) and the capital of the newly created Greek empire, under the rule of the Ptolemies. . . . Concerning the fact that Egypt was the greatest education centre of the ancient world, which was also visited by the Greeks. . . . Plato in the Timeaus tells us that Greek aspirants to wisdom visited Egypt for initiation, and that the priests of Sais used to refer to them as children in the Mysteries." George James cited a long list of the fathers of Greek philosophy who, as students, had visited Egypt for the purpose of their education-Thales (525 .C.E.), Pythagoras, Democritus, Plato, and Aristotle. George James also stated that "any invading army would first loot the Royal Library of Alexandria and then would turn their attention to the Menephtheion at Thebes (Grand Lodge of Luxor, center of the world-wide African University system, The Mystery System). They would also visit the cities of Memphis and Heliopolis and likewise loot their libraries and temples. . . . The Greeks (i.e., Alexander the Great, Aristotle's school and the succeeding Ptolemies) converted the Royal Library of Alexandria into a research centre, by transferring Aristotle's school and pupils from Athens to this great Egyptian Library, and therefore the students who studied there received instructions from Egyptian priests and teachers, until they died out. . . . the subjugation of Egypt by Alexander the Great in 330 B.C. had checked the further development of Greek civilization on its native soil. . . . this school (University, Library of Alexandria) of philosophers, mathematicians and astronomers. Here for the next 700 years, science had its chief abiding place." Yet at the time of Herophilos (325-280 B.C.) the Greek capture of the Egyptian royal libraries had just taken place and scholars such as Herophilos had recently arrived in Egypt to study under the indigenous Egyptian scientists and to study and translate the preexisting books written earlier by these African scholars.

Thus, when we read of the discoveries of Greek scientists and philosophers from the time of Pharoah Amasis onward there exists the very great possibility that their discoveries were not their own but the teachings of their Egyptian professors. This would particularly be the case with Herophilos, so called first discoverer of the pineal gland. He actually resided in Egypt at the Greek University and Library of Alexandria, which had been formed from the confiscated vast libraries of ancient Egypt and the libraries of priest-scientists from the various colleges of Egypt. Importantly, Herophilos localized the soul in the brain's ventricular system. Yet, upon viewing pictures of the unwrapping of Pharoah Tut-ankh-amun's head (Fig. 9)[16] there was found a golden bird laid across the top of the crown of the head with outstretched wings covering the front of the head and the body of the bird along the center line of the head. This may have been a symbolic statement of the actual African knowledge of the location of the soul being in the brain's ventricular system because the shape of the bird closely resembles the top-view appearance of the system, lateral ventricles similar to the outstretched wings, body similar to the third and fourth ventricles. The pineal gland is located anatomically at the posterior end of the third ventricle and the pituitary gland is present at the anterior end of the third ventricle.[28, 31] Modern science has now discovered that though pineal hormones are released into the blood they are concentrated primarily in the cerebrospinal fluid (C.S.F.) that flows through the brain ventricular system.[41, 42] Again, the symbolism of the bird found atop Pharoah Tut-ankh-amun suggest that such facts may have been known by Africans over 3,300 years before modern science's rediscovery of the same and 1,000 years before Herophilos. The third ventricle has long been called the vault of initiation. Certainly, it is most critical to consider that the ancient Egyptians not only knew of the psychological operation of what they term the spirit, soul, and mind but had also defined the physical location and perhaps physiological operation of this trinity.

Subtle and more direct indications of the original discovery of the location and importance of the pineal gland are indicated by several other sources. First, the Egyptians defined the purpose of education to be the freedom of the soul. The grades of students in their educational system were divided into neophyte, intelligence, and sons of light. The latter two higher grades of students were distinguished by their ability to develop Nous, mind or inner vision. This was the ability to have access to the greater mind, that 99% of one's mind that one is unaware or unconscious of, the personal unconscious mind, soul and spirit. Critically, to have inner vision suggests that one must also have an eye for inner vision, an inner or third eye. According to the ancient Egyptian myth, Horus fought his evil uncle Seth to avenge the death of his father Osiris. In battle Horus' eye was torn to pieces, but by magic Moon God, God of writing, assembled the pieces. This eye of Horus was the third eye, a regenerated or transformed eye (process of initiation), the sound eye, Udjat, the eye of magic.[35] An eye transforms light, spirit, into more dense forms of matter that have informational content such as neurotransmitters, indoleamines, and polypeptide hormones which have been rediscovered by modern scientists. Yet, we find several Egyptian references to the Eye of Horus' relationship to sunlight—I am Horus and I have come forth from the Eye of Horus (Uraeus-Pineal Gland). I am Uatchet (Uraeus, Eye of Horus) who comes forth from Horus. I am Horus and I fly up and perch myself upon the forehead of Ra in the bows of his boat which is in heaven (Book Of The Coming Forth By Day, Book Of The Dead). She (Uatchet, Uraeus or Pineal) riseth up on the left side of thy head, and she shineth from the right side of thy temples without speech; they rise up on thy head during each and every hour of the day as they do for their father Ra (sun), the bandage of Nekheb was laid upon the forehead of every carefully prepared mummy, and The goddess Uatchet cometh unto thee in the form of the "living Uraesu", to annoint thy head with their flames (Book Of The Coming Forth By Day, Book Of The Dead).[35]

The outstanding works by the modern African scholar Dr. Yosef ben-Jochannan, *The African Origins of The Major Western Religions,*[43] *Black Man's Holy Black Bible,*[44] and *We, The Black Jews*[45] have revealed how much the world's major religions, including Christianity have borrowed from the religions of Africans, particularly the ancient Egyptians. Thus, it should come as no surprise to find in Genesis 32;27-32[34] that it was at *Peniel* (pineal gland) that Jacob (mental slave, neophyte, dwelling in ignorance, symbolic of the undeveloped unconscious or entrapped within the physical body (the contained mind, soul, spirit) met the Angel of God (soul, spirit). During the wrestling bout which ensued, he ascended from his former state of lower consciousness and was transformed into Israel (liberated mind, soul, spirit). It was at Peniel that Jacob saw God face to face and his life was preserved or renewed: "And Jacob called the name of the place *Peniel,* for I have seen God face to face, and my life is preserved." Phylogenetically, the pineal gland is actually in humans a modified eye. In the lower life forms such as amphibians and reptiles, western fence lizard, the pineal is present as a parietal or third eye on the top of the forehead.[31, 35] In the higher life forms such as mammals the pineal withdrew into the head embrologically, converting from a physical eye into a light transducer which converts light into hormonal signals that can actually change the form and function of the physical body and levels of consciousness (spirit, soul, mind, body).

The pineal hormones melatonin and serotonin operate as hormonal keys that unlock the door to the unconscious mind, dreams. Melatonin is known to initiate dreams by activating the locus coeruleus. It is known that ancient Egyptians did practice dream analysis and hypnosis.[29, 30, 36] The recent rediscovery of the concept of the unconscious, hypnosis, and dream analysis, partially attributed to Sigmund Freud, should also be credited to the ancient Egyptians.[48-53] A photograph of the desk of Sigmund (Fig. 10)[49] does reveal a large number of Egyptian statues including one of the God Osiris, God of the Underworld or unconscious,

Figure 12. Katherine S. Gilbert, Ed., *Treasures of Tutankhamun* (Metropolitan Museum of Art, New York, 1977, p. 99).

confirming an African knowledge of the unconscious thousands of years before the time of Freud.

A consideration of the pineal gland and melatonin does lead one to raise the question of ancient Egyptian symbolism in relation to the importance of their own Black skin color.[46, 47] Of the myriad of physiological functions of pineal melatonin there are at least two major roles that act directly upon physical Blackness, melanin. First, melatonin maintains and promotes the various shades of skin color by its effects upon the pigment cell, melanocyte, at the skin dermal-epidermal junctions. Second, melatonin initiates dreams by its action upon the locus coeruleus.[54] The locus coeruleus is black because it contains large amounts of melanin, the same chemical that produces skin color which in this case is found within the very structure of the brain. Furthermore, the locus coeruleus is the twelfth and uppermost in a chain of twelve pigmented brain nucleii found in the brain stem. These are the substantia nigra with its associated nucleus brachialis pigmentosus and nucleus paranigralis. The other nine nucleii are either part of a neuromelanin column or adjacent to the neuromelanin column. They are: locus coeruleus, nucleus intracapularis subcerleus, nervi trigeini, mesencephasius, pontis centralis oratis, tegmenti pedennculoponticus, parabrachialis, medialis dorsomotor and retro ambigualis. The name locus coeruleus literally means black dot. Locus is a latin word, stlocus locum meaning point of dot. Coeruleus is derived from the Sanskrit word *caeruleus yamas* meaning black. Additionally, it should be noted that the symbol black dot as an actual image does appear in the Egyptian hieroglyphic name for the Sun God Ra.[47] The third eye or Eye of Horus contains the same symbolic image, black dot, as the black pupil through which light enters the eye of inner vision. Similarly, the entrance to the Egyptian temple usually had two obelisks, whose tops were crowned by the pyramidial point, the ben-ben or pyramidion, an all-black cap stone. Pyramids often contained a similar black cap stone, the pyramidion. Thus, it was the first point of the pyramid-temple site or obelisk-temple site to receive sunlight as the sun arose from darkness on each new day and symbolizing that light first enters through a doorway of darkness (pyramidion, pupil) when entering the temple of the human body.[47]

The symbolism of the crown should be placed in the context of the stream of African philosophical thought that stretches from the pre-dynastic Memphite cosmology through the post dynastic heirs of ancient Egypt, Dogon Cosmology. The Memphite cosmology is a stone inscription found at Memphis that had been rewritten by the Ethiopian-Egyptian Pharaoh Taharqa (690-664 B.C.E.) of the 25th dynasty who said he had copied the text from an ancient inscription of his ancestors. The language and arrangement of the text is of the form used at the beginning, before the dynastic period of Egypt. The text states that the Primate of the Gods Ptah (mind) was the first to emerge from the primeval waters of Nun in the form of a Primeval Hill. Closely following the Hill, the God Atom also emerges from the waters and sits upon the Hill.[11] The Hill is another name for the human body, whereas Atom can be correlated to the concept of the sun. Of course the top of the hill would be the human head. Symbolically this is the basis for the Egyptian statement of the Eye of Horus, the Black doorway or pupil, pyramidion, eye on the mountain, through which light first enters the human temple or body. At this point one can be left in wonder, daring to glimpse the possible historical significance of such a statement and reflecting on the possibility that this is a very ancient memory. For this may have been a concept impressed upon the minds of early humans in the ancestral Great Lakes region of North East Africa in the watery regions at the base of the Mountain of the Moon. Similarly, the great emphasis of the Egyptians upon the crown of the head, the heaved up place or heaven, symbolically pictured as the winged scarab, whose body is like the crown of the skull when viewed from the top (Fig. 11). This may speak to an ancient African awareness of the importance of the enlargement of the cerebral cortex in man as compared to mammalian and primate ancestors. Nonetheless, the statue of Pharaoh Tutankhmun emerging from the primeval water of Nun (Fig. 12) is a direct reference to the Memphite Cosmology of religion, historical evolution of humanity, and daily experience of all humans in the drama of life, the struggle to free the spirit, soul, and mind through a conscious awareness of their operation and the liberation thereby from the body and unconscious state. For just as there was an original sea of the watery regions of the Great Lakes from which humanity did emerge in Africa, so too there exists an internal sea within the human body, the blood stream and cerebro spinal fluid of the brain's ventricular system.

This review of the symbolism of the crown, jewels and tableau of the ancient Egyptian African Pharaoh of the 18th dynasty, Tut-ankh-amun, has found evidence of the ancient African knowledge of the pineal gland. These ancient Africans appear to have had knowledge of the pineal anatomy, its psychological effects, and its physiological relationships with other parts of the brain's structure through the cerebrospinal fluid-filled brain ventricular system. Apart from being symbols of political power over a unified nation of African people they functioned on another level of meaning. They were symbols of potential psychological unity within the grasp of each citizen of the nation. It appears that these Africans knew that the pineal gland contained chemical keys that could unlock various levels of consciousness that would yield operative awareness of the personal mind, soul, and spirit. Furthermore, this triune concept of spirit, soul, and mind appear to have been central concepts found throughout various layers of their educational system. The stated purpose of their educational system was to free the soul from the finite consciousness of the body. Thus, it is reasonable to expect that such a people would have developed an extraordinarily elaborate symbolism around such issues.

References

1. Ghalioungui, Paul, *The House of Life, Per Ankh, Magic And Medical Science in Ancient Egypt*, B.M. ISRAEL, Amsterdam, 1973, p. 127.

2. Leek, F. Filce, *The Human Remains from the Tomb of Tutankhamun*, V, Tutankhamun Tomb Series, Griffith Institute, University Press, Oxford, 1972.

3. ben-Jochannan, Yosef A.A., *Tutankhamun's African Roots, Haley et al., Overlooked?*, Alkebu-lan Books and Education Materials Association, New York, 1978.

4. Lamy, Lucie, *Egyptian Mysteries, New Light on Ancient Spiritual Knowledge*, Crossroad, New York, 1981, pp. 44, 45.

5. West, John Anthony, *Serpent in the Sky: The High Wisdom of Ancient Egypt*, Harper & Row, New York, 1979, p. 17.

6. Gilbert, Katherine Stoddert Ed., *Treasures of Tutankhamun*, Metropolitan Museum of Art, New York, 1976, p. 99.

7. Murname, William J., *The Penguin Guide to Ancient Egypt*, Penguin Books, New York, 1983, p. 47.

8. Romer, John, *Valley Of The Kings*, Michael Joseph Ltd., London, 1981, pp. 245-76.

9. Piankoff, Alexandre, *The Shrines of Tut-Ankh-Amon*, Bollingen Series XL, Princeton University Press, 1977, pp. 128-31.

10. Budge, Ernest A. Wallis, *Tutankhamen, Amenism, Atenism and Egyptian Monetheism*, Bell Publishing Company.

11. James, George G.M., *Stolen Legacy*, Julian Richardson Associates, San Francisco, 1976, pp. 139-51.

12. ben-Jochannan, Yosef A.A., *Black Man of the Nile and His Family*, Alkebu-lan Books and Education Materials, New York, 1981.

13. Griaule, Marcel, *Conversations with Ogotemmeli*, An Introduction To Dogon Religious Ideas, International African Institute, Oxford University Press, New York, 1965, pp. 16-23.

14. King, Richard D., Private photograph, Cairo Museum, Cairo, Egypt, Group Lecture Tour with Dr. Yosef ben Jochannan, 1983.

15. Private photograph, Cairo Museum, Cairo, Egypt.

16. Leek, op. cit., plate V.

17. Leek, op. cit., plate X.

18. Leek, op. cit., plate XI.

19. Budge, E.A., Wallis, *The Gods of the Egyptians*, Volumes I and II, Dover Publications, New York, 1969.

20. Guralink, David B. and Friend, Joseph H. Eds., *Webster's New World Dictionary of the American Language*, The World Publishing Company, New York, 1968, p. 1477.

21. Jacobi, Jolande, *The Psychology Of C.G. Jung*, Yale University Press, New Haven, p. 39.

22. Ibid, p. 40.

23. James, op, cit., p. 27.

24. James, op, cit., p. 32.

25. James, op, cit., p. 68.

26. James, op, cit., pp. 123-124.

27. Lamay, Op. cit., pp. 24, 25.

28. Reiter, Russel J., *The Pineal Gland* vol. I-III, CRC PRESS, Inc., Boca Raton, Florida, 1981.

29. Wurtman, Richard J., Moskowitz, Michael A., "The Pineal Organ, Part I," The New England Journal of Medicine, 296:23, 1977, p. 1329.

30. Wurtman, Richard J., Moskowitz, Michael A., "The Pineal Organ, Part II," *New England Journal of Medicine*, 296:24, p. 1977.

31. Smith, Ivor, "Indoles Of Pineal Origin: Biochemical and Physiological Status," *Psychoneuroendocrinology*, Vol. 8, no. 1, 1983, pp, 41-60.

32. Reiter, Russel J., "The Pineal Gland: An Intermediary Between the Environment and the Endocrine System," *Psychoneuroendocrinology*, Vol. 8, no. 1, 1983, pp. 31-40.

33. Cardonali, David P., "Molecular Mechanisms of Neuroendocrine Integration in the Central Nervous System: An Approach Through the Study of the Pineal Gland and Its Innervating Sympathetic Pathway," *Psychoneuroendocrinology*, Vol. 8, no. 1, 1983, pp. 3-30.

34. King, Richard D., "Uraeus: From Mental Slavery to Mastership," *Uraeus*, Vol. I, no, 3, 1978, pp. 22-35.

35. King, Richard D., "The Pineal Gland Review," Fanon Center Publication, Los Angeles, 1977.

36. Hobson, J. Allan, Mc Carley, Robert W., "The Brain as a Dream State Generator: An Activation Synthesis Hypothesis of the Dream Process," *American Journal of Psychiatry*, 134:12, 1977, pp. 1335.

37. Carman, John S., et al., "Negative Effects of Melatonin on Depression," *American Journal of Psychiatry*, 133:10, 1976, pp. 1181.

38. Moskovitz, Charlene, Moses, Hamilton, and Klawans, Harold L., "Levodopa-Induced Psychosis: A Kindling Phenomenon," *American Journal of Psychiatry*, 135:6, 1978, p. 669.

39. Reiter, Russel J., *The Pineal Gland*, vol. I, CRC Press, Inc., Boca Raton, Florida, 1981, p. 3.

40. James, op, cit., pp. 41-51.

41. Mess, B, et. a., *Melatonin, Cerebrospinal Fluid, Pineal Gland Interrelationships, Brain En-*

docrine Interaction II, The Ventricular System, Karger, Basel, 1975, p. 335.

42. Barr, Frank E., *Melanin and the Mind-Brain Problem*, Institute for the Study of Consciousness, 2924 Benvenue Ave., Berkeley, California, 1982.

43. ben-Jochannan, *African Origins of the Major Western Religions*, Alkebu-Lan Books, New York, 1970.

44. ben-Jochannan, *The Black Man's Religion*, Alkebu-Lan Books Associates, New York, 1976.

45. ben-Jochannan, *We The Black Jews*, Alkebu-Lan Books Associates, New York, 1982.

46. King, Richard D., "Black Dot, Part I," *Uraeus*, Vol. 2, no. 1, 1980, pp. 18-32, 43.

47. King, Richard D., "Black Dot, Part II," *Uraeus*, Vol. 2, no. 3, 1982, pp. 4-22.

48. Sulloway, Frank J., Freud, *Biologist of the Mind, Beyond The Psychoanalytic Legend*, Basic Books, Inc., New York, 1979, p. 366.

49. Engelman, Edmund, Berggasse 19: *Sigmund Freud's Home and Offices, Vienna 1938:* The Photographs of Edmund Engelman. With an Introduction by Peter Gay. Captions by Rita Ransohoff, Basic Books, New York, 1976.

50. Mac Hovec, Frank J., "Hypnosis Before Mesmer," *American Journal of Clinical Hypnosis*, Vol. 17, no. 4, p. 215.

51. Tompkins, Peter, *The Magic Of The Obelisks*, Harper & Row, New York 1981.

52. Shadow, Kenneth, *Cults of the Shadow*, Samuel Weiser, New York, 1976.

53. James, op, cit., p. 134.

54. Jouvet, M. and Delorme, F., "Locus Coeruleus and Paradoxical Sleep," C.R. Soc. Biol (Paris), vol. 159, 1965, pp. 895-899.

55. Olswezki, J. and Baxter, D., *Cytoarchitecture of the Human Brain*, Stern and Birjelow, editors, J. Rodgers, New York, 1954.

56. Bazelon Mary and Feinchel, Gerald M., et al., "Studies on Neuromelanin I, A Melanin System in the Huamn Adult Brainstem," *Neurology*, vol. 17, 1967, pp. 512-19.

57. Marsden, C.D., "Pigmentation in the Nucleus Substantiae Nigrae of Mammals," *Journal of Anatomy*, vol. 95, 1961, pp. 256-262.

58. Feinchel, Gerald M. and Bazelon, Mary, "Studies on Neuromelanin II, Melanin in the Brainstems of Infants and Children," *Neurology*, vol. 18, 1968, pp. 817-820.

59. Schere, H.J., "Melanin Pigmentation of the Substantia Nigra in Primates," *Journal of Comparative Anatomy*, vol. 71, 1939, pp. 91-95.

60. Lewis, Charlton T. and Short, Charles, *Harpers Latin Dictionary, A New Latin Dictionary*, American Book Company, New York, 1907, pp. 262, 1074.

61. Rev. Means, Sterling, M., *Ethiopia: The Missing Link in African History*, 1945.

62. Dury, Victor, *Ancient History of the East*, vol. 1, p. 21.

63. Mookadi, Badha K., *Hindoo Civilization*, p. 33.

64. Rashidi, Runoko, "Ancient India. The Eastern Bastion Of the Ethiopian Empire," Lecture, Amenta Conference, Compton, California, August 1981.

65. Russell, G.V., "The Locus Coeruleus," Tex. Rep. Biol. Med., Vol. 13. 1955, pp. 939-88.

66. Finch, Charles, Lecture, Amenta Conference, Compton College, Compton, California, October 1983.

67. Gilbert, op. cit., plate 22.

KEMETIC CONCEPTS IN EDUCATION

Asa G. Hilliard III

> *As to the man without experiences, he does not listen, he does nothing at all. He will see knowledge where there is ignorance, he will see profit where there is loss; he makes all kinds of errors, taking always the side opposite to what is praiseworthy. In that way, he lives on what is perishable. His food is evil speech, as to which he marvels. He lives everyday on what the wise know to be mortal, flying from what is best for him, because of the multitude of efforts which present themselves to him each day.*
>
> —Chapter 41, *Book of Ptah-Hotep*
> (Myer, 1900, pp. 294-5)

Long before the colonization of the African continent by European nations, and long before the first recorded invasions of the African continent by any nation outside the continent, Africans had developed the most sophisticated system of education to be found in early records. Those records show that the African system of education, especially its classical expression in ancient KMT (later called Egypt by the Greeks), was the parent of other systems of education, especially early European education in Greece and Rome (James, 1956; Babbitt, 1969).

> Witness to this also that the wisest of the Greeks: Solon, Thales, Plato, Eudoxus, Pythagoras who came to Egypt and consorted with the priests, and in this number some would include Lycurgus also. Eudoxus, they say, received instruction from Chonuphis of Memphis, Solon from Sonchis of Sais, and Pythagoras from Oenuphis of Heliophis. Pythagoras, as it seems, was greatly admired, and he also greatly admired the Egyptian priests and, copying their symbolism and occult teachings incorporated his doctrines in enigmas. As a matter of fact, most of the Pythagorean precepts do not at all fall short of the writings that are called Hieroglyphics . . .
>
> —Plutarch

Long after invasions of and colonizations in ancient Africa by outside nations, Africans maintained sophisticated systems of education. They maintained sophisticated systems appropriate to their environment even under harsh rural conditions. We can still see some of those systems today in traditional communities. It was these systems that were the priority targets of colonizers. Only when they were destroyed would Africans be weakened and confused to the point of serious vulnerability (Griaule, 1972; DuBois, 1969; Ngubane, 1979; Jahn, 1961; Erny, 1973).

Much of the present indigenous African education system is a part of a "secret" oral tradition, as was the case in Ancient KMT (Harley, 1970; Griaule,

1972; James, 1976; DuLubicz, 1978). Knowledge was "secret" only in the sense that advanced technical ideas and skills would be taught only after a rigorous program of study had been mastered. This was nothing more than a recognition of something important about the learning process. It would mean little to give "secret" knowledge to an unprepared learner. He or she would not understand it.

Over the full course of African history, a number of African civilizations and nations were destroyed by external conquests (Ngubane, 1979; Williams, 1974; Rodney, 1974; Padmore, 1969). This has led such writers as Armah (1979), to describe in *Two Thousand Seasons*, the nearly 2,000 years of destruction and decline of African nations, mainly by outside invaders.

Any examination of education in Ancient KMT must take into account this relationship of Africa to the rest of the world, especially to its conquerors. Yet because of the traditional ignorance, neglect, defamation, and destruction of African history and culture by outsiders over centuries, the reclamation and restitution of African history today is a very difficult task.

Education Under Black African Rule

Within the time available to me today, my main purpose is to present a brief description of parts of the education system of ancient KMT when it was under native African leadership. While the population of KMT was somewhat mixed ethnically and racially even in the early kingdoms, it was southern black African leadership that founded KMT and governed it during its golden ages. For example, out of thirty dynasties or kingdoms, it was during the first seven dynasties that most of the pyramids were built. It was during the 18th dynasty that the most magnificant temples and tombs were built. It was during the 25th dynasty that there was a restoration of ancient ways. These were native African dynasties. Generally we may say that the native dynasties were Dynasties One through Twelve, Dynasty Eighteen, and Dynasty Twenty-Five. The Nineteenth and Thirtieth dynasties did have large scale building programs that imitated earlier native African culture. They added nothing new. Rameses II of the nineteenth dynasty did increase the scale of some architecture during his rule, but it was in essence the same type of architecture that his predecessors had created.

Operating Framework

The following statements will set forth the operating framework for this article. The limitations on the length of this presentation preclude a detailed review of supporting documentation for each of the following points. However, a more detailed treatment of evidence for these assertions has been presented elsewhere (Hilliard, 1984).

- According to archaeological finds, the oldest hominoids in the world lived in Africa several million years before they appeared anywhere else in the world. Most of the bones of ancient man were found in sites that cluster around that great central eastern African lake Nyanzaa (named Lake Victoria by the Europeans) on the equator. Only in the last one million years do we find that hominoids were on other continents.
- The oldest recorded civilization to date is Nile Valley civilization.
- The oldest nation on record to date was the Nubian nation Ta Seti, located to the south of KMT. Remember also, it was a king of the south or Upper KMT that united KMT and founded its First dynasty.
- KMT was Africa's greatest recorded African classical civilization.
- KMT was the natural extension of inner-African culture.
- There was in ancient times and there remains today a cultural unity between KMT and the rest of the African continent.
- The native African populations were a Negroid people.
- Ancient African nations influenced other civilizations worldwide.
- KMT was a black African nation during its most important development periods.
- Africans in the African diaspora, including the Americans and the Carribean retained and still retain varying degrees of African culture. That culture is reflected in family patterns, language, religious belief systems, artistic creativities, etc.

Sources of Evidence

While few historians have written specifically about Kemetic education, there is a good deal of direct and indirect evidence that helps us to bring a good picture of it into focus. The sources of evidence include the following:

- Sacred texts written in mdw ntru (renamed Hieroglyphics by the Greeks): Pyramid texts, papyri, coffin texts, etc.
- Monuments: Pyramids, tekenu (renamed obelisks by the Greeks), stellae.
- Carvings.
- Paintings.
- Pottery.
- European "classical" writers, some of whom were eyewitnesses (Greek and Roman).
- The ancient and contemporary cultural practices of inner-Africa (religion, family practices, symbolic structures, educations, etc.), when compared to those of ancient KMT are very similar.

Foreign (Asian) Invasions as the Destruction of High Culture

Given the brief time that is allotted to this presentation, I have decided to begin my description of Kemetic education at one of the peak periods of its development, the New Kingdom, the 18th Dynasty. This was the Kingdom that included Thutmoses III, the great conqueror; Akhenaton, the world's first apostle of non-violence and who is falsely regarded as the originator of the idea of monotheism; Hatshepsut, the most famous woman to rule KMT or any other ancient nation as a "King;" and the popular but inconsequential young pharaoh "King Tutankamen." These were native Africans who, led by Sequenenre the Southerner of the late 17th dynasty, had expelled the Asian Hyksos invaders from KMT and re-established African rule.

It is very important to note that these Asian Hyksos invaders, also called shepherd kings, represented a dramatic interruption in the creative Kemetic cultural traditions. They were alien and made no recognizable lasting contribution to the culture of KMT, even though they ruled for five dynasties.

> These invaders, now generally called Hyksos, after the designation applied to them by Josephus (quoting Manetho), themselves left so few monuments in Egypt that even their nationality is still the subject of much difference of opinion; while the latent character of their supremacy for the same reason, are equally obscure matters. The documentary materials bearing on them are so meager and limited in extent, that the reader may easily survey them and judge the question himself . . . (Breasted, 1937, p. 29).
>
> The Hyksos left no literary evidence of their occupation of Egypt. Indeed, they left practically no large monuments at all. What we know about them has been painfully gleaned from a host of scarabs—those beetle shaped amulets so characteristic of Egypt—cylinder seals, and a few other isolated objects; a tiny sphinx with royal head and a semetic face in the act of clawing to death an Egyptian; a dagger with remarkable representations of animals on the handle; a fragmentary writing pallet. . . . Perhaps the only truly "monumental" relics of the invaders are several blocks from a stone building found at Gebelein, a few miles south of Thebes, which contained the names of the Kings, Khyan and Apophis Owoserre" (Steindorff, 1957, pp. 25-26).

After this long cultural lull, the native 18th Dynasty came as a revival of the African culture of the first twelve dynasties, and indeed the culture of the pre-dynastic period.

Kemetic Education

The center of 18th dynasty government was at Wa-Set, or Wo-Se', meaning in Kemetic "The Septer." Wa-Set was renamed "Thebes" by later Greek invaders. It was renamed "Luxor" by still later Arab invaders. In Wa-Set were two gigantic temples that contained the most highly developed education systems on record from ancient times.

One temple, the Southern Ipet (place), now called by the Arabic name the "Temple of Luxor," was located in the south of the city of Wa-Set. It was connected to the largest temple of ancient times, the Ipet Isut, called Karnak by the

Arabs. These magnificent buildings existed long before there was a Greece, and even longer before Greeks would conquer KMT under Alexander the Great. Nearly a thousand years after the Greek invasion, the essentially Asiatic Arabic population under Islam would take over KMT.

Ipet-Isut meant "the most select of places," or "the holiest of places." It was both a center of religion and education, since the two could not be separated in the minds of the Kamites. It housed an elite faculty of priest-professors. It has been estimated that at one time there were more than 80,000 students at all grade levels studying at Ipet Isut University (Abdullah, 1984). Temples were at the center of religion, politics, and education.

Ipet-Isut was like all other lesser temples in KMT's Nile Valley. Every temple had a faculty and a library (Hurry, 1928). This was true, not only in the 18th dynasty or New Kingdom, it was also true in the oldest Kingdoms as well, kingdoms that flourished, before the invasions. For example, libraries were an important part of Old Kingdom culture.

> In one of the tombs at Gizeh, a great functionary of the sixth dynasty . . . takes the title of "Governor of The House of Books." This simple mention thrown incidently between two or more elevated titles would be sufficient in fault of others coming to show us the extraordinary development at the time of Egyptian civilization. Not only had they a literature, but that literature was also large enough to fill libraries, its importance was so great that to one of the functionaries of the court was especially attached the preservation of the royal library. . . . In a later writing, Professor Maspero says this liberation was of the time of Shepseska. He was the sixth King of the fourth dynasty . . . (Myer, 1900, p. 20).

The faculty were called Hersetha or "teachers of mysteries," and were divided into departments (Myer, 1900), as follows: (1) Mystery Teachers of Heaven (astronomy and astrology); (2) Mystery Teachers of All Lands (geography); (3) Mystery Teachers of the Depths (geology); (4) Mystery Teachers of the Secret Word (philosophy and theology); and (5) Mystery of Pharaoh and Mystery Teachers who examined words (law and communication).

Ancient KMT was a high-tech society. It required literal armies of educated people. The first step in the formal process of general education was training as a scribe, a highly honored profession. The route to sacred or secular office was through the scribal schools.

Scribes began their work by copying existing great works. The Mdw Ntr (Hieroglyphics) expressed the great ideas of the age. There was no Dick, Jane, and Spot here—no Mickey Mouse and Donald Duck, no Cinderella, and Jack and the Beanstalk, no Goldilocks and the Three Bears. Scribes were introduced to serious matters from the outset. Though they may not and probably did not understand fully what they were copying initially, gradually they came to know the greatest historical and spiritual tradition in the history of mankind.

The process of education was not seen primarily as a process of acquiring knowledge. It was seen as a process of the transformation of the learner who progressed through successive stages of rebirth to become more godlike. Disciplined study under the guidance of a master teacher was the single path to becoming a new person.

The education system was an open admission system that was not tied to heredity.

> There is not a son for the Chief of the Double White House; there is not an heir for the Chief of the Seal (Myer, 1900, p. 165).

The "Double-White House" was the Pharaoh's capital. In other words, in order to be educated, the Pharaoh's children, like all others had to follow the difficult path of hard study on their own. For example, Amenhotep, son of Hapu, was of lowly birth. However, he is identified as the architect-priest who designed the basic plan of the great temple of Ipet-Isut (White, 1970, p. 86).

Kemitic educators were first and foremost serious students of natural phenomena, especially in the native African dynasties. It was the long, painstaking study of everything in nature that led Kamites and other Africans to the belief in the essential unity of all things in the universe, and to a belief in one supreme God. This belief was held in KMT from earliest times. According to the great Egyptologist, E.A. Wallis Budge, who studies all the ancient Kemetic literature, the study of that literature reveals that there was never a time when Kamites did not believe in one Great God (monotheism). This God was nameless, incomprehensible, and self-created (Budge, 1973, p. xxiii). Kamites believed that any facet of nature could be studied to cover principles of nature's operations, or put another way, aspect of God. This allowed for the use of many natural objects as *symbols* of divine principles. It was the ancient Kamites' attempt to live in harmony with nature's principles, or God's manifestations (not many gods or polytheism), that led them to develop the earliest moral teachings and forms of worship to institutionalize those teachings.

Anyone who reads the ancient texts will detect the universal preoccupation of native Africans with the sacred. The overall aim of education is exemplified by the NTRU (diving principles) Tehuti and Maat. Tehuti (renamed Thoth by the Greeks) was the masculine wisdom principle of God. Tehuti also represented writing and learning. Maat was a feminine principle of God and represented truth, justice, and righteousness. By following such pathways as these and others, Kamites hoped to become more like the Supreme Creator, who was hidden.

Some students of ancient KMT have described the education system as "practical," as lacking in a desire to pursue "knowledge for its own sake," as if the "pursuit of knowledge for its own sake" represented a higher and more advanced concept than "practical" education. Kemetic education can be described as *functional*, a blend of *theory and practice*, a *wholistic* education. I remain unconvinced that "education for its own sake" or "learning for the love of learning" is a more lofty goal than education to become more like the Supreme Creator. Put another way, should education be for its own sake or for God's sake?

The European Response to Kemetic Education

Ancient KMT was conquered first by Asians, later by Europeans and finally by an Arabic-Asian population. However, under Greek rule, beginning with Alexander the Great in 323 B.C. and lasting through the Roman Ceasars to the time of Roman Emperor Justinian circa 6th century A.D., a strange thing happened. Before the Greek invasion, Greek students and settlers had been going to KMT for years to learn religion, architecture, and the arts and sciences. For example, the Parthenon on the Acropolis is merely a late copy of African architecture like the Southern Ipet and Ipet Isut Temples which had been developed in KMT at such places as Wa-Set. Yet even after winning their wars with KMT, Greece and Rome became and remained captives of Kemetic culture, especially its religion and education, for nearly 650 years!

It took years of calculated struggle for Romans to destroy Kemetic education. These struggles were initiated by rulers with such edicts as those issued by Theodosius, 380 A.D., and Justinian, 527 A.D. They had to burn down African temples or universities, and destroy or tame the priest-professors to destroy the leadership of KMT. Kemetic religion and education was led by a priesthood that was not Roman. Emperors from Constantine on wanted no foreign leaders as competition, especially for the minds of the people. Christianity became a state religion with a native Roman leadership.

All over KMT today, one can see the results of Greek and Roman conquerors' efforts to copy the culture that they conquered. They rebuilt African temples (church/schools) and joined the African religion. They carved their own images on the African temples. They showed themselves being blessed by African Gods, wearing African clothes and performing African ceremonies. A visitor to KMT today must wonder as he or she gazes on the many massive African temples that were rebuilt by the Europeans, why did they go to such trouble? Noble Europeans even had their bodies mummified in the African way! They took home the African religion of Isis, Osirus, and Horus. It remained very popular and prominent until suppressed by the royal edicts. Even then the influence of Africa remained. For example, the city of Paris, France is named for Isis (Par Isidos or Place of Isis). Notre Dame Cathedral is actually built on the site of the older Temple of Isis!

The last Kemetic college, Philae at the First Cataract, was closed under orders from Justinian in 527 A.D. After this, the classical education of KMT died out or went underground.

Many of the Kemetic educational concepts did not die. They remained in more or less disguised form in the education systems of European conquerors. George G.M. James, in *Stolen Legacy* (1956), has examined traditional histories of philosophy and has shown as did Plutarch (Babbitt, 1969), that many of these authors acknowledge that the wisest of the Greeks were students of African teachers in Kemetic universities. They were given a *liberal arts* education which became the prototype for later Greek and Roman education systems. In Greece, "the Trivium" of grammar, rhetoric and logic were practiced. In Rome, "the Quadrivium" of arithmetic, astronomy, geometry, and music were added. Taken together, these were the "seven liberal arts," the foundation of western higher education. They also remain in the traditional education systems of Nile Valley migrants to all other parts of the African continent.

Conclusion

Our reasons for looking at the ancient Kemetic system of education are many The following reasons are but a few of them:

- Kemetic education is our best window on ancient African education continent-wide.
- Kemetic education is the parent of "western" education and therefore it must be understood if ancient and modern western education is to be understood.
- Kemetic education is a system that can and, in my opinion, should provide guidance for the organization of the education of our people today.

Morehouse men, African Americans have been asked over the years to sit as spectators in silence, in awe, in wonder, and in admiration of the ancient and modern cultures of other peoples. We have not been asked to follow that ancient African dictum, "Man, know yourself!" Were we truly to know ourselves, we would be able to use our own traditions and experiences as the basis for creative problem solving in today's world. To do otherwise is to become cultural schizophrenics, split personalities, trying vainly as DuBois has said, to view the world through the eyes of others, who look on us with amused pity and contempt, "while we chase gods not our own" (Bengu, 1975).

Many of those who view us thus have been partners in the design of an educational process that has withheld from us our birthright, a knowledge of ourselves. It has been said, "He who steals my purse steals trash. But he who steals my good name, steals that which does not make him rich but makes me poor indeed." But "truth crushed to the ground" will rise again. In the words of Gerald Massey:

> Truth is all potent with its silent power
> If only whispered, never heard aloud
> But working secretly, almost unseen,

Save in some excommunicated book;
'Tis as the lightning with its errand done
Before you hear the thunder.

Morehouse Men, you have a special opportunity and a special responsibility—an obligation. It is not enough for you to be bright and competent. You must also have purpose and direction. It is not enough for you to "make it" on your own—to save yourself. As the character Abena says in Armah's novel, *Two Thousand Seasons* (1979), "There is no self to save without the rest of us." Morehouse Men, Know Yourself!

References and Selected Bibliography

Abdullah, Mahmoud (1984). Egyptologist and Tour Guide. Seti I Travel, Luxor, Egypt.

Aldred, Cyril (1965). *Egypt To The End of The Old Kingdom*. New York: McGraw-Hill.

Armah, Ayi K. (1979). *Two Thousand Seasons*. Chicago: Third World Press.

Babbitt, Frank C. (Translator) (1969). *Plutarch's Moralia*, volume 5. Cambridge: Harvard University Press.

Bengu, S.E.M. (1975). *Chasing Gods Not Our Own*. Pietermaritzberg, Natal Republic of South Africa: Shorter and Shooer.

Breasted, James Henry (1937). *A History of Egypt from the Earliest Times to the Persian Conquest*. New York: Charles Schribner's Sons.

Budge, E.A. Wallis (1977). *The Dwellers on the Nile*. New York: Dover Publications (first published 1926).

Budge, E.A. Wallis (1973). *Osirus and the Egyptian Resurrection*. New York: Dover Publications (first published 1911).

Cerny, Jaroslav (1947). *Paper and Books in Ancient Egypt*. London: published by H.K. Lewis & Company, Ltd. (for the University of London).

Diop, C.A. (1978). *Cultural Unity of Black Africa*. Chicago: Third World Press.

DuBois, Felix (1969). *Timbucktu the Mysterious*. New York: Negro Universities Press (first published 1896).

Erny, Pierre (1973). *Childhood and Cosmos*. New York: Black Orpheus Press.

Freud, Sigmund (1967). *Moses and Monotheism*. New York: Vintage (first published 1939).

Gay, John. *Red Dust Tracks on the Road*.

Graves, S.P. (1913). *Education Before the Middle Ages*. New York: McMillan.

Griaule, M. (1975). *Conversations with Ogotemneli*. Oxford: Oxford University Press.

Haskins, R.W. (1844). *The Arts, Sciences, and Civilization, Anterior to Greece and Rome*. Buffalo: A.W. Wilgus.

Hilliard, Asa G. III (1984). *Pedagogy in Ancient KMT*. Paper presented to the Ancient Egyptian Studies Conference, Los Angeles.

Hurry, J.B. (1928). Imhotep: Vizier and Physician of King Zoser and Afterwards the Egyptian God of Medicine. London: Oxford University Press.

Jackson, John G. (1974). *Introduction to African Civilization*. Secaucus, N.J.: Citadel Press.

Jahn, Jahneinz (1961). *Muntu: The New African Culture*. New York: Grove.

James, George G.M. (1976). *Stolen Legacy*. San Francisco: Julian Richardson.

Laurie, S.S. (1902). *Historical Survey of Pre-Cristian Education*. London: Longmans, Green and Company.

Myer, Isaac (trans.; 1900) *Oldest Books in The World: An Account of The Religion, Wisdom, Philos-*

ophy, Ethics, Psychology, Manners, Proverbs, Sayings, Refinement, Etc., of the Ancient Egyptians. New York: E.W. Dayton.

Mertz, Barbara (1978). *Redland, Blackland: Daily Life in Ancient Egypt*. New York: Dodd Mead Company.

Mokhtar, G. (1981). *General History of Africa To Ancient Civilizations of Africa*. Berkeley, California: University of California Press.

Lamy, Lucie (1981). *Egyptian Mysteries: New Light on Ancient Spiritual Knowledge*. New York: Crossroads.

Montet, Pierre (1964). *Eternal Egypt*. New York: New American Library.

Padmore, George (1969). *How Britain Rules Africa*. New York: Negro Universities Press (first published 1936).

Rodney, Walter (1970). *How Europe Underdeveloped Africa*.

Schwaller de Lubicz R.A. (1978) *Symbol and The Symbolic*. Brookline, Mass.: Autumn Press.

Schure, Edward (1973). *The Mysteries of Ancient Egypt: Hermes/Moses*. Blauvelt, New York: Multimedia Publishing Corporation (first published 1889).

Smith, William A. (1955). *Ancient Education*. New York: Philosophical Library.

Smith G. Elliott (1916). *The Influence of Ancient Egyptian Civilization in The East and in America*.

Steindorff, George and Keith C. Seele (1957). *When Egypt Ruled the East*. Chicago: University of Chicago Press.

Turner, Lorenzo (1942). "Some Contacts of Brazilian Ex-slaves with Nigeria, West Africa," *Journal of Negro History*, vol. 27, no. 1, pp. 55-67.

White, J.E. Manchip (1970). *Ancient Egypt: Its Culture and History*. New York: Dover.

Williams, Chancellor (1974). *The Destruction of Black Civilization*. Chicago: Third World Press.

Wilson, John A. (1956). *The Culture of Ancient Egypt*. Chicago: University of Chicago Press.

EGYPT AND ETHIOPIA IN THE OLD TESTAMENT

Charles B. Copher

In the King James and Revised Standard Versions of the Bible, the word "Egypt" (Mitzraim in Hebrew) along with cognates, occurs some seven hundred forty times in the Old Testament.[1] The word translated Ethiopia and/or Cush (Cush in Hebrew) along with cognates, and including three instances of duplication in the references, appears fifty-eight times in the King James Version. In this version the translation "Ethiopia" is used thirty-nine times; "Cush" (untranslated) with cognates, nineteen times. The numerous references to Egypt led one Old Testament scholar to remark, "No other land is mentioned so frequently as Egypt in the Old Testament. . . . To understand Israel one must look well to Egypt."[2]

The occurrences of the words are in several types of the Old Testament literature including the Pentateuch, or five books of the Law, the historical books, the books of prophecy, and in the poetical-wisdom books, but not in all the thirty-nine books that constitute the Protestant Old Testament. Additionally, the literature in which the references occur dates from all periods in the literary history of the Old Testament, and deals with all periods of Old Testament history—from the time of the Hebrew patriarchs (ca. 1800 B.C.) down to and including the Hellenistic period in Biblical history (332-141 B.C.).

In this essay the main references to Egypt are classified and presented under seven headings as follows:

- As the name of a person.
- In narratives of the Hebrew patriarchs and Joseph.
- In narratives of the enslavement, Moses, and the exodus.
- With reference to the Hebrews having been brought out of Egypt.
- In prophetic oracles.
- Egypt in historical relations with Israelites-Judahites-Jews.
- In poetical-wisdom literature.

References to Ethiopia/Cush are arranged and discussed under the following five captions:

- As a term of identification.
- As a geographical reference.
- In prophetic oracles.
- Ethiopia/Cush in historical relations with Judahites.
- In poetical-wisdom literature.

Egypt

Egypt (Mitzraim) as the Name of a Person

Four times Egypt appears in the Old Testament as the name of a person (Genesis 10:6), 13f. duplicated in I Chronicles 1:8, 11). In these instances Egypt is stated to be the (eponymous) ancestor of the Egyptian people and of peoples descended from them. Important to note among the descendants are the Philistines, a fact that may well point to Egyptian relations with the island of Crete.[3]

In Narratives of the Hebrew Patriarchs and Joseph

Beginning in Genesis, chapter 12:10 and continuing through the end of the book, there are seventy-nine occurrences of the word Egypt. These are contained in the accounts of the three Hebrew patriarchs, Abraham, Isaac, and Jacob, and of Joseph. Recounted are Abraham's going down to Egypt with his entourage during a time of famine in his adopted home, the land of Canaan; and the bestowal of riches upon Abraham by the Pharaoh who had taken Abraham's professed sister, but really his wife, into his harem, and the Pharaoh's expulsion of Abraham upon his learning through plagues that Sarah was Abraham's wife and before he had had intercourse with her. It is recounted further that Abraham had an Egyptian maid, Hagar, by whom he sired his first-born son, Ishmael, for whom Hagar obtained an Egyptian wife (Genesis 16:1, 3; 21:9). Isaac is said to have been instructed not to go down to Egypt (Genesis 26:2).

The references with regard to Jacob are interwoven with the accounts concerning Joseph. They relate that during a time of famine in Canaan Jacob learned that food was available in Egypt whither his favorite son, Joseph, had been sold some years previously. After reestablishing relations with Joseph, Jacob moved with his entire family to Egypt. There he died, but he was buried in Canaan, mourned by Egyptians as well as by Hebrews (Genesis 50:3-13).

The narratives that recount the story of Joseph contain the largest number of references to Egypt in the book of Genesis. In what is really a series of stories there is narrated Joseph's being sold as a slave in Egypt to an Egyptian officer whose wife attempted to seduce him; his refusal to cohabit with the woman on moral and religious grounds, and consequent imprisonment on the false charge of attempted rape; and his interpretation of the Pharaoh's troublesome dreams through a God-given ability in consequence of which the Pharoah elevated him to a position second only to his own. Further, the Pharoah gave him an Egyptian wife, Asenath, by whom he had two sons, Manasseh and Ephraim. As the Pharaoh's vice-regent, so the stories continue, Joseph was placed over the fiscal affairs of Egypt in which position he enabled the country to survive seven years of famine which followed seven years of plenty, with sufficient food for export. Moreover, Joseph obtained the whole of the land of Egypt for the Pharaoh's personal possession. Upon his death Joseph was embalmed but not buried in Egypt. His body was kept unburied in anticipation of the Hebrews' return to Canaan where his burial place was to be.

A question arises: To what extent are the narratives of the patriarchs and Joseph records of actual historical events? In reply John Bright in his book, *A History of Israel,* writes that neither upon the basis of the Biblical chronology nor upon the basis of extra-Biblical evidence can one place the patriarchs (and Joseph) within any particular century or centuries. Neither can they be identified as individual personalities. Continuing, he states that it is impossible to relate any person or event in Genesis 12-50 to any person or event otherwise known (in Egyptian history) thereby establishing a synchronism.[4] Similar statements are made by other liberal scholars such as Henry Thomas Frank who in his book, *Bible, Archaeology, and Faith,* states "We have no direct reference outside the Bible to any Biblical figure before the monarchy"—that is, before 1000 B.C.[5] Additionally, Emanuel Anati in his book *Palestine Before The Hebrews,* asserts that "The Biblical accounts do not provide the missing links which would enable us to place the kings and their people (here with reference to Egypt and Ethiopia) in a precise historical framework."[6]

Despite such statements as the foregoing, Biblical historians, on the bases of the Biblical narratives and archaeology, do arrive at definite and positive answers—one liberal, the other conservative. Seeing at least some historical value in the Biblical accounts, the liberals view Abraham, Isaac, and Jacob as heads of tribal movements rather than as father, son, and grandson who succeeded each other as the head of a single family group. Many associate the sale of Joseph into Egypt with the Hyksos period (ca. 1720-1550 B.C.).[7]

On the other hand, taking the Biblical narratives as actual historical accounts, the historical accuracy of which is guaranteed by the Bible's being literally the Word of God, conservative scholars are able to give exact dates for the patriarchs and Joseph as individual persons, and to relate them to specific persons and events in Egyptian history. Thus, conservatives are able to say dogmatically that Abraham was in Egypt between 2091 and 1991 B.C.; that Jacob went with his family to Egypt around 1876 B.C.; and that the Pharaoh who "knew not Joseph" was a Hyksos ruler rather than one of the 18th or 19th dynasties.

Specifically, Merrill F. Unger in his book, *Archaeology and The Old Testament* is able to state categorically that the patriarchs were in Palestine contemporaneously with the Middle Kindgom in Egypt under the Twelfth dynasty (2000-1780 B.C.). He associates Jacob and Joseph with some Pharaoh of his dynasty, Amenemes I-IV or Senworset I-III and places the Hebrews in Egypt during the Hyksos period (1780-1546 B.C.). He places their enslavement in Egypt during the reign of Amenemhet II (1841-1797 B.C.) approximately twenty-five years prior to the end of the Twelfth dynasty.[9] In very substantial agreement with Unger and Wood is Charles F. Aling in his book, *Egypt and Bible History.*[10]

In Narratives of the Enslavement, Moses, and the Exodus

Eighty-one times Egypt is referred to in the accounts of the enslavement of Hebrews in Egypt, of Moses, and of the exodus from Egypt. In these accounts, as may be observed in those concerning the patriarchs and Joseph, Egypt is referred to most often as the *locus* of events.

Following a recounting of the enslavement of the Hebrews for security reasons subsequent to Joseph's death by a Pharaoh who knew nothing of Joseph there is given an account of the birth of Moses into a Hebrew family and his adoption by a daughter of the Pharaoh. This is followed by a second account which tells of Moses' identification with the Hebrews upon his attainment of adulthood, his murder of an Egyptian taskmaster, and his consequent flight from Egypt to Midian. In this latter land, as the account continues, Moses was identified as an Egyptian, married and sired two sons, remained for forty years during which time he worked for his father-in-law as a shepherd, and received a call from the God of the Hebrew fathers under a hither-to unknown name, Yahweh, to return to Egypt in order to free the Hebrew slaves. In turn Moses returned to Egypt where with his brother Aaron he labored for forty years to obtain release of the Hebrews. During this time, God sent a series of plagues which affected the Egyptians but not the Hebrews in order to induce the Pharaoh to free the Hebrews. Through a final plague, the death of the first-born of all the Egyptians, God forced the Pharaoh to give in. Upon second thought, however, after the Hebrews were well on their way out of Egypt, the Pharaoh sent his army in pursuit only to have it drowned in the waters of a sea through which the Hebrews passed on dry land.

With respect to the enslavement of Hebrews in Egypt, Moses, and the Exodus and their relationships to actual history, we have the same situation as that concerning the patriarchs and Joseph.

Liberal scholars are able to see an enslavement of a few Hebrews, perhaps under Ramses II (1290-1224), Moses as an actual person who fought for the liberation of his people, and an exodus of a few thousand at most during the reign of Ramses II or of his son, Merneptah (1224-1214 B.C.)[11]

On the other hand, conservative scholar Leon Wood [12] states that the Pharaoh who "knew not Joseph," and placed the Hebrews in bondage was the first Hyksos ruler, around 1730 B.C., seventy-five years after Joseph's death. Moses was born in 1526, during the reign of Thutmose I (1539-1514). The order to kill the Hebrew babies was given by a ruler of the 18th dynasty. Hatshepsut was the princess who adopted Moses, and Moses and Thutmose III (1452-1450) grew up as rivals in the court. Moreover, Thutmose III would have been the Pharaoh who oppressed the Hebrews and who died during Moses' exile from Egypt; Moses and Aaron dealt with Amenhotep II; and the exodus of some 2,000,000 Hebrews occurred under Amenhotep (1450-1425) (1441).

It may be remarked in passing that the fact that the Pharaohs of the 18th dynasty were Black may account for some of the anti-Black Biblical interpretations of the Jewish rabbis as set forth in the Talmud and Midrashim.

With Reference to Hebrews Having Been Brought Out of Egypt

By far the largest group of references of a single kind to Egypt in the Old Testament have to do with the Hebrews having been brought or led out of Egypt, one hundred thirty-five in number. These references appear in twenty of the thirty-nine books that make up the Old Testament. The largest number appears in the book of Exodus (31) followed by the second largest in the book of Deuteronomy (23). The rest of the Pentateuch, the book of Leviticus and Numbers, contains twenty. Other instances are contained in the historical books (37), the Psalms (4), and in seven of the prophetical books (20). In the main, the passages in which the references are located fall into three groups: those that assert the event as having taken place; those that are reminders of the event, and those that call for praise in remembrance of the event. On another hand, these references are in addition to numerous ones that refer back to the "mighty acts of God" performed in Egypt on behalf of the Hebrews.

In Prophetic Oracles

One hundred eighty-three times Egypt is referred to in eleven of the sixteen books of the prophets (including the book of Daniel). Primarily these references are in the form of oracles or are contained in oracles. However, some occur in or as historical accounts within some of the prophetical books. Still others consist only of allusions to Egypt. In descending numerical order the number of references are as follows: Jeremiah, 62; Ezekiel, 48; Isaiah, 37; Hosea, 13; Amos, 7; Zechariah, 5; Micah, 4; Daniel, 4; Joel, 1; Nahum, 1; and Haggai, 1.

In the ensuing presentation the chronological order in which the prophets lived, and presumably the dates when the various prophecies in the books, in the main, were delivered and/or written down are observed. It is to be noted that the historical periods ranged from around 760 B.C. to 164 B.C.

The Book of Amos (760-750 B.C.). The references in Amos have to do with God's having brought the Hebrews out of Egypt, and with comparing the doom that is to befall Israel with that which had fallen upon Egypt (chapters 2:10, 3:1; 3:9; 4:10; 8:8; 9:5; 9:7).

The Book of Hosea (750-721 B.C.). Five types of oracles with reference to Egypt are to be found in the book of Hosea: that in which the prophet asserts that God has been Israel's God since the days of enslavement in Egypt; that which deals with God's having brought Israel out of Egypt; that in which the prophet harshly criticizes Israel for seeking Egypt's help; that in which the prophet declares that because of her sins Israel will return to Egypt; and that in which the prophet declares that because God cannot ultimately give her up she will return from Egypt (chapters 2:15; 7:11; 7:16; 8:13; 9:3; 9:6; 11:1; 11:5; 11:11; 12:1; 12:9; 12:13; 13:4).

The Book of Isaiah, chapters 1-39 (742-682 B.C.). That portion of the book of Isaiah which is attributed to Isaiah ben Amoz, Chapters 1-39 in the main, and which dates from 742 B.C. to 682 B.C., contains four important anti-Egyptian prophecies and one pro-Egyptian prophecy. The pro-Egyptian prophecy, however, may date from as late as the Hellenistic period (332-141 B.C. in Old Testament history).

The first anti-Egyptian oracle pronounces doom upon Egypt; it is contained in Chapter 19:1-17.[13] The second consists of a symbolic prophecy acted out by the prophet as for a period of three years (715-712 B.C.) he went about naked and barefoot. By his actions he proclaimed that Egypt (and Ethiopia) shall be led away as captives of war by the Assyrians, and stated that those who trust in the Egyptians and Ethiopians will be dismayed and confounded (Chapter 20). The Third, which dates also as does the second from the period when the Ethiopian dynasty ruled Egypt, warns the people of Judah against going down to Egypt for help (chapter 30:1-18). Oracle number four among the anti-Egyptian prophecies, contained in chapter 31:1-3, repeats the message of the third.

The pro-Egyptian oracle (chapter 19:18-26) foresees a day when Israel's God will be worshipped in Egypt by the Egyptians, and when Egypt along with Israel and Assyria will be blessed.

The Book of Isaiah, chapters 40-55 (540 B.C.). Within the chapters of the book of Isaiah that are believed by numerous critical scholars to date from the period of the Babylonian exile (597-538 B.C.) are two oracles which refer to Egypt. The first of these (chapter 43:1-7) is a message of comfort for Judah, promising to give to Cyrus the Persian ruler Egypt (and Ethiopia along with Seba) as a ransom for the people of Judah in exile. The second (chapter 45:14-17) promises that the Egyptians (along with Ethiopians and Sabeans) will become subject to the Judahites and recognize their God.

The Book of Micah (735-700 B.C.). Micah's four references to Egypt have to do with God's having brought Israel out of Egypt; with the people of Assyria and Egypt coming to Judah; and with God's doing marvelous things as when Israel first came out of Egypt (chapters 6:4; 7:12; and 7:15).

The Book of Nahum (612-600 B.C.). Nahum's one reference to Egypt (chapter 3:8-9) equates the forthcoming destruction of Nineveh, capital of the Assyrian empire, with the fall of No-Amon (Thebes) which the prophet states fell despite aid from Egypt, Ethiopia, Put, and Lubim. The fall of Thebes occurred in 663 B.C., toward the end of the Twenty-fifth Ethiopian dynasty.

The Book of Jeremiah (626-582 B.C.). As noted above, the book of Jeremiah contains the greatest number of references to Egypt among the prophetical books, sixty-two. Within the book there are five prophecies directed against the Egyptians; one prophecy favorable to the Egyptians; two prophecies against the people of Judah some of whom have fled to Egypt; and five historical accounts that tell of events involving Egypt which occurred during and immediately after the last days of the Kingdom of Judah (609-582 B.C.). In the succeeding discussion the prophesies are dealt with; the historical accounts are treated under the next caption.

The first anti-Egyptian prophecy (chapter 2:14-37) upbraids the people of Judah for having trusted in Egypt (and Assyria) instead of having trusted in God, and prophesies that they shall be put to shame by the Egyptians even as they had been by the Assyrians. The second (chapter 9:25f.) includes Egypt among other "uncircumcised" peoples who are to be punished by God. In chapter 43:8-13 the third anti-Egyptian oracle, spoken by Jeremiah in the Egyptian city of Tahpanhes, proclaims doom upon the Pharaoh and upon Egypt. Anti-Egyptian oracle number four prophesies an ill fate for Pharaoh Hophra (chapter 44:30). And the fifth, which consists of the whole of chapter 46 except for part of one verse, pronounces doom upon Egypt and Pharaoh Necho at the hands of Nebuchadrezzar, King of Babylon. This prophecy did come true when in 568 the Babylonian ruler did invade Egypt. The prophecy favorable for the Egyptians is composed of verse 26b, chapter 46. It states that after Egypt's destruction by Nebuchadrezzar the country shall be inhabited as in olden times.

Chapters 24:8-10 and 44:1-29 contain the anti-Judahite oracles. The objects of the oracles are those people of Judah who remain in Canaan; and those who have fled to Egypt, now living in the Egyptian cities of Migdol, Tahpanhes, Memphis, and in the land of Pathros (Upper Egypt) because they now serve other gods.

The Book of Ezekiel (593-570 B.C.). The forty-eight references to Egypt in the book of Ezekiel are distributed among three types of prophecies. Those of the first type are pronounced against the people of Judah because they are seeking help from Egypt or because the ancestors committed idolatry during the period of Egyptian enslavement. The second type, consisting of the whole of chapters 29-32, primarily, is directed against Egypt. The third type, represented only by one brief oracle hidden away in chapter 29:13-16, prophesies restoration of Egypt after a period of forty years, albeit as a very powerless nation that recognizes the Lord as God.

An oracle in chapter 17:11-21 adversely criticizes the King of Judah for sending ambassadors to Egypt for help against the King of Babylon. Chapter 19 consists of a lament over former King Jehoahaz who had been taken captive by Pharaoh Necho to Egypt in the year 609 B.C. (See also II Kings 23:30-34, duplicated in II Chronicles 36:1-4). In chapter 20 appears an oracular reply by the prophet to certain of the elders of the Judahite people in Babylonian exile who came to inquire of the Lord. Ezekiel states that God would have destroyed the fathers for their idolatry in Egypt but for His name's sake. And in chapter 23 the prophet castigates the people of Judah for having (allegorically) committed adultery with the Egyptians formerly as well as presently.

As noted, the whole of chapters 29-32 consists of prophecies concerning Egypt, all of which except one are anti-Egyptian. In these Egypt's coming destruction by Nebuchadrezzar is predicted which prediction came to reality[14] as we have noted in 568 B.C., under reference to Jeremiah, chapter 46.

The Book of Haggai (520 B.C.). Haggai's one reference to Egypt (chapter 2:5) reminds the people of the restored Judahite community in Jerusalem of the convenant made with them (the fathers) when they came out of Egypt.

The Book of Joel (ca. 350 B.C.). Joel's prophecy, contained in chapter 3:19, and anti-Egyptian, asserts that Egypt (along with Edom) will become desolate because of violence done to Judah.

The Book of Zechariah (ca. 300-200 B.C.). The five references to Egypt in the book of Zechariah appear in those sections of the book that most critical scholars date in the Hellenistic period (332-164 B.C.). They occur in two kinds of passages that hold out hope for the Jews. In the first it is prophesied that Jewish exiles shall be brought back from the land of Egypt while at the same time Egypt's power will be eliminated (chapter 10:10-11). The second states that a plague will come upon the Egyptians if they fail to come up to Jerusalem in order to observe the Feast of Booths (chapter 14:18-19).

The Book of Daniel (165-164 B.C.). In chapter 11 of the book of Daniel several verses which make reference to Egypt are to be found. According to critical literary-historical scholars, verse 8 refers to Ptolemy III who captured the fortress of Seleucia and brought back much booty to Egypt. Further, verse 9 is said to have reference to the king and country of Egypt. Verses 40-45 predict that Ptolemy will provoke a war in which Antiochus, the Seleucid ruler, will conquer Libya, Egypt, and Ethiopia, but will perish along the seacoast.

Egypt in Historical Relations with Israelites-Judahites-Jews

This topic was both an exclusive and an inclusive peculiarity. It excludes what some regard as historical acounts in the narratives concerning the patriarchs and Joseph; and of the enslavement, Moses, and the exodus—all of which are found in the Law books. It deals with the data in the "historical" books. Further, it does not include some forty-four references to Egypt in the books of Joshua, Judges, and Samuel which, for the most part, refer to the enslavement in and exodus from Egypt. On the other hand, the topic does include data of a historical nature found in some of the prophetical books as noted above. In some cases this latter material duplicates information given in the historical books; in others it supplements, as is indicated.

In toto, there are one hundred eighteen references to Egypt in the historical books. Those in the books of I and II Kings (including duplicate passages in II Chronicles, Isaiah, and Jeremiah) deal with nine matters, as follows: (1) the marriage of Solomon to the daughter of a Pharaoh (I Kings 3:1; 9:16); (2) Solomon's trade with Egypt in horses and chariots (I Kings 10:28f., duplicated in II

Chronicles 1:16f.; 9:28); (3) Hadad the Edomite's flight to Egypt from David, reception by the King of Egypt who gave him a sister-in-law for wife, and Hadad's return to Edom after David's death (I Kings 11:17-21); (4) Jeroboam the Ephraimite's flight to Egypt from Solomon where he remained under the protection of Pharaoh Shishak until Solomon's death whereupon he returned to Israel (I Kings 11:40f., 12:1ff., duplicated in II Chronicles 10:2); (5) Shishak's invasion of Judah and placing it under tribute (I Kings 14:25, expanded in II Chronicles 12:2-9); (6) Hoshea King of Israel's seeking help from So (?) King of Egypt against the Assyrians (II Kings 17:4); (7) The Chaldean Rabshekah's speech to the people of Judah about their unwise reliance upon Egypt for help (II Kings 18:21ff., duplicated in Isaiah, chapter 36); (8) Egypt's domination of Judah by Pharaoh Necho, including Necho's defeat of King Josiah, his dethronement of King Jehoahaz, and his installation of Jehoiakim as King of Judah, during the period 609-605 B.C. (II Kings 23:29-24-7, duplicated and expanded in II Chronicles 35:20-36:4); and (9) Flight of Judahite refugees to Egypt (II Kings 25:26, expanded in Jeremiah 43:1ff.). An additional historical reference appears in Jeremiah, chapter 37:5-7. It reports the coming of an Egyptian army to assist Judah against the Chaldeans, and the prophet's prediction that the army is about to return to Egypt.

In regard to Solomon's marriage to an Egyptian princess it is notable that of his reputed seven hundred wives and three hundred concubines she is the chieftess. More is said about her than about all the others. It is more than interesting to note that the author of II chronicles (chapter 8:11) makes the following statement concerning her, in addition to what is stated in II Kings, "and Solomon brought up the daughter of Pharaoh out of the city of David unto the house that he had built for her; for he said, my wife shall not dwell in the house of David King of Israel, because the places are holy, whereunto the ark of the Lord hath come."[15]

Scholars variously assess the significance of the marriage and of the capture of the city of Gezer by the Pharaoh who gave it to Solomon as a dowry for the princess. One view holds that the marriage indicates the superiority of Solomon's empire over the Egyptian kingdom of that time.[16] Another sees the capture of Gezer by the Pharaoh as an attempt to reassert Egyptian power in Asia.[17] In addition there are questions in regard to the identity of the Pharaoh. It seems clear that he was a ruler during the Twenty-First dynasty (1090-940 B.C.). Some scholars believe that he was not a Pharaoh over all Egypt, but merely a prince who ruled in the eastern Delta region. On the other hand there are those who identify him with Psusennes II (ca. 984-950 B.C.);[18] while still others identify him with Siamun, next to the last of the Twenty-First dynasty rulers (ca. 976-958 B.C.).[19] Solomon's trade in horses and chariots between Egypt and Asia Minor is confirmed by archaeology.

The flight to Egypt by Hadad the Edomite during David's reign and that of Jeroboam during the reign of Solomon shows that Egypt was a haven of safety and support for adversaries of Judah during those times. It appears that the

Pharaoh of Hadad's day sought to discourage his return to Edom in order to reassert independence from Judah during the time of Solomon.[20] On the other hand, Shishak (Sheshonk) founder of the Twenty-Second dynasty (940-745 B.C.) might well have given encouragement to Jeroboam toward the end of weakening Judah.[21] The preceding conjecture is supported by the fact that in the fifth year of Rehoboam's reign Shishak invaded Judah and forced her to pay tribute. This invasion is attested by Shishak's own record which is engraved on a pylon that he erected at the temple of Karnak. This record indicates that he invaded not only the Kingdom of Judah but that of Israel as well; and represents a reassertion of Egyptian power in Asia.[22]

The Reference to King Hoshea's seeking help from So, King of Egypt, against the Assyrians makes for a number of problems. Chief among these is the identity of So. Some view the name as being that of a Pharaoh, variously identified with Sibe, a petty king of the East Delta;[23] with Seve or Shabaka who at the time was a commander of Egyptian forces under his father Pianki;[24] or probably Tefnakhte of the Twenty-Fourth dynasty.[25] Others see the name as referring to a place: thus So is taken to be the Hebrew rendering of the Egyptian word Sais.[26] Marcel Taperruque of France in "La Bible Et Les Civilizations Du Nil" is among those who claim that So cannot be identified.[27]

Concerning Pharaoh Necho II's domination of Judah, this lasted only during the period 609-605 B.C. After 605, as the Bible indicates (II Kings 24:7) the Egyptian ruler did not come out of his land, for the King of Babylon had taken from the River of Egypt unto the River Euphrates all that pertained to the King of Egypt.

In Poetical-Wisdom Literature

Within the poetical-wisdom books of the Old Testament are six references to Egypt of great significance. The first of these appears in Psalm 68:31 where it is declared (according to the King James Version translation) that princes shall come out of Egypt. In four passages (Psalms 78:51; 105:23, 27; and 106:21f.) Egypt poetically is called the "land of Ham." The sixth reference is in Proverbs 7:16 wherein advice is given to a young man against consorting with an adulteress who has decked her bed "with fine linen from Egypt."

Ethiopia/Cush

As a Term of Identification

Four times the word "Cush" appears in the Old Testament as the name of a person (Genesis 10:6, 7, 8, duplicated in I Chronicles 1:8, 9, 10; and Psalm 7). In the first three instances the person is stated to be the first son of Ham, one of Noah's three sons, the (eponymous) ancestor of various peoples located in Africa and Southwest Asia, and the particular father of Nimrod who founded cities in Mesopotamia. In the fourth it appears as the name of a Benjaminite in the title of the Psalm.

In the form of "Cushite" the word appears twice in Numbers 12:1 as the identifying characteristic of a woman whom Moses is said to have married. This designation is applied again in Jeremiah 38:7, 10, 12, where Ebed-Melech, an officer in King Jehoiakim's court, is described as being an Ethiopian, or as it is in Hebrew a Cushite. And in II Samuel 18:21-32 the designation "The Cushite" (Cushite with the definite article) is applied eight times to a courier in David's army. "Cushi" as the name of a person appears once in Jeremiah 36:14ff. where it is given as the name of the great-grandfather of Jehudi, another member of King Jehoiakim's court. The name appears a second time in Zephaniah 1:1 wherein it is stated that a person of that name was the father of the prophet and a descendant of one Hezekiah, presumably a former king of Judah and therefore a member of the dynasty of David.

With references to Moses' having married a Cushite woman, White scholars generally, liberal and conservative, may take passing notice but never make inferences relative to a Black component within the ancient Hebrew populace.[28] Some attempt to explain the reference away as having nothing to do with a Black person, as did the ancient Jewish rabbis who interpreted the passage symbolically. It was upon the basis of the rabbinical interpretation rather than the Bible itself that Cecil B. DeMille in the movie "The Ten Commandments" could portray Moses' wife as White.[29] Taking the Biblical text at face value, and even ignoring Josephus' report that Moses married an Ethiopian princess,[30] the passage can be harmonized with Zipporah's, though a Midianite, having been the wife referred to. Cushites lived in Arabia and elsewhere in Asia as well as in Africa.

The presence of a Cushite in David's mercenary army (II Samuel 18:21-32) led H. Preserved Smith in his commentary on *The Books of Samuel* to refer to him as a "negro" who was "naturally a slave."[31] A far better description lies in the fact that David employed Philistine mercenaries who had come from Crete where Black troops had been in service since early Minoan times, having come from Ethiopia and Egypt.[32]

Ebed-Melech (Jeremiah 36:14ff.) and Jehudi, great-grandson of one Cushi (Jeremiah 38:7ff.) demand great attention. Interestingly and strangely only one White scholar of whom I am aware has mentioned them as members of the Judahite court during Jeremiah's time. This scholar, H. Jagersma, in his recent history of Israel directs the reader to an article published in Howard University's *Journal of Religious Thought*, and written by Professor G. Rice of Howard on "Two Black Contemporaries of Jeremiah."[33]

As a Geographical Reference

Six times Ethiopia/Cush appears as a place name for an apparently distant land located in some instances south of Egypt. In Genesis 2:13 it is given as the name of a place around which the River Gihon flows. Twice in the book of Esther (chapters 1:1 and 8:9) the name appears as one of two extreme boundaries of the Persian empire. In Isaiah 18:1 reference is made to a land that lies beyond the rivers of Ethiopia and that sends ambassadors by the Nile. The prophet Ezekiel pronounces doom upon Egypt that shall reach to the border of Ethiopia (chapter 29:10); and in II Chronicles 21:16 an invasion of Judah by Arabians who live near the Ethiopians is reported.

In Prophetic Oracles

Ethiopia/Cush is referred to in prophetic oracles within the books of Isaiah, Jeremiah, Ezekiel, Daniel, Amos, Nahum, and Zephaniah. Herein the references are dealt with according to the chronological order of the prophet's appearance in history except in the case of two passages in the book of Isaiah, and in the case of the prophet and book of Daniel.

The Books of Amos (760-750 B.C.). In Amos (chapter 9:7) the prophet compares the Israelites to the Ethiopians, stating that they are equal in God's sight.

The Book of Isaiah (742-682 B.C.; 540 B.C.). In Isaiah (chapter 20) Ethiopia is included with Egypt as the object of a prophecy of doom, as was noted in the discussion under Egypt.

From a later date, around 540 B.C., are two oracles which appear in the so-called Second Isaiah (chapters 43:3 and 45:14). Again, as noted in the discussion under Egypt, the passage in which the first of the verses appears contains a message of hope for Judahite exiles. According to it Ethiopia (along with Egypt and Seba) will be given in ransom for them. And still again as was noted in the discussion under Egypt, verse 14 of chapter 45 appears in a prophecy that predicts subservience of Ethiopia, Egypt, and the Sabeans to the restored people of Judah.

The Book of Zephaniah (626 B.C.). Zephaniah contains two references to Ethiopia: one in an oracle that states the destruction of Ethiopia along with several other nations (chapter 2:12), and one in an oracle that foresees the time when worshippers of God who lived beyond the rivers of Ethiopia will bring offerings to Jerusalem (chapter 3:10). The latter passage may refer to Judahites in dispersion or to native Africans who will be converted to Israel's religion.

The Book of Jeremiah (626-582 B.C.). In chapter 13:23 the prophet uses the unchangebility of the Ethiopian's color to argue that the people of Judah cannot change their sinful ways, while in chapter 39:15-18 he pronounces a blessing upon Ebed-Melech the Ethiopian because he trusted in God. And in Chapter 46:9 the prophet includes the Ethiopians among the peoples who had been helpless in aiding the Egyptians against the Chaldeans in the Battle of Carchemish (605 B.C.).

The Book of Nahum (612-600 B.C.). As noted in the discussion under Egypt, the one reference to Ethiopia in the book of Nahum (chapter 3:9) includes

Ethiopia as one of our countries that supported the Egyptian city of Thebes but were unable to prevent its fall in 663 B.C. to the Assyrians.

The Book of Ezekiel (593-570 B.C.). An oracle of doom pronounced primarily upon Egypt in chapter 30 includes Ethiopia three times as being also the object of destruction (verses 4, 5, and 9); and in chapter 38:5 Ethiopia is included among several nations that the prophet says shall be destroyed.

The Book of Daniel (165/164 B.C.). Chapter 11:43 includes the Ethiopians among those whom Antiochus will conquer, as noted in the discussion under Egypt.

With the inclusion of the account of the Queen of Sheba's visit with Solomon (I Kings 10:1-10, 13, duplicated in II Chronicles 9:1-10, 12); and of the reference to Ophir in I Kings 10:11-12); duplicated in II Chronicles 9:10-11, there are possibly six instances in which Ethiopia/Cush appears in historical relations with the Kingdom of Judah. That of the Queen's visit would chronologically be the first, while the reference to Solomon's trade with Ophir would be the second, both occurring during Solomon's reign, roughly 960-922 B.C. The third instance is recorded in II Chronicles 12:13 wherein it is reported that Ethiopians were in the army of Shishak, the Pharaoh who invaded Judah during the reign of King Rehoboam, already referred to under the discussion of Egypt. (See also I Kings 14:25-26 in which passage there is no reference to Ethiopians in Shishak's army.) The next two references to Ethiopia/Cush are given only in II Chronicles (chapter 14:9-15 and 16:8) wherein the author states that there was an invasion of Judah by one Zerah the Ethiopian who was defeated by King Asa (913-873 B.C.). The sixth instance occurs with reference to Tirhakah (Taharqua) (II Kings 19:9, duplicated in Isaiah 37:9, but not mentioned in II Chronicles) who is said to be king of Ethiopia and who is coming to assist Judah against the Assyrians.

Relative to the visit of the Queen of Sheba with Solomon, Edward Ullendorff in his volume *Ethiopia and The Bible* regards the event as historical and locates Sheba in either Southwest Arabia or the Horn of Africa.[34] Josephus in his *Antiquities* states that she was Queen of Ethiopia and Egypt, Ethiopia referring to the land immediately south of Egypt, centered in Meroe.[35] On the other hand, the author of *Black Heroes In World History* (Biographies From Tuesday Magazine) regards the Queen as having her capital in Axum (Abyssinia or modern Ethiopia), but with her kingdom including Southwest Arabia.[36] With this view William Leo Hansberry was in agreement, upon the basis of his notes edited by Joseph E. Harris;[37] as is the Reverend Jacob A. Dyer in his booklet, *The Ethiopian in the Bible*.[38]

Father Mveng of the Cameroun argues that the Queen is to be identified as the Queen of Saba which in (most) ancient times, going back to the Twelfth dynasty in Egypt (1991-1786 B.C.) was the capital of the Kingdom of Cush, and that Saba is to be identified with Meroe.[39]

Whether Ophir, with which land Solomon traded should be included in this essay is debatable. Leon Wood notes that four different locations have been suggested, only one of which is in Africa: Southwest Arabia, Southeast Arabia, Somaliland, and Supara in India.[40] To these four must be added a location established by Father Mveng, namely the region of Zimbabwe[41]—a location that perhaps would take the land out of the boundaries of Ancient Ethiopia. Outstanding scholars among the liberal Biblical historians opt in favor of Somaliland.[42] Unger decides on modern day Yemen and the African coast,[43] while Wood favors India.[44]

The identity of Zerah the Ethiopian makes for still another problem in history. As Keita Tarharka Sundiata notes in his book, *Black Manhood: The Building of Civilization by the Black Man of the Nile*, Zerah was identified by Jean F. Champollion with Osorkon I, second King of the Twenty-second dynasty, (ca. 914-874).[45] This view has now been largely abandoned. Professor Harry M. Orlinsky regards him as head of an Egyptian army,[46] then as the probable leader of Arabian Bedouin tribes.[47] John Bright thinks that he might have been a commander of Egyptian mercenary troops left behind by Shishak.[48] In substantial agreement with Bright is Leon Wood who regards Zerah as an Ethiopian, likely a military leader under Osorkon I.[49] Closely akin to Orlinsky's latter view is that of J.M. Meyers who thinks that he may have been an Ethiopian, or an Arabian from Cushan who was an adventurer in the Pharaoh's pay.[50]

In Poetical-Wisdom Literature

Ethiopia is referred to three times in the poetical-wisdom literature of the Old Testament: in Job 29-19 where reference is made to the topaz of Ethiopia; in Psalm 68:31 which states that Ethiopia shall soon stretch out her hands unto God; and in Psalm 87:4 where Ethiopia is mentioned along with other places of renown.

Summary Observations

The foregoing study discloses that Egypt and Ethiopia figure in the most ancient traditions, and in the literature of the Hebrews-Israelites-Judahites-Jews from all periods of Old Testament history. It reveals further that the two countries, especially Egypt, are referred to in a majority of the books that constitute the Protestant Old Testament. It notes that almost without exception the references to the two countries are negative in nature. Apart from the few pro-Egyptian/Ethiopian passages that were noted, and a passage in Deuteronomy 23:7 wherein it is stated that you are not to abhor an Egyptian because you were a sojourner in his land, there is hardly anything good said about either country.

Further still, the study demonstrates that Egypt was involved in Old Testament history from earliest times, and that Ethiopia figured in that same history from the beginning of the Twenty-fifth, Ethiopian dynasty.

That of the some seven hundred forty references to Egypt most are in the main of a negative nature should be no surprise. How could it be otherwise, considering the fact that the Egyptians were the oppressors, and the memory of Egyptian oppression was kept alive throughout the generations. Yet, an ambivalent love-hate relationship with or attitude toward Egypt existed throughout Old Testament history. Egypt across the years was a haven of refuge, so that even in New Testament times the author of the Gospel according to Matthew could tell of Jesus' escape to Egypt, then use Hosea 11:1 as a reference to Jesus' return from the land.

Notes

1. This number makes allowance for duplication.
2. John Paterson, "The Old Testament World," in *The Bible and History*, ed. by William Barclay (Nashville and New York: Abingdon Press, 1968, p. 39.
3. See, for example, R.K. Harrison, *Old Testament Times* (Grand Rapids, Michigan: William B. Eerdmans Publishing Company, 1970), pp. 171ff.
4. Op. cit. (3rd ed. Philadelphia: Westminster Press, 1981), p. 83.
5. Op. cit. (Nashville-New York: Abingdon Press, 1971), p. 64.
6. Op. cit. (New York: Alfred A. Knopf, 1963), p. 377.
7. For such views, see, for example, John Bright, op. cit. p. 87; H. Jagersma, *A History of Israel in the Old Testament Period*, translated by John Bowden from the Dutch (Philadelphia: Fortress Press, 1979), p. 46; and Theodore H. Robinson, *A History of Israel*, Vol. I (Oxford: Claredon Press, 1932), p. 63.
8. Op. cit. (Grand Rapids, Michigan: Zondervan Publishing House, 1954), p. 107ff.
9. Leon Wood, *A Survey of Israel's History* (Grand Rapids, Michigan: Zondervan Publishing House, 1970), p. 33ff.
10. Op. cit. (Grand Rapids, Michigan: Baker Book House, 1981.
11. See liberal historians such as Bright, Jagersma, and Robinson, op. cit.
12. Wood, op. cit., pp. 83ff. Aling holds similar views.
13. Ira Maurice Price, Ovid R. Sellers, and E. Leslie Carlson, The Monuments and the Old Testament (Philadelphia: The Judson Press, 1958), p. 282, state that Isaiah 19 describes the distress of Egypt under the Assyrians during the period of the Ethiopian dynasty.
14. In passing, it may be noted that these prophecies of Ezekiel, all dated between 587-570 B.C., serve as an excellent historical commentary on the glory of ancient Egypt and Ethiopia, and on Egypt's origins in the South. Further, they serve as a good theological commentary on Egypt from a Judahite point of view. Further still they set forth an exact prediction of Egypt's future as it will become under the Persians and others.
15. The Chronicler, writing between 400-250 B.C., thinks that this *Hamite* would contaminate both the dynasty of David and the holy places.
16. For a contrary view, see Robinson, op. cit., p. 246, and Unger op. cit., p. 221. Frank, op. cit., p. 164, and Bright, op. cit., p. 212, support the view.
17. See Bright, op. cit., and Frank, op. cit.
18. Frank, op. cit.
19. See Bright, op. cit., p. 212; Aling, op. cit., p. 121; Siegfried Hermann, *A History of Israel in Old Testament Times*, trans. by John Bowden from the German (Philadelphia: Fortress Press, 1975), p. 183 and others.

20. Frand, op. cit.

21. Ibid.

22. See, George A. Barton, *Archaeology and the Bible* (7th ed. Philadelphia: American Sunday School Union, 1937), pp. 28, 456f., and others.

23. Price et al., op. cit., pp. 261f.

24. See Elmer W.K. Mould, *Essentials of Bible History* (rev. ed. New York: Ronald Press Company, 1951), p. 251. In agreement with Mould is E. Mveng, "La Bible Et L'Afrique Noire," in *Black Africa and The Bible*, ed. by E. Mveng and R.J.Z. Werblowsky (New York: Anti-Defamation League of B'nai B'rith, 1972). Mveng refers to Smabaka as the Black founder of the Twenty-Fifth dyansty.

25. Bright, p. 275

26. Ibid.

27. Mveng and Werblowsky, op. cit.

28. An exception is Merrill F. Unger, op. cit., p. 136. For a Black African Scholar's apt discussion of the subect one should see E. Mveng's article cited above.

29. See Henry S. Noerdlinger, *Moses and Egypt* (Los Angeles: University of Southern California Press, 1956), p. 70 for a discussion.

30. See *The Works of Flavius Josephus*, translated by William Whiston, A.M. (Hartford, Conn.: S.S. Scranton Co., 1903), "Antiquities of the Jews," Book II chapter X, p. 76.

31. Henry Preserved Smith, *The Books of Samuel*, Vol. VIII of *The International Critical Commentary*, ed. by Charles Augustus Briggs, Samuel Rolles Driver, and Alfred Plummer (New York: Charles Scribner's Sons, 1899), p. 359.

32. See Harrison, op. cit., for an Egyptian origin of Minoan Cretan civilization; and especially Joseph E. Harris, ed., *Africa and Africans as Seen by Classical Writers: The William Leo Hansberry African History Notebook*, Vol. II (Washington, D.C.: Howard University Press, 1977), p. 136.

33. H. Jagersma, op. cit., p. 175.

34. Edward Ullendorff, op. cit. (London: Oxford University Press, 1968), pp. 130ff.

35. Op. cit., Book VIII, Chapter VI, p. 253.

36. Op. cit., p. 2.

37. Joseph E. Harris, ed., *Pillars in Ethiopian History: The William Leo Hansberry African History Notebookl, Vol. I (Washington, D.C.: Howard University Press, 1974), p. 59.*

38. Op. cit. (New York, Washington, Hollywood: Vantage Press, 1974), pp. 27ff.

39. Footnote info missing

40. Op. cit., p. 292.

41. Op. cit., p. 27.

42. For example, William Foxwell Albright, Archaeology and the Religion of Israel (New York: Doubleday and Company, Inc., 1969), p. 130; Bright, op. cit., p. 215; Frank, op. cit., p. 138.

43. Op. cit., p. 225.

44. Op. cit., p. 292.

45. Op. Cit. (Washington, D.C.: University Press of America, 1979), p. 272.

46. In *Ancient Israel* (Ithaca, New York: Cornell University Press, 1954), p. 103.

47. In *Understanding the Bible Through History and Archaeology* (New York: Ktav Publishing House, Inc., 1972), p. 177.

48. Op. cit., p. 235.

49. Op. cit., p. 341f.

50. Reported by Bright, op. cit., p. 235.

THE KAMITIC GENESIS OF CHRISTIANITY

Charles S. Finch

We have the impression in modern times that Christianity burst suddenly on an unsuspecting, morally decrepit world like the full-grown, fully-armored Athena from the brow of Zeus. Avowedly, it sprung out of the Jewish tradition but was considered to be a higher dispensation than Judaism. That there were perceptible shadings of the Platonic philosophical tradition is also readily acknowledged but again, Christianity is seen to occupy a higher plane. In spite of this "conventional wisdom," a painstaking examination of the question reveals yet another root, one which demonstrates that the way for the establishment of Christianity was paved not merely over the course of centuries but of millenia. In this vein, Gerald Massey traces the Christ myth back 10,000 years B.C. to the lands drained by the Nile River on the continent of Africa.[1] Even if we were to yield to more conservative reckonings, it is clear that there is at least a 4500-year connection that leads to Christianity out of Africa and through ancient Egypt or Kemit (Km't). It is this that we propose to explore because the evidence, carefully considered, begins to force upon one the conclusion that the Kamitic[2] influence was the preponderant one, that what became historical Christianity was largely an elaboration and re-working of Kamitic religious and symbolic ideas. Such a premise is shattering in the way only a long-buried truth can be when it is once again brought to light. This is undoubtedly an heretical and blasphemous idea to modern Christian divines but early on, canonical or "official" Christianity buried a great many truths under the blanket of "heresy." To propose that Christianity was Kamitic in origin must seem to some to be turning Christianity upside down on its head; rather it is setting Christianity right side up on its feet.

While we cannot do an exhaustive background treatment of Egyptian religion—its pantheon, myths, and cosmogony—it is necessary to sketch in some of the more important divine actors in the religious drama that connects Christianity to the pre-extant Kamite mythos. For it is demonstrable that the religious concept of the "Christhood" was worked out first in the profoundly important and influential drama of Osiris. The Egyptian name of Osiris is "Asar," which, when broken down its components, "As-ar," can be translated as "born of or created of Isis (Ast)" and this identifies him in one of his aspects as the son of Isis. He was originally a vegetation or corn god identified with the principle of growth. He was also a lunar god, as alluded to in his earthly reign of 28 years which is the conventional lunar cycle; a god of the vine, having taught men the science of viticulture; a dying god, murdered and dismembered into 14 pieces by his brother

Figure 1. The Annunciation, Conception, Birth, and Adoration of the Child.

Set; and lastly and most importantly a resurrected god, having in one phase of the myth been reconstituted and revivified by his wife-sister-mother Isis and in another phase by his son and fulfiller, Horus. As the god of resurrection he is the Judge of the Dead, Lord of Eternity, and the hope of every person for rebirth after death.

The second important deity in the Osirian drama is Isis, whose Egyptian name "Ast" means "throne, seat, or abode."[3] She is the greatest goddess of the Egyptian pantheon, the veritable Great Mother embodying all of the positive feminine attributes as gestator, bringer-forth, nurturer, protector, and perserver. She is the Virgin Mother of Horus, the sister-wife of Osiris, and the ideal of the true and faithful consort. She mourns Osiris in his death and seeks his dismembered body all over the land so that, in the end, she may gather it together and re-instill it with life.[4] She is the goddess of the corn and grain, a lunar goddess, a star goddess identified with Sirius. In her lunar aspect she is often pictured as the Great Cow and in her stellar aspect she is called the "Queen of Heaven."[5]

Horus is the third principle in the drama. His earliest representation is as the infant son of Isis sitting in her lap suckling her breast. Another early aspect of him is as the twin brother of Set. In this schema, Horus is the personification of light and Set the personification of darkness. Horus and Set, though not originally so, become mythically the warring twins and, as the avenger of his father's murder, Horus is Set's implacable enemy. In his solar aspect, Horus is styled the "son of Ra" and is the youthful, rising sun that conquers the dragon of darkness. Indeed the Egyptian form of his name, "Heru," forms the root of the word "hero." In the epic literature of the ancient world, the hero is almost invariably the youthful solar champion who slays the dragon of darkness. Horus or Heru is the prototype of this legendary hero. As the son of Osiris, Horus is also the one who is perfected and glorified.

Lastly, there is the god Set who is an enigmatic figure because although he was at first a benevolent god, he becomes the Great Adversary and Arch-Enemy during the ascendancy of Osiris. He is the personification of war, conflict, destruction, dessication, and death. His abode is the desert and his color is red. He is the

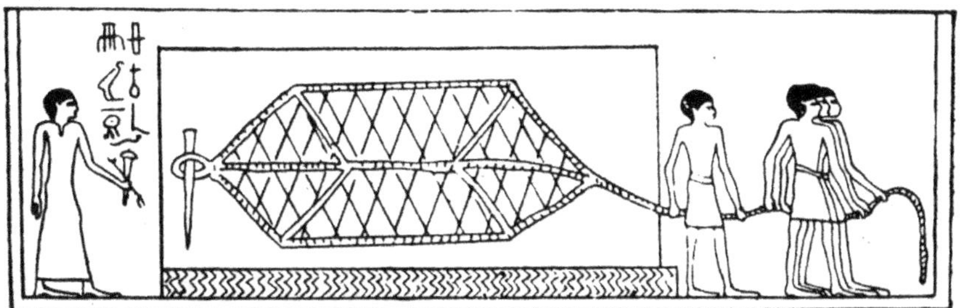

Figure 2. The Four as Fishers for Horus.

Evil One who enviously murders his kingly brother Osiris and threatens the existence of his infant son Horus.

By delineating the mythological and symbolical aspects of the principle actors in the Osirian drama, certain parallels to the Christian drama commend themselves to our attention. Osiris and Horus are in a sense one, that is aspects of each other. This "composite" entity Osiris-Horus is the archetype of the Gospel Jesus. Comparing the Kamitic archetypal figure to Christ we have a being who is born of a Virgin Mother, contends against the Adversary, embodies the vine, is the "bread of life" (Osiris as corn god), and personifies the dying god who is resurrected and reigns as the Judge of the Dead and Lord of Eternity. Comparing Isis to the Virgin Mary we see that she is the virgin mother who brings forth the divine child. Set compares with Satan, the Evil One. Indeed, Set gives his name to Satan as "Set-an:" "Set," as we have seen, is the destructive power and "an" in the Egyptian language is a mark of emphasis.[6] However, there are more than just parallels and interesing analogies to be plumbed and we can begin to systematically link up the Kamite mythos, as personified by the Osirian drama, and Gospel Christianity.

Horus in some of his earliest aspects is often represented as lame and deformed; he is "Horus the imperfect" because he is born of the Mother only, *without the Fatherhood.*[7] However, in a later phase he is a type of divine perfection because he is born of both a divine mother *and* a divine father. Similarly, Jesus in his Christhood is a type of perfection because he is "of the Father" as well as the mother. The Nativity itself seems to come right out of an Egyptian original. In the Temple of Amen at Luxor, there is a group of four vignettes depicting the birth of the infant pharoah, who as the god-kind or divine king is an avatar of Horus. In the first scene, Thoth, the announcer and messenger of the gods, proclaims to the royal mother the impending birth of a son who is descended from the god Amen and will reign as the divine king. In the first chapter of Luke, verses 26-38, the messenger angel Gabriel announces to Mary the impending birth of a divine king,[8] the Son of God. In the second scene of Luxor, the

Figure 3. A schematic of the Zodiac in the Temple of Hathor circa 100 B.C. This temple was a rebuilt version of an earlier Temple of Hathor built on the very same site, circa 1,600 B.C.

god Kneph, who personifies Breath as Spirit, holds the ankh, the symbol of life, to the mouth of the royal mother, indicating that she is conceiving by the power of Spirit. In the Gospel of Matthew, Mary is made pregnant by the "power of the Holy Spirit."[9] In the third scene at Luxor, the divine child is born corresponding to the birth of the divine child at Bethlehem. In the final scene at Luxor, the gods gather around the infant to praise and adore him. In the second chapter of Luke, verses 13-14, the heavenly hosts gather above the infant Jesus to praise and adore him.

It is axiomatic Jesus the Christ was associated with the sun and assumed most

Figure 4. The Soul of Osiris, incarnate in a Ram, as worshipped at Busiris, Philae, etc.

of the attributes of the solar gods of antiquity. We can understand this better with reference to the solar nativity. The birthday of Horus in his solar aspect was December 25th. That day is the first day after the winter solstice on December 21st that the sun begins to ascend toward its zenith at the summer solstice on June 21st. Certain non-Gospel traditions place the birthplace of Jesus in a cave and metaphorically speaking, the nadir of the sun at the the winter solstice is termed "the cave." The sun begins to rise from its "cave" around midnight on the eve of December 25th and can be said to be "born in a cave." Between 2410 and 255 B.C., on the morning of December 25th, the constellation Virgo, "the Virgin," was on the eastern horizon as the sun rose and so the sun could be said to have been "born of the Virgin." These dates precede the rise of historic Christianity

Figure 5. Horus in Pisces.

and the celestial allegory applies, at this juncture in time, to the Horus, the solar prototype. In light of this, the undeniable solar character of Jesus Christ becomes all the more evident when we take into account that the later Christian fathers *changed the original* birthdate of Jesus on January 6 to December 25. The astronomical character of the Nativity is given further substance by consideration of the star Sirius, which is the brightest star in the heavens. Edward Carpenter tells us that some three thousand years ago, Sirius

> stood on the southern meridian (and in more southerly lands than ours this would be more nearly overhead); and that star—there is little doubt—is the Star in the East mentioned in the Gospels. To the right, as the supposed observer looks at Sirius on the midnight of Christmas Eve, stands the magnificent Orion, the mighty hunter. There are three stars in his belt which . . . lie in a straight line pointing to Sirius . . . A long tradition gives them the name of *the Three Kings.*[10] (emphasis mine)

The ancient Egyptians identified Sirius with Isis on the one hand and the jackal-headed Anubis on the other. Sirius, in his character as Anubis, was from time immemorial the Kamite announcer, herald, and guide. In the Kamite scheme, Sirius announced the birth of the sun to the "Three Kings" in Orion's belt.

Figure 6. (a) Tet with the head of Osiris. (b) A priest supporting Tet with the head of Osiris.

There is yet additional evidence that links up the Kamite and Christian versions of the Nativity. In the Osirian drama, Set, as a ploy against Horus, accuses him of bastardy and his mother Isis of harlotry because Horus has no living father. Seb, the "chief magistrate" of the gods, who in one aspect is the "foster-father" of Horus, rules in favor of Horus through the intercession of Thoth, the Messenger. Similarly, in the first chapter of Matthew, the conception of Mary without a known father causes her betrothed Joseph to consider repudiating her because of harlotry. However, an angel of the Lord intercedes in Mary's behalf and Joseph, like Seb before him, accepts the verdict in favor of the divine child and becomes the "foster-father" of Jesus.

The Kamite astronomical mythology can aid us in further uncovering the role in Jesus the Christ as a solar figure. Both the Christian Easter and the Passover out of which it derives are equinoctal festivals, that is, they commemorate the spring equinox which was one of the most important events in antiquity. The Passover only in a superficial sense refers to the angel of death "passing over" the homes of the Hebrews in Goshen smeared with the blood of the lamb. It also refers to the sun, in its path along the ecliptic, "passing over" the celestial equator at the spring equinox when night and day are of equal length. The celestial equator is an infinite extension into space of the terrestial equator; the ecliptic

Figure 7. Representations of the "Opening of the Mouth."

is the apparent path of the sun as it moves from its nadir (or "cave") at the winter solstice to its zenith at the summer solstice. In the northern hemisphere, the day is shortest at the winter solstice and longest at the summer solstice, attaining perfect equilibrium with the night at the equinoxes. At the spring equinox, the sun undergoes a "second birth" as the length of the day exceeds that of the night. Moreover, the sun at this time, on its ecliptic path, "crosses" (or "passes over") the celestial equator. The ecliptic and the celestial equator form a point of crossing, i.e., a "cross." At that point, the sun is fixed on a celestial cross, hence it is "crucified." In addition, the celestial equator forms a broad arc through space which can be figuratively represented as a "mount" or a rounded "calvarium," Latin for "skull." This then is the source of the imagery of the Christian crucifixion on Mount Calvary (Golgotha). It is on the celestial Calvary that the sun is momentarily suspended (crucified) at the crossing. These are the facts of astronomical mythology, worked out over a period of milleniums by the Kamite astronomer-priests in the lands drained by the Nile. These ancient savants projected onto the heavens a complete symbolic representation of their mundane world so that earth and heaven were mirrors of each other.

For uncounted generations lost in the dim mists of pre-historic antiquity, the Kamite astronomer-priests painstakingly mapped out all of the visible sky. They used typological nature symbols to create markers to help them chart the heavens. One product of this careful labor is the Zodiac which the modern world inherited from the priests of Kemit.[11] It is indubitably clear that the Zodiac, and the science of its interpretation, profoundly affected the political, social, and historic events of antiquity and its indelible imprint is still part of our modern consciousness in ways we are only dimly aware of. The heavenly Zodiac was pictured as a great circular "clock" divided into twelve equal arcs or signs. The

Figure 8. Anubis anointing the mummy of Osiris with Isis giving directions.

Zodiac could only be charted in the sky after the Great Year had been determined. To explain the Great Year, one has to appreciate that the axis of the earth is tilted about 23 degrees from vertical or true north. Given this tilt, there is a "wobble" effect of the earth's north axis in relation to true north. As the earth revolves around the sun, the earth's north axis slowly revolves around true north, taking 25,868 years (26,000 in round numbers) to effect a complete revolution. This is the Great Year. As this slow; 26,000-year revolution occurs, the equinoxes appear to move slowly backward in relation to their position in the signs of the Zodiac. The 2,155-year presence of the spring equinox in each Zodiacal sign constitutes an "age." This 2,155-year figure is arrived at by dividing the length of the Great Year, 25,868, by twelve, the number of signs in the Zodiac. In the year 2410 B.C., the spring equinox moved into the Zodiacal sign of Aries the Ram out of the sign of Taurus the Bull. This inaugurated the "Age of Aries" and the Ram and its related symbols, the Lamb and the Shepherd, became the avatar of the age. Some 2,155 years later, the spring equinox in its backward precession moved into the sign of Pisces the Fishes in 255 B.C. which inaugurated the Age of Pisces whose avatar was the Fish(es). During the Arian Age, the Ram or Lamb figures as the dominant religious symbol of the world and the Jewish Passover ritual, using the lamb as the sacrificial victim whose blood saved the Children of Israel from the wings of Death, was a product of the Age of Aries. The traditional skewering of the Paschal Lamb on

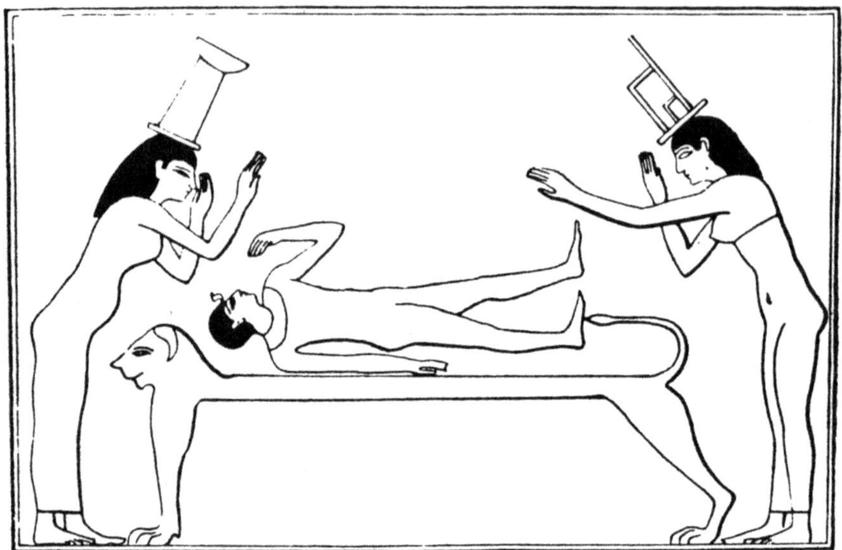

Figure 9. Isis and Nephthys bewailing the death of Osiris. From a bas-relief at Philae.

the spit is a form of crucifixion which commemorated the sun's "crucifixion" on the "cross" of the equator and ecliptic in the sign of the Ram (Lamb). When one age supersedes the previous one, the dominant symbol generally has enough power to carry over to the succeeding age. Thus in the 32nd chapter of Exodus, verses 4-5, we find the Children of Israel worshipping the golden calf, the avatar of the preceding Taurean age. The anger of Moses at the impiety of the Israelites when he descends from Mt. Sinai is largely due to their worship of a discarded avatar, one that had been superseded by the Ram. Christianity, rising during the Age of Pisces, incorporated as its symbol the Fish(es). Throughout the New Testament, fish symbolism abounds and as if to put to rest any doubt on the matter, Jesus himself emphatically states, "This is a wicked generation. It demands a sign and the only sign that will be given it is the sign of *Jonah*" (emphasis mine).[12] Now Jonah was swallowed by a great fish and hence is identifiable as *the Fish-Man*. Jesus then is clearly establishing himself as the avatar of the Piscean age in the process of connecting himself to the Fish-Man. True to pattern, however, the messiah of the Piscean age incorporates the older form of the avatar and so is also regarded as the Lamb, who by his sacrifice "takes away the sins of the world," and as the Good Shepherd. In fact, the oldest form of the Christian crucified savior figure is not that of a man but of a lamb. The crucifixion of the sun as Ram or Lamb at the spring equinox is inherited from the incredibly old Kamite religion, which was adopted by the Jews and passed on as a remnant of the former Age to Christianity. It is easy enough to trace a parallel process in

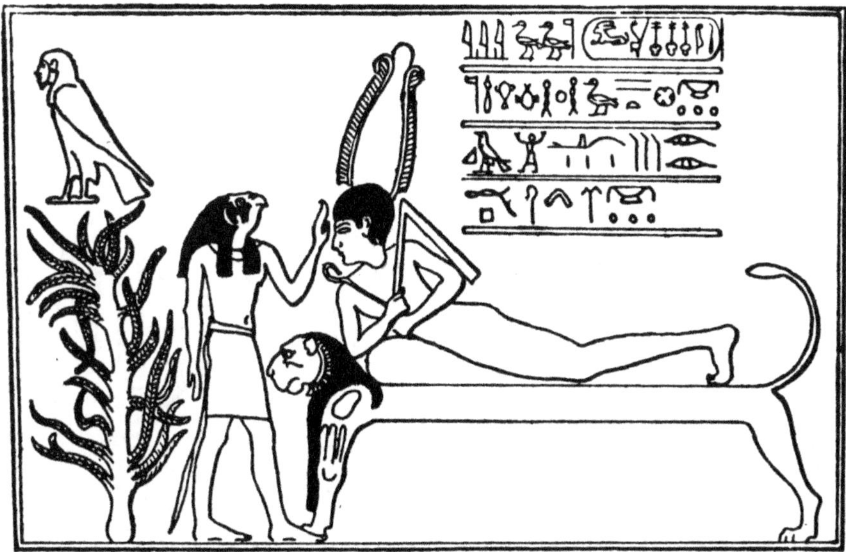

Figure 10. **(a)** ***Extreme left*****: The soul of Osiris on the Erica tree. (b)** ***Right*****: Osiris of Hermopolis of Lower Egypt rising from his bier at the command of Horus.**

Egypt. Egyptian dynastic history begins in the Age of Taurus the Bull and the dominant gods of the time are Ptah of Memphis, whose symbol is the bull, the Osiris of Abydos, who is also identified with the bull. Between 2400 and 2100 B.C., with the advent of the Age of Aries the Ram, the god Amen and his patron city Thebes rise to the fore and command the dominant place in the Egyptian state religion. Amen's symbol is the ram and the older bull-gods, Ptah and Osiris, give way. However, Osiris, never really relinquishes his central place in the religious sensibilities of the ancient Egyptians and gradually, in one form or another, he is identified with all the other gods in the pantheon. As "Asar-Sa" he is literally "Osiris the Shepherd" and so partakes of the Ram symbolism.[13] Lastly, after the beginnings of the Piscean age in 255 B.C., Egypt embraces the religion of the Piscean avatar, Christianity, but without disestablishing the old religion. We sum up by saying that Jesus Christ was the Piscean avatar symbolized by the Fish(es) who was the continuation of the earlier Kamitic avatars and who thus inherited the symbols of the previous age in his manifestations as the Lamb and the Good Shepherd.

We can continue the process of unlayering the Kamite astronomical symbolism in the Gospels. We have now established some sure ground for asserting that Jesus assumed the attributes of the sun gods of antiquity whose prototype was Horus. The solar character of Jesus is further exemplified by the Palm Sunday procession of Jesus into Jerusalem on the back of an ass, his way strewn by palm branches. One of the earliest Kamite personifications of the sun-god was

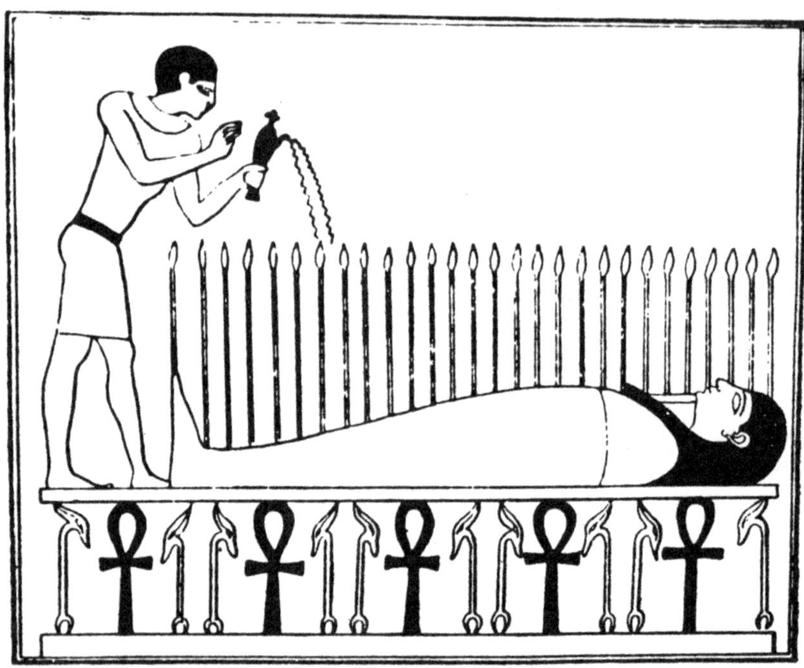

Figure 11. Osiris-Nepri, with wheat growing from his body. From a bas-relief at Philae.

Aiu who was the ass-headed god. He is a form of Ra, the sun, and is represented as the golden ass who carries the disk of the sun on his head between his ears.[14] The palm branch, Gerald Massey informs us, is a type of time, with the two equal sides of the branch representing the equality of day and night at the equinox. Jesus riding the ass to the scene of his ultimate crucifixion is a figure of the sun moving toward the equinox (symbolized by the palms) at the Easter or Passover where he will be "crucified" on the "cross" of the equator and ecliptic. In another phase of Kamite mythology, the ass was identified with Set; this evil character of the ass is recounted in a hymn to Ra in which the priest recites ". . . may I smite the Ass; may I crush the evil one . . ."[15] Thus at another level of symbolism, Jesus perched on the back of the ass may represent his supremacy over Satan, i.e., of the sun (Horus) over darkness (Set).

The cross, the outstanding and fundamental symbol of Christianity, is itself incomparably old as a Kamite symbol. In the form of the ankh, known as the "crux ansata," it is the symbol of life, uniting masculine and feminine images. The earliest Christians adopted the ankh as their symbol of the cross. It is interesting to note, as an aside, that in a number of West African religions, the crossroads is a place charged with numinous power because it represents the place of union between human and divine, material and spiritual, living and dead. We find some

Figure 12. Christ in Glory. Coptic Art (*left*). St. George and the Dragon (*right*).

sense of this in the Egyptian Tet cross, which is a conventionalized image of the Tree and which represents the backbone of Osiris. Gerald Massey states that the Tet cross is a type of the eternal and signifies death and the dead, i.e., those who have "crossed over."[16] When the Tet cross is erected, Osiris, the dead god, is raised up, "suspended" as it were from his backbone, and thereby reigns as the resurrected one, Lord of Eternity:

> At a very early period Osiris was assimilated to the Tet and the ceremony of "setting up" the Tet became the equivalent of the reconstitution of the backbone and the body of Isiris generally.[17]

In the cross, then, a number of symbols converge: it is a type of stability and everlastingness, a nexus between the living and the dead, an image of resurrection, and the cosmic moment of the equinoctal "crossing."

In Christian dogma, the death of Jesus is stereotyped as a Roman-style crucifixion on Mount Calvary. However in the Book of Acts in the New Testament, it is explicitly related that Jesus was hanged from a gibbet, rather than being nailed to a cross.[18] There is a strange parallel here to the mythical history of the Yoruba god Shango.[19] Shango rules as one of the first, if not the first, kings of the Yoruba nation of Oyo. He becomes alienated from his subjects who persecute him and drive him from the throne. In his despair, he hangs himself from a tree (of which the Tet cross is a type), and then falls into a large hole in the

Figure 13. Jesus Christ. This representation of Jesus is on the obverse side of a coin whose front has a likeness of Justinian II.

ground. Eventually, he ascends into heaven on a chain, a type of the ladder of Ra upon which the beatified souls ascend into heaven, and becomes a powerful orisha or god who is the personification of lightning and thunder. Of further interest is the fact that Shango's avatar is the ram. The common elements shared by Jesus and Shango command attention: the kingly status (Jesus as the "king of Israel"); the persecution by one's own people; the death by hanging; the descent into the lower world (" . . . he descended into Hell . . ."), the ascension into heaven by an act of self-resurrection; the imagery of a man who becomes divine; the identification with the ram (lamb). These are all conspicuous parallels that suggest much.

As one reads the Gospels one is struck by how various episodes and characters recall details from Kamite mythology. It is noted in several of the Gospels how Jesus cured a blind man by rubbing spittle on his eyes.[20] In the Osirian drama, the blind Horus has his sight restored to him by Thoth rubbing spittle into his eyes. In the 7th chapter of Mark, verses 8-9, the evangelist relates a story of a deaf and dumb man who has his speech restored to him:

> They brought to him (Jesus) a man who was deaf and had an impediment in his speech . . . He took the man aside away from the crowd, put his fingers into his ears, spat, and touched his tongue. Then, looking up to heaven, he sighed, and said to him, 'Ephphatha!' Which means 'Be opened.'

This can be compared to passages in Budge's edition of the *Book of the Dead*, more properly called the "Book of the Coming Forth By Day," which describe the well-known ceremony of resurrection known as the 'opening of the mouth':

> Horus hath opened thy mouth . . . 'Thy mouth was closed up' . . . Kher-heb says: 'Open the mouth and the two eyes . . .'[21]

In the ancient Kamite conception, to be dead was to be deaf and dumb, i.e., without "the Word," which called everything to life. The opening of the mouth restores the Word to the dead, i.e., the one who is "dumb," and restores life. In the Gospel of the Evangelist John we see the identification of the Word with the Christ. In the first verse, John writes "In the Beginning was the Word, and the Word was with God, and the Word was God." In the 14th verse, he informs us that the "Word was made flesh" in the person of Jesus Christ. Osiris too was the "great word," that is, "the word of what cometh into being and what is not."[22] According to E.A. Wallis Budge, "Osiris the Word spake the words through all things in heaven came into being from non-existence."[23] In addition, "Because he was the first man who raised himself from the dead, he became the type and symbol and hope of every dead man."[24] In the Kamite cosmo-conception, the power of life and re-birth rested in the Word which was commanded, indeed personified, by Osiris. In the funerary ritual, the Kher-heb priest says over the deceased, who seeks immortality through identification with Osiris, "Thy voice shall never depart from thee, thy voice shall never depart from thee."[25]

As a religion, Christianity is almost entirely built around the messiahship of Jesus Christ. As we might expect, the archetypal messiah is found in the Kamite religion in the person of Horus. The word "Messiah" is Hebrew and signifies the "anointed one" who is the expected king and deliverer. After the failure of the Jews to establish the earthly kingdom under the messiah, Christians changed the expectation of an earthly kingdom to one of a heavenly or spiritual kingdom under the messiahship of Christ. The root of the word "messiah" can be found in the Egyptian word "mes" which means "to give birth," "to be born anew," "child," or "son."[26] As a proper noun, "Mes" is the "chief prince" and "Mesu" is a man's name.[27] The terminal "ia" in Egyptian is the particle of exclamation, which emphasizs the emotive content, and when added to "Mes" gives "Mes-ia." The Mes-ia is thus the "Great Prince" or "Great Man" while still retaining the connotation of rebirth and the sonship. This corresponds very well with the sense inherent in the term "messiah" as used by Christians and Jews. Moreover, the Egyptian deity "Iah" was the great prototype of the Hebrew Yahweh and "mesIah" would translate as "son of Iah" or Yahweh. Again, this conveys almost exactly the sense of the Judaeo-Christian messiahship. Finally, Gerald Massey informs us that Horus was the "messu"[28] which means "anointed." The genesis of the messiah concept is thus to be found in the Kamite world.

As the messiah, Jesus was the "kristos" or Christ. This word "kristos" or Christ means "anointed in Greek and is a direct translation of the Hebrew word "messiah." In Egypt, the "krst" or "karast" was the *anointed* mummy identified as the reborn, re-arisen Osiris. Jesus in his Christhood is the re-arisen anointed one, showing that the Egyptian "krst" and the Greek "kristos" are virtually identical. This is exemplified in another way by the story of Lazarus in the Gospel of John, chapter 11, verses 1-44. Lazarus is the dead brother of the two sisters Martha and Mary who mourn him. They prevail upon Jesus to minister to him and he reassures them by saying "I am the resurrection and I am life." He goes to the tomb of Lazarus and calls to him, "Lazarus come forth." The reawakened Lazarus rises up and comes out of his tomb swathed in linen bandages, i.e., in "mummified" form. Osiris is the dead brother of the two sisters Isis and Nephthys who mourn him. He is, as we have seen, the archetypal mummy wrapped in linen bandages and in this form is called Asar-Taiti, that is, "Osiris the Mummy."[29] It is Horus who is called upon to minister to Osiris and, with the two sisters in attendance, reanimates and reawakens the dead body. This is pictured in scenes where the mummified Osiris slowly rises to an upright position from his funeral bier. In the pre-extant Kamite version, it is the sisters who exhort the dead god to "Come forth to thy house!"[30] The connection is secured by examining the name "Lazarus." Its root is "azar" which is "asar," the name of Osiris. "L" is the Semitic definite article which means "the." The terminal "us" is the Egyptian "as" which means "to call" or "to hail."[31] Literally, "Lazarus" means "the Osiris called (forth)."

Central to the practice of the Christian religion is the re-enactment of the sacrifice of Jesus as the eucharist, i.e., the giving of his body and blood in the form of bread and wine "so that sins may be forgiven" thus enabling the communicant to conquer death. This sacrifice is formalized and consecrated in the Mass. The word is the same as the Egyptian "mes" "the evening bread" or "the evening supper."[32] The analogy to the Last Supper is obvious. Jesus is the "bread of life" and the eating of his "body" is a form of mystic communication with the deity. The Pyramid texts of the 6th dynasty (circa 2600-3000 B.C.), shed light on the eucharistic feast of Christianity. In the so-called "cannibal hymns," the dead pharoah Unas is said to eat the bodies of the gods and drink their blood.[33] The imagery employed is quite graphic and may even be a hold-over from a more primitive time when the ancestors of the dynastic Egyptians did indeed partake ritualistically of human flesh and blood. But it is also quite evident that in the Pyramid texts—the graphic imagery notwithstanding—the rendering is allegorical, for it is to receive the magical and divine potency of the gods that the manes

Figure 14. Black Madonna from Nuria, Spain. She is called "The Queen of the Pyrenees."

Unas is said to "eat them." He becomes as the gods themselves by partaking of their essence. The eucharist of Christianity is but a refinement of this idea.

Osiris, in one of his earliest aspects, is a corn or grain deity, i.e., that from which the daily bread is made. In one representation we see him lying flat and stalks of grain growing out of him;[34] his sacrifice through his death and dismemberment allows the grain to grow. As is Jesus, he is the "bread of life," and the breaking of the eucharistic bread during the Mass (or "mes") recalls the dismemberment of the body of Osiris. The other aspect of the Mass is the drinking of the blood of Christ in the form of wine. Now Osiris is the god of viticulture and the wine is, on the one hand the "spirit" of the grape on account of its intoxicating properties (hence the term "spirits" to denote alcoholic liquors) and, on the other hand, is the "blood" of the grape. Since as the divine viticulturist he is the personification of the grape, to drink wine is to partake of the blood and spirit of Osiris. Jesus, in the Gospels, changes the water into wine. This imagery is also Kamitic. In a prayer in behalf of the deceased to Ra, the priest is made to say, "his water is wine like that of Ra."[35]

In the 14th chapter of the Gospel of John, verse 6, Jesus tells Thomas "I am the way; I am the truth and I am life; no one comes to the father except by me." Osiris is called the "Lord of Maat"[36] which means that he is "Lord of Truth." As "Asar-Neb-Ankh"[37] he is literally the "Lord of Life." No one in the Kamite schema comes to Father Ra in his boat of the sun except by Osiris, the Great Judge. It almost begins to appear that the figure of Osiris-Horus was lifted bodily out of the Kamite mythos and deposited intact in the New Testament Gospels.

The figure of the Virgin Mary, as we have seen, also emanates from Kamite typological antecedents. The word "meri" in ancient Egyptian means "beloved" or "one who loves or is loved."[38] The goddess Meri-f-ua is a guardian of Osiris making her a form of Isis, and we have already noted the identity of the Virgin Mary and the Virgin Isis. Mary is also identifiable with the Kamitic goddess Hathor whose Egyptian name, "Het-Her," means "house, mansion, or temple of Horus," Thus she is a form of the mother of Horus. In one of her aspects she carries the epithet "meri" as "Hathor-Meri" or "Hathor the Beloved." Hathor is often personified as a dove and the Evangelist John relates that he sees the Holy Spirit coming down on the head of Jesus in the form of a dove.[39] Massey states that the Hathor dove is a type of rebegetting spirit and in *Natural Genesis* says:

> In the *Legenda Aurea*, at the assumption of Mary the Christ addresses his mother as his dove, and says, "Arise my mother! My dove! tabernacle of glory, vase of life, celestial temple."[40]

As noted above, the "Het" in the Egyptian name for Hathor means "temple" or "tabernacle." Christian tradition thus identifies Mary as a type of the Egyptian goddess Hathor. An additional Kamitic connection is revealed in the Gospel of

Luke where both Mary and her kinswoman Elizabeth have divine visitations that result in the impregnation of both of them.[41] Elizabeth gives birth to John who in his adult career becomes "the voice crying in the wilderness" proclaiming, "Prepare a way for the Lord; clear a straight path for him." In the Osirian drama, both Isis and her kinswoman (sister) Nephthys conceive by Osiris. Nephthys gives birth to Anubis whose title is the "opener of the way" and who, as illustrated in the Dogon cosmology, is the "master of the first speech (word)" and thus a form of the "proclaimer."[42]

The Great Adversary in the Kamitic schema is Set who as "Set-an" gives his name to the Judaeo-Christian Satan. As we have seen, Set's color is red which is consistent with the anthropomorphic representations of Satan in medieval Christian iconography depicting him as a red, horned being with cloven hooves and a tail. Set was sometimes personified as a goat in ancient Egypt so we see that the conventionalized notions of the Christian Satan and the Egyptian Set concur.

It is hard, if not impossible, to escape the conclusion that the New Testament was a re-worked Kamitic document or, at least, had its ultimate genesis from Kamitic sources. This being the case, it shouldn't surprise us to learn that, according to the Acts of the Apostles, the first gentile convert to Christianity was the Ethiopian minister of Candace, the Queen of Cush, who was baptized by the Apostle Philip. Nor should it surprise us to learn that early Christianity was nurtured and kept alive by the "desert Fathers" of Egypt who bequeathed the monastic tradition to later Christianity. Moreover, if we examine the *first human* representations of Jesus the Christ, he is pictured as a black man with woolly hair.[43] In addition, the Isis cult, in which Isis is depicted as a Black-colored African goddess holding the black infant Horus in her lap, became one of the most important and influential religions in the Roman empire. Roman legions carried this figure of Black Isis holding the Black infant Horus all over Europe where shrines were established to her. So holy and venerated were these shrines that when Christianity invaded Europe, these figures of the Black Isis holding the Black Horus were not destroyed but turned into figures of the Black Madonna and Child. Today these are still the holiest shrines in Catholic Europe.

A brief word should be said about the "historical Jesus." Though this deserves a fuller treatment, it is beyond the scope of this article.[44] It is by now well-established that, outside the Gospels themselves, there is no authentic independent record or witness to the actual existence of Jesus as described in the Gospels for the first four generations after his supposed death by crucifixion. As G.R.S. Mead has opined, "The very existence of Jesus appears to have been unknown" by the commentators and historians in the Greek, Roman, and Jewish world of the 1st century.[45] Given the manifestly mythic character of Jesus as shown by our discussion and given that his entire history seems to have been drawn from prototypes in Kamitic sources, it isn't any wonder. In 120 B.C., a man was born of a woman named Miriam and an artisan named Joseph who took the name Jeshu ben Pandera. He eventually became a member of the Essene brotherhood, which is the pre-Christian Jewish sect that *directly* gave rise to historic Christianity. The most important Essene center was Egypt and it was there that Jeshu ben Pandera spent many years under the tutelage of an Essene sage named ben Perachia. When he left Egypt, Jeshu was apparently well-versed in the mystic sciences of Egypt because he began to travel through Palestine, teaching, healing the sick, and performing "wonders." He was arrested by the Jewish authorities, accused of practicing magic, convicted, and *hanged on the Passover* in the town of Lydda in 70 B.C. when he was about 50 years of age. This is the real history of a man who was evidently a great teacher and healer and the path of the "historic Jesus" leads back to him and him alone. As the author has stated before in another context,[46] perhaps the vast savior mythology, already in place in the Kamite world for thousands of years, coalesced in the Piscean Age around the person of this obscure but remarkable Essene sage.

The whole process of re-establishing the Kamitic presence in world history is rather akin to looking at a crystal in the light: when the light strikes it from one direction, you see the crystal in one stereotyped way. The moment the light shines from a different angle, things are seen and appreciated in the crystal which were not apparent before. Only the perspective has changed. The world and its history are like that crystal: all that it takes is another kind of light and another kind of vision to see things that were there all along and only apparently hidden from view.

Notes

1. See Massey, Gerald, *Natural Genesis*, 2 vols., London: Williams and Norgate, 1883, passim, and *Ancient Egypt*, 2 vols., New York: Weiser, 1970, passim.

2. The word "Kamitic" is taken from "Km't" which was the ancient Egyptians' name for their country and means "the Black Land." "Kamitic" is used here to specifically refer to the cultural products of Egypt and her cognate Nile Valley civilizations, Ethiopia and Cush. However it also refers to the cultural ethos of African civilization in its broadest sense in time and space. In the context of this article, "Kamitic" is used interchangeably with "Egyptian."

3. Budge, E.A. Wallis, *An Egyptian Hieroglyphic Dictionary*, vol. 1, New York: Dover Publications, 1978, pp. 78-81.

4. See Neumann, Erich, *The Origins and History of Consciousness*, trans. by R.F.C. Hull, Princeton: Princeton University Press, 1970, plate 29 after page 240.

5. This is a term given to Isis by Apuleius in the 11th book of his Metamorphosis (Golden Ass).

6. Budge, op. cit., p. 56.

7. Consult the works of Gerald Massey—*Book of Beginnings, Natural Genesis*, and *Ancient Egypt*, passim—for an extensive treatment of this. See also Erich Neumann's *The Great Mother: An Analysis of an Archetype*.

8. *In these verses of Luke, the angel Gabriel is made to say (of Jesus), "... he will be king over Israel forever; his reign shall never end."* *The New English Bible*, New York: Oxford University Press, 1971.

9. Ibid., "The Gospel According to Matthew," 1st Chapter.

10. Carpenter, Edward, *Pagan & Christian Creeds*, New York: Harcourt, Brace, & Co., 1921, pp. 29-30.

11. See Lockyer, Norman, *The Dawn of Astronomy*, Cambridge: M.I.T. Press, 1964, pp. 18-19 for a discussion and reproduction of the Egyptian Zodiac as represented at the Temple of Hathor at Denderah.

12. See the 12th chapter of Matthew, verses 38-40 and the 11th chapter of Luke, verses 29-30, *Bible* . . ., op. cit.

13. Budge, op. cit., p. 87.

14. See Budge, ibid., p. 109; see also Budge, *Gods of the Egyptians*, vol. 2, New York: Dover Publications, 1969, p. 367.

Budge, E.A. Wallis, *The Book of the Dead*, New York: Dover Publications, 1967, p. 248.

16. Massey, *Natural Genesis*, vol. 1, op. cit., p. 448.

17. Budge, E.A. Wallis, *Osiris: The Egyptian Religion of Resurrection*, vol. 1, New Hyde Park: University Books, 1961, p. 52.

18. "Book of Acts," chapter 5, verses 30-31, *Bible* . . ., op. cit.

19. See Frobenius, Leo, *The Voice of Africa*, vol. 1, trans. by Rudolf Blind, New York: Benjamin Blom, Inc., 1968, pp. 204-227 for a discussion of several versions of the myth of Shango; see also Beier, Ulli, *Yoruba Myths*, London: Cambridge University Press, 1980, pp. 20-32.

20. "Gospel According to Mark," chapter 8, verse 24, *Bible* . . ., op. cit.

21. Budge, *Book of the Dead*, op. cit., p. 268. After reviewing this manuscript, the author's wife Mrs. Ellen Finch pointed out that there is a perfectly natural explanation for the "opening of the mouth" symbolism. The first sign of life in a newborn infant is when he *opens his mouth and cries*. The newborn cry then is the "first word." This explains perfectly the symbolic reasoning behind the Egyptian "opening of the mouth" ceremony performed over the dead person about to undergo rebirth. In order for the rebirth to occur, the dead manes has to open his mouth and utter the Word ("cry") just as the newborn infant does. This can be amplified further by noting that physiologically the newborn cry is preceded by an inrush of air or breath; air and breath are synonymous with "spirit" in the Kamite conception so that the "opening of the mouth" in the funeral ritual presupposes that the spirit re-enters the dead manes and reanimates or revives it in the resurrection. Few if any authors have given an adequate or coherent explanation of the "opening of the mouth" ceremony and I am indebted to my wife for helping me understand the matter more clearly than I ever did before. Note: Kher-heb was a type of funerary priest; "Kher-heb" translates literally as "purveyor of the word."

22. Budge, *Osiris* . . ., op. cit., p. 79.

23. Ibid.

24. Ibid., pp. 79-80.

25. Budge, *Book of the Dead*, op. cit., p. cxxxix.

26. Budge, *Hieroglyphic Dictionary*, op. cit., pp. 321-322.

27.Ibid., p. 323.

28. Massey, *Ancient Egypt*, vol. 1 op. cit., p. 217.

29. Budge, op. cit., p. 88.

30. Frazer, James George, *Adonis, Attis, Osiris*, vol. 2, New Hyde Park: University Books, p. 12.

31. Budge, op. cit. p. 79.

32. Ibid., p. 323.

33. See Lichteim, Miriam, *Ancient Egyptian Literature*, vol. 1, Berkeley: University of California Press, 1973, pp. 36-38.

34. Budge, *Osiris* . . ., op. cit., p. 58.

35. Ibid., p. 104.

36. Ibid., p. 308.

37. Budge, *Hieroglyphic Dictionary*, op. cit., p. 86.

38. Ibid., p. 310.

39. "Gospel According to John," chapter 1, verse 32, *Bible* . . ., op. cit.

40. Massey, *Natural Genesis*, vol. 2, op. cit., p. 417.

41. "Luke," chapter 1, verses 5-56, *Bible* . . ., op. cit.

42. In *Conversation with Ogotemmeli* by Griaule, Marcel, New York: Oxford University Press, 1965, pp. 16-23, we have almost a complete exposition of a West African (Dogon) Kamitic cosmogony whose connections to ancient Egypt are unmistakable. According to the blind Dogon sage Ogotemmeli, the first (divine) son is the jackal who obtained mastery of the "first word" and "ever afterward he was able to reveal to diviners the designs of God." This jackal is clearly the Dogon Anubis—the earliest form of the guide and messenger—who is thus the prototype of John the "proclaimer" of Jesus.

43. See Murray, Margaret, *the Splendour That Was Egypt*, New York: Philosophical Library, 1949, plate XCIII on page 252.

44. For a thorough examination of the philological and historiographical questions surrounding the historical Jesus, see Mead, G.R.S., *Did Jesus Live 100 B.C.*, London: Theosophical Publishing Society, 1903.

45. Ibid., p. 48.

46. See Finch, Charles S., "The Works of Gerald Massey: Studies in Kamite Origins," *Journal of African Civilizations*, vol. 4, no. 2, November 1982, p. 63.

Additional References

Bonwick, James, *Egyptian Belief and Modern Thought*, Indian Hills: Falcoln's Wing Press, 1956.

Clark, R.T. Rundle, *Myth and Symbol in Ancient Egypt*, London; Thames and Hudson, 1978.

Deren, Maya, *Divine Horsemen: The Voodoo Gods of Haiti*, New York: Dell Publishing Co., 1970.

Doane, T.W., *Bible Myths and Their Parallels in Other Religions*, New York: Truth Seeker Co., 1948.

Higgins, Godfrey, *Anacalypsis*, 2 vols., New Hyde Park: University Books, 1965.

Jackson, John. G., *Mjn, God, and Civilization*, New Hyde Park: University Books, 1972.

Jahn, Jahnheinz, *Muntu*, trans. by Marjorie Grene, New York: Grove Press, 1961.

Jung, Carl Gustav, *Aion*, trans. by R.F.C. Hull, Princeton: Princeton University Press, 1979.

Mead, G.R.S., *The Pistis Sophia*, Secaucus: University Books, 1974.

Mead, G.R.S., *Thrice Greatest Hermes*, 3 vols., London: John Watkins, 1949.

Szekely, Edmond Bordeaux, *The Essene Gospel of Peace*, 3 Books, San Diego: Academy of Creative Living, 1972-1978.

Tompkins, Peter, *Secrets of the Great Pyramid*, New York: Harper & Row Publishers, 1971.

THE NILE VALLEY PRESENCE IN ASIAN ANTIQUITY

Runoko Rashidi

Upon examining the roots of Asian history, its human and prehuman beginnings, its numerous advanced high cultures, one invariably finds Black faces and African foundations. The earliest hominids to populate Asia were regional varieties of Homo Erectus. This would include those fossil remains labeled Peking and Java Man. Both collections of fossils have established datings of up to 500,000 B.P. Homo Erectus fossil remains from Africa, particularly Kenya, however, range back as far as 1.6 million years. By this period our distant ancestors had lost most of their body hair, possessed a dark pigmentation, and wore a crown of tightly curled or wooly hair. Over a half-million years ago, having domesticated fire and aware of basic methods of transporting food and water, Homo Erectus was ready to begin his Asian trek. On the route he carried his highly distinct physical features; features which could only have been altered to any significant degree over an extremely long period of time.[1]

The first modern humans, Homo Sapiens Sapiens, we can identify in Asian history were diminutive blacks, commonly labeled pygmies and negritoes, and originally birthed in east-central Africa, the continental cradleland. New and controversial finds in this region, and southern Africa as well, may give them an antiquity of up to 100,000 years. Their migrations out of Africa were gradual processes, beginning in all probability more than 50,000 years ago. These little blacks were on the move at the time and eventually spread to the far corners of the earth. What their impact was on the high-cultures which followed, characterized by metallurgy, urban dwelling, agricultural science, advanced scripts, etc., has neither been fully measured nor appreciated.

These small blacks, essentially hunters and gatherers, can be traced in Asia from Iran to the Philippines. Archaeologist/historian Gaston Maspero finds them well represented in early Elam, and describes them, ". . . as short and robust people of well knit figure with brown skins, black hair and eyes, who belonged to that Negritic race which inhabited a considerable part of Asia in prehistoric times."[2] In south India their remnants are exemplified by the Kadar and Uralis. Other members of this early human family have survived in the Andaman Islands in the Bay of Bengal. Western anthropologists have gone to great lengths to explain the presence of these Andamanese, whose numbers do not exceed 20,000. One account has them as the descendants of a shipwrecked crew of African slaves. In southeast Asia, in Thailand and Malaysia, the little blacks are called Sekai. Their case is similar to that of the Andamanese and the little blacks of the

Figure 1. Male citizen of Susa.

Philippines, the Aeta, in that there are only a few thousand of them. In southern China, particularly in Yunnan province, accounts of "black dwarfs" persisted well into the third century.[3] In Taiwan they were known as "little black man" and only disappeared about one hundred years ago.[4]

The next ethnic type to populate and dominate Asia were the Austrics, best exemplified by the aboriginal people of Australia. Like their small predecessors they are generally regarded, in anthropological circles, as examples of the most primitive forms of humanity, and they too have only survived in the most isolated areas, e.g. deserts, mountains and islands.

Besides a common language, the Austric family is distinguished by short stature and straight to wavy hair, and appear to have reached their zenith over 15,000 years ago. There is little evidence of their possession of written languages, and efforts at clear documentations of their early history have been formidable undertakings.

Albert Churchward calls this group the Nilotic negroes and includes within it the Ainu of Japan. The Ainu, according to Churchward,

> . . . are of the same original race and type as the Australian Aborigines and their beliefs correspond with the rituals of ancient Egypt . . . Their skulls are of the same shape and average capacity as the Australians and Nilotic negroes.[5]

The Austric family, together with the smaller blacks, fused with the early whites to form the west Asian ethnic group usually called Semites, and groups related therewith.

> Anthropologically and culturally speaking, the Semitic world was born during protohistoric times from the mixture of white and black skinned people in Western Asia.[6]

> This community of physical type, possibly already disturbed, was finally altered by the spread of the Armenoid type of peoples akin physically to men of that type, who penetrated from the highlands into the lowlands at a period in Asiatic history yet to be determined, and who by hybridizing in different degrees with their predecessors brought the welter of physical types which confront every student of ethnology of the region stretching from Cape Cormorin to Kurdistan . . .[7]

The Austrics constituted an important element in the early populations of southern Arabia, with their skeletal remains also having been unearthed in ancient Mesopotamia. In south Asia they proliferated, and are six million strong today in east-central India, where they are known as the Munda and Kolarians. A Munda sub-group, the Gonds, form the root word of the semi-mythical submerged continent of Gondwanaland, reputed to have formed an extensive land bridge joining east Africa with south Asia. The Veddas of Sri Lanka are also an

Figure 2. Bronze female figure from Mohenjo-Daro excavations, 3rd millennium B.C. (Naji).

Austric remnant population and represent the longest continued occupation of any of the island's ethnic types.

Having very briefly reviewed the first hominid and modern human populations of Asia, it now seems appropriate to examine the Nile Valley impact on Asian civilization. Here again the evidence supporting the Nile Valley foundations of Asian high-cultures is substantial, for as the larger blacks began their move into the continent in protohistoric and historic times, they took the major components of their culture with them.

Early observers, such as Ephorus, point out that "the Ethiopians occupied all the southern coasts of both Asia and Africa."[8] Homer described the blacks as divided and "dwelling at the ends of the earth, towards the setting and rising sun."[9] Strabo adds that the Greeks " . . . designated the whole of the southern countries towards the ocean . . . on the coasts of both Asia and Africa as Ethiopia."[10] Of course Herodotus comments on the blacks of Asia, distinguished from the blacks of Africa only by their straight hair.[11]

Uthman Amr Ibn Bahr Al-Jahiz, a brilliant black scholar, writing in the 9th century, and himself part of the African diaspora in Asia, included among the black populations:

> . . . the Ethiopians, the Berbers, the Copts, the Nubians, the Zaghawa, the Moors, the people of Sind, the Hindus, the Qamar, the Dabila, the Chinese, and those beyond them . . . the islands in the seas . . . are full of Blacks . . . up to Hindustan and China.[12]

A millennium later, John Baldwin, one of the leading 19th century advocates of early Ethiopian diffusions into Asia echoed Al-Jahiz:

> It is now admitted that a people of the Cushite or Ethiopian race, sometimes called Hamites, were the first civilizers and builders throughout western Asia, and they are traced, by the remains of their language, their architecture, and the influence of their civilization, on both shores of the Mediterranean, in eastern Africa and the Nile Valley, in Hindustan, and in the islands of the Indian Seas.[13]

The Biblical genealogy of the races of man as outlined in Genesis, places Kanaan, one of the sons of Ham, the Biblical progenitor of the Blacks, at the heart of the Phoenician city-states.[14] The Phoenicians enter history prominently early in the third millennium B.C. They were the advanced naval power of their time and maintained a large degree of control and influence on the Palestine/Lebanon sea coasts through the heyday of imperial Rome.

As new populations entered the region the Phoenicians began a colonization process that included Khart-Haddas, or Carthage. One of the major Phoenician cities, Byblos, provides the name for the Christian Bible.

Robert Graves traces the origins of the Kanaanites, or Phoenicians, to

Figure 3. Modern photo of a Dravidian woman, whose ancestors erected the civilizations of the Indus Valley (Naji).

Uganda.[15] If that were not enough we might add that the Kanaanites were successors in Palestine/Lebanon to the Natufians, a clear and distinct African People.[16]

Southern Arabia

In southern Arabia too there is a black foundation, which once dominated the entire peninsula and has yet to be eradicated. The blacks were however pushed into and isolated in Arabia's southern extremities, e.g. Hadramaut. A considerable number of scholars and travellers have consistently pointed these facts out:

> To the Cushite race belongs the oldest and purest Arabian blood, and also that great and very ancient civilization whose ruins abound in almost every district of the country.[17]

> The people of Arabia belong to two distinct and apparently quite different races. The common idea of the Arab type . . . is a tall, bearded man with a clean-cut, hawk-like face. The Arabs of South Arabia are smaller, darker, coarser featured and nearly beardless. All authorities agree that the Southern Arabs are nearly related by origin to the Abyssinians. Yet strange to say it is the Egypto-African race who are the pure Arabs, while the stately Semite of the north is Mustrab . . . Arab by adoption and residence rather than by descent.[18]

Anthropological studies place the early south Arabians in antiquity's black belt. In this scheme of things they would occupy a place intermediate between Africa's upper Nile Valley populations and those of the Dravidians of southern India. When the Kushite blacks entered the region, sometime after 4000 B.C., they found other blacks, the Austrics, already in possession of the land. At a later date, towards the end of the third millennium B.C., Indo-Europeans or Semites, perhaps both, broke southward, and in the face of fierce resistance, settled amongst and heavily intermixed with the earlier inhabitants.

> The south Arabs represent a residue of Hamitic populations which at one time occupied the whole of Arabia. To account for the round-headness and certain Caucasian traits we have had to postulate migration and miscegenation . . . The dark-skinned indigenes of South Arabia may have been round-headed and, at a later date, Hamites from Africa and round-headed Caucasians may have invaded their land and their marriage beds. For aught we know, many racial waves may have spread southwards or northwards in long past times.[19]

The language of the ancient south Arabians, and the Mahra of today, can also be placed in our black belt. George Rawlinson, a Biblical scholar and one of the pioneering savants of west Asian scripts, regarded the vocabulary of south Arabia's Mahra and the Galla of Abyssinia as living relics of that used by the Kushite nations of old.[20]

The kingdoms of southern Arabia were particularly prosperous from about

Figure 4. Typical southern Indian depiction of the Lord Shiva, principal deity of modern south India (Naji).

1200 B.C. thru the early centuries of the common era. One of these kingdoms, Saba, was at least part of the domain of Makeda, the legendary Queen of Sheba, called Bilqis in the Koran.

The region's wealth was derived from the large-scale export of incense, and its geographical position as a safe haven for the numerous ships involved in the trade of luxury items from east to west. Of course the role of the blacks in the fostering of Islam must not be overlooked. Al-Jahiz in fact asserts that Abd Al-Muttalib, grandfather of the Prophet Muhammad, was "black as the night and magnificent."[21]

Sumer and Elam

Ancient Sumer, which has also been called Shinar, Chaldea, Babylon and Babylonia, is the first major high-culture of Asia. Extending over southern Mesopotamia, it has in fact been projected as the birthplace of civilization itself. This conclusion however would appear to be the result of a combination of simple ignorance and scholastic racism. Sumer actually seems nothing less than a Nile Valley offshoot, its citizens calling theselves the "blackheads."

I do not argue that Sumer was exclusively peopled by Blacks or that the Africans were the only early ethnic entity in the area, but in respect to Sumerian civilization, the black contribution was decisive.

The Sumerian account of the fish-headed god Oannes, who appears at the mouth of the Persian Gulf as a civilizing agent and begins the dawn of Sumer, may be only symbolic of a gradual movement of blacks from the upper Nile Valley into and along the coasts of southern Arabia, and slowly arriving in southern Mesopotamia before continuing on gradually to the north and east. This seems the only logical explanation for the frequency of not simply African, but particularly Nile Valley physical and cultural remains.

The exacting results of craniological research, linguistic studies, and comparative studies of the region's religious and philosophical beliefs, provide irrefutable proofs of Sumer's Nile Valley origins. Eyewitness accounts, the early predominance of the lower Mesopotamian city of Kish, apparently only a modification of the Nilotic Kush, and comparisons of Sumerian and Nile Valley physical sciences, detail a pattern of similarities which far exceed the realm of coincidence and chance.[22] Genesis also makes Sumer a Nilotic colony when it identifies the mighty hunter Nimrod, the original Sumerian, as a son of Ethiopia or Kush.[23]

Having sprung into view early in the third millennium B.C., by the late 17th century B.C., the once powerful Sumerian city-states had been largely overwhelmed by non-Africoid nomadic tribes. Confined for a time to the Kingdom of the Sea Land at the base of the Persian Gulf, their last national entity, the Sumerian Blackheads were the victims of the sweeping migrations and resulting tur-

Figure 5. Colossal bust of the Buddha from the Champa high-culture of 11th-century Vietnam. "The religion of Buddha, of India, is well known to have been very ancient. In the most ancient temples scattered throughout Asia, where his worship is yet continued, he is found black as jet, with the flat face, thick lips, and curly hair of the negro" (Godfrey Higgins, 1836; photo by Naji).

moil in this highly critical period of west Asian history. Ultimately the black-heads were absorbed into new populations or dispersed to new regions. Yekubi, a 9th century historian, in discussing Abyssinia and the Sudan, states that "The sons of Ham, sons of Noah, at the time of the division of the sons of Noah, migrated west from the land of Babil (Mesopotamia/Sumer), and crossed the Euphrates toward the sunset."[24] It should also be of note that the Biblical patriarch Abraham journeyed forth from Ur, the most important of all the Sumerian cities, as the Kingdom of the Sea Land was falling. It is uncertain then whether Abraham should be identified as a Sumerian refugee seeking a safe abode for his family and followers, or part and parcel of the massive Semitic and Caucasoid intrusions that facilitated Sumer's demise.

Although Sumer perished as a national entity, its civilizing influence remained. The various nations that followed could only build on her foundation. Her tutorial relationship with her successors was very similar to that of the Egyptians with Greece and Rome.

Ancient Elam, which enters history about 3000 B.C., shared Sumer's eastern border and political destinies. Elam's capital was Susa, generally held to be the home of the mighty Memnon, the great black warrior-king. The story of Memnon was one of the most widely circulated of a non-Hellenic hero in the world of antiquity. In addition to the reference of Quintus and the illusions of Homer, Memnon is referred to by Hesiod, Virgil, Ovid, Pindar, Diodorus Siculus, Aeschylus, Pausanias, Strabo, and Appolonius among others. Arctinus of Miletus composed an epic poem, *Ethiopia*, in which Memnon was the leading figure. Diodorus records that Memnon led a combined force of ten thousand Susians, and an equal number of Ethiopians, along with two hundred chariots to the aid of the beleaguered Trojans. According to one account:

> Priam had by now persuaded his half-brother, Tithonus to send his son Memnon the Ethiopian to Troy . . . Tithonus governed the province of Persian for the Assyrian king Teutamus, Priam's overlord . . . he was black as ebony but the handsomest man alive, and like Achilles wore armour forged by Hephaestus. Some say that he led a large army of Ethiopians and Indians to Troy by way of Armenia.[25]

Memnon distinguished himself in battle and momentarily checked the Greek onslaught before suffering a mortal wound. The Greco-Trojan conflict, c. 1270 B.C., long regarded as only a myth, was given a firm historical foundation by Schliemann in the 19th century. Troy's strategic position on the northeast coast of Asia Minor must have made her an important western port for the Susians, and it is only logical for them to have come to her aid in such a desperate commercial situation. This is a highly important point in the study of the African story in early Asia, for having firmly established their presence, our initial premise, we must then proceed to determine exactly what they did once there. Very exciting are the possibilities of actual blood ties linking the Susian and Trojan royal

Figure 6. Central portion of the Bayon, Angkor. Kampuchea, 12th century (Naji).

families; ties which may well have been similar to those of the Ethiopians and Egyptians in the major periods of Nile Valley history, e.g. the 17th and 18th Egyptian dynasties.[26] The fact that Memnon led a combined force of blacks, i.e. Susians and Indians, presumably Africoid, Nilotic Kushites or even Egyptians, could well represent an early example of a confederation of black nations assisting a sister nation and political ally in a time of national crisis.

All of the accumulated evidence points to a west Asia absolutely alive with Black people. Strabo, for example, makes note of an African presence extending from Syria northward into central Turkey.[27] The *Armenian Geography* applies the name Ethiopia to the whole territory from the rivers Tigris to the Indus.[28] Moses of Chorene, the Armenian historian, identifies Belus, a term usually used by the Greeks, with Nimrod, and adopts a genealogy for him only slightly different from Genesis. In this case Nimrod, or Belus, is the grandson of Kush and the son of Egypt. In both instances Nimrod/Belus is descended directly from the Nile Valley.[29]

The racial affinities of the Colchians have been another source of anguish and frustration for western academia. For the ancients this was not the case. Herodotus, for example, regarded Colchis, the possessor of the Golden Fleece in Greek mythology, as an Egyptian colony established during the military campaigns of Senusert III, c. 1860 B.C. He not only points to the Colchians' black skin and wooly hair, but also to their oral traditions, language, methods of weaving and circumcision practices. It should be added that Herodotus was not the only observer to comment on the Colchians' racial and cultural affinities.[30] Well after Herodotus' time, c. 450 B.C., the Colchians maintained the distinct physiognomy he ascribed to them. St. Jerome, writing during the fourth century calls Colchis the second Ethiopia.[31] Sophronius, patriarch of Jerusalem, over two hundred years later, describes an Ethiopian presence in the same region.[32] Even today, in the same district about which Herodotus wrote, exists a numerically minute, black-skinned and wooly haired community.[33] Colchis is perhaps then the best example of the remarkable tenacity of the blacks of Asia and their ability to survive in a frequently hostile environment.

Intermediate between Elam and the Indus Valley lies a region formerly known as Gedrosia, "land of the dark folk," and known today as Baluchistan, the archaic spelling of which, Beloochistan, is reminiscent of Belus/Nimrod.

The Indus Valley

In the 1920's discoveries of large mounds in Pakistan's Indus Valley led to the excavations of two long abandoned urban centers. Ancient documents gave some indication of their existence, but the full extent of the civilization they represented had not even been guessed at. The two cities, Mohenjo-daro in Sind and Harappa in western Punjab, had been constructed along old river beds and possessed multiple level houses enhanced by sophisticated wells, drains, and bathrooms complete with toilets.

In 1931 another city, Chanhu-daro, somewhat closer to the mouth of the river Indus, was excavated. We are now aware of a staggering one thousand Indus valley sites, covering a cultural area of more than 1100 miles east to west and 800 miles north to south, all of which are pre-Aryan. The revelation of the Indus Valley civilization, constructed and developed by the south Indian Dravidians, descendants of the Nile Valley, has led to a complete revision of Indian history.

Although the Indus Valley civilization reached its zenith about 2400 B.C., essentially identical cultural remains, centered around argicultural communities in Baluchistan, have been carbon dated to the beginning of the fourth millenium. The identification of a Dravidian language, Brahui, in eastern Baluchistan, would also support the idea of a gradual movement towards the east of the same people who had earlier settled in Arabia, Mesopotamia and Iran. Spurred on perhaps by increasing populations or the encroachment of northern nomads, the west Asian Blacks swept into the region and, quickly realizing its vast agricultural potential, dramatically applied their long-evolved technologies towards its exploitation.

The mature state of the Indus high-culture seems to have popped up fully developed. This is the case in site after site. Indus cities were constructed with a remarkable uniformity, characterized by consistent grid plans of straight streets, with standardized kiln-burned and mud bricks utilized as the principal building materials. There appears to have been no major architectural innovations for a time span exceeding six centuries.

Of the many Indus Valley sites, ranging from the river Oxus deep in central Asia, to Lothal, near the Gulf of Gambay, north of Bombay, Mohenjo-daro and Harappa are by far the largest and most thoroughly excavated. They were the centers of the Indus complex, and may have alternated as the administrative capitals. More specific information has been denied us because of the virtually undeciphered Indus script. In spite of extensive research by countless scholars the language remains a mystery, the resolution of which could result in a tremendous leap forward.

Much has been said about contacts of the Indus with other territories. The Indus was in fact a center of wide spread commercial activities. Long distance trade is indicated by finds of lapis lazuli from Afghanistan at several Indus sites. Ongoing trade relationships, initially by land and later by sea, between Mesopotamia and the Indus began in the third millennium and continued intermittently for centuries. The port city of Lothal, at the southern end of the Indus complex, had a foreign exchange so developed that it constructed an artificial dock, measuring 955 x 121 ft., to receive ships and handle cargo.[34] This is the oldest artificial dock in the world. At the end of the second millennium. B.C. Lothal also had close trade and cultural contacts with Susa.[35]

A layover zone and an important religious center between the Indus and

Mesopotamia was Dilmun, on the eastern coast of the Arabian peninsula, extending from Bahrain to Oman. A series of recent excavations have revealed the skeletal remains of a largely indigenous yet eclectic culture that combined elements from the Indus to the west that heretofore had been ignored.

The post 1900 B.C. period reflects a steady decline in the Indus cities. High on the list of contributing factors were the gradually diminishing agricultural returns due to over-cultivation. Another element was an increase in flooding due to tectonic disturbances in the lower Indus Valley. Both of these elements, combined with increasing human and cattle populations, led to forced migrations into India proper, and a gradual abandonment of the Indus cities. Hot on the heels of the migrating blacks were northern nomads who had never seen a city, had no appreciation of sedentary life, and were to fundamentally alter the course of Indian history.

The Aryans were of the same ethnic and cultural type as the Kassites, Mitanni, Hurrians and Dorians. They were representative of the Indo-European family of languages and came originally from central Europe or south Russia. When burst upon the scene, early in the second millennium B.C., they literally sent the world reeling. The outpouring of the Mongol hordes across Eurasia in the 13th and 14th centuries might be the closest analogy.

The Aryan intrusions into south Asia began about 1900 B.C. and continued intermittently to about 800 B.C. They ultimately swept across all of northern India. They named their conquered territories Aryavarta, land of the Aryan. Their conquest however was not easily accomplished. Generally on the defensive, the blacks fought back valiantly. Whether or not they received the kind of assistance referred to earlier in respect to Memnon and Troy, we simply do not know. There is the story of the Ethiopian king Ganges, conveyed by Samuel Purchas, "who with his Ethiopian army passed into Asia and conquered all as far as the River Ganges . . ."[35a] Apollonius of Tyana also makes mention of a King Ganges whom he regarded as ruler of both the Ethiopians of the Nile Valley and India as well.[36] Eusebius preserves a tradition that "in the reign of Amenophis III, a body of Ethiopians migrated from the country about the Indus, and settled in the Valley of the Nile."[37]

The fullest documentation for the Aryan conquest of northern India is from the book of hymns called the Rig Veda. The Rig Veda was composed by the Brahmans or priests, and represents the sum total of the early Aryan experience. Besides the religious aspect of the Rig, probably introduced by the conquered Dravidians, it is absolutely rampant with violence and racial overtones. The blacks are referred to as Dasas, Dasyus, and Simyus, and the major Aryan deities, particularly Indra, are repeatedly called upon to slay the detested enemy:

> Indra, invoked by many, and accompanied by his fleet companions, has destroyed the Dasyus and Simyus who dwelt on earth, and distributed the fields to this white worshippers.[38]

> Indra has destroyed the town of the Dasyus . . . cast thy weapon against the Dasyu, and increase the vigour and fame of the Arya.[39]
>
> Indra protects his Arya worshipper in wars. He flays the enemy of his dark skin, kills him, and reduces him to ashes.[40]
>
> Cast thy dart, knowingly Thunderer, at the Dasyu, increase the Arya's might and glory . . .[41]

It is also in the Rig Veda that we find the first documentation of the racially oriented caste system.[42] The four castes are supposed to have sprung from god Brahman. The Brahmins, composed of the poets and priests, were identified with color white and derived from the god's mouth. The Kshatriya, the administrative and military caste, were linked with the color red and came from Brahman's arms. The Vaisya were identified with yellow and came from the thighs of Brahman. They were the mercantile caste and apparently the recipients of a greater degree of racial intermixture. The conquered Blacks formed the Sudra caste. They were identified with the color black and issued from Brahman's feet. They were almost entirely dispossessed and were destined to serve as the perpetual slaves of the higher castes. The Sanskrit term for caste, Varna, literally means color. As the centuries progressed the caste system became more regimented. As the intensely hostile racial relations began to soften the term Aryan became the personification of all that was noble: Sudra, all that was debased.[43]

Buddhism, arising in the sixth century B.C., appears as a natural reaction to Brahminism. It placed no emphasis on caste and experienced its greatest popularity in the central, eastern and southern regions of India, heavily populated by the blacks who had retreated before the Aryan hordes.

A number of theories have been enunciated in respect to the origins of Buddha and Buddhism. Diop, for example, surmises that Buddha was an Egyptian priest fleeing the persecution of the Persian autocrat Cambyses.[44] Edward Moore, writing about two hundred years ago, makes a similar, almost guilty, observation.

> Some statues of Buddha certainly exhibit thick Ethiopian lips; but all wooly hair; there is something mysterious, and unexplained connected with the hair of this, and only of this, Indian deity. The fact of so many different tales having been invented to account for his crisped, wooly head, is alone sufficient to excite suspicion, that there is something to conceal—to be ashamed of; more than meets the eye.[45]

For Godfrey Higgins the truth was self-evident. Higgins subscribed to the belief in a series of Buddhas, all of whom were black. "That the Buddhists were Negroes, the icons of God clearly prove."[46]

By the sixth century B.C. the blacks of India had begun a strong resurgence and Buddhism was not its only expression. Mahapadma Nanda, for example, of Sudra origin, rose as the champion of the oppressed and established a dynasty of his own. Nanda was so ruthless in his endeavors that he earned the title of "the exterminator of the Kshatriya race . . ."[47] The short-lived Nanda dynasty was followed by another of longer duration, the Mauryan.

The Mauryan dynasty was also of Sudra origin and came in the aftermath of the withdrawal of Alexander's expeditionary forces, c. 320 B.C. The dynasty's founder, Chandragupta, stepped into the political vaccuum and rapidly expanded his control of a region far exceeding that of the Nandas.

The greatest ruler of the Mauryan dynasty was Ashoka, a highly compassionate man who introduced a series of humanitarian reforms which were quite radical for the time. Initially aggressive and warlike, Ashoka came to abhor violence and promoted an atmosphere of religious tolerance. The following statement reflects the mature Ashoka:

> There is no better work than promoting the welfare of the whole world. Whatever may be my good deeds, I have done them in order to discharge my debt to all beings.[48]

During Ashoka's illustrious reign Buddhist missionaries were sent both to the east and west. This may account for the highly Africoid depictions of the Buddha in southeast Asia.

After the fall of the Mauryan dynasty African cultural ideals were rigidly maintained in the far south of India among the Dravidians, the builders of the Indus Valley civilization. The Cholas, Pallavas and Pandyans were only three of the powerful kingdoms which could not be conquered by the Aryans or anyone else. The Dravidian kingdoms, in fact, often carried the war into the heart of Aryavarta. When Dravida was subdued it was done under the guise of religion, this made possible through the inclusion of clearly African concepts and deities, including Shiva, Vishnu, Kali and Krishna.

Elements of both Brahmanism and Buddhism are apparent in the Dravidian colonies established in southeast Asia during the years of Black rule. Funan, Angkor and Champa, for example, reflect profound Dravidian influences, particularly in its iconography and architecture.

Funan represents the earliest known kingdom in southeast Asia. Its builders were known as Khmers, a name that recalls the Egyptian Kam, the black. The major temple was identified with Mount Meru, again bringing us into touch with India and the Nile Valley. The Funan Kingdom was in motion by 300 A.D. and enjoyed great power. Discovery of Roman coins at a Funanese site demonstrates how far reaching their commercial activity was. The Chinese describe the Funanese men as "small and black."[49]

Angkor succeeded Funan by the sixth century. The African deity Shiva, first identified in the Indus Valley, was the greatest god. Each temple possessed two libraries and scholars were highly regarded. Constant innovation and vigilance of the region's highly advanced irrigation systems and dams were the basis of its prosperity.

Both Thailand and Vietnam produced prominent black communities, as depicted in its Buddhist sculpture and architecture, the most Africoid in the world. The fate of the black kingdoms of southeast Asia must be tied to the rising influx of Mongoloid Asians from the north. The issue of black/yellow racial and cultural relations is so critical that it must be developed as a special area of study. It is of particular concern to African scholars.

China and Japan

There is evidence of substantial populations of Blacks in early China. Archaeological studies have located a black substratum in the earliest periods of Chinese history,[50] and reports of major kingdoms ruled by Blacks are frequent in Chinese documents.[51] The black presence in ancient China is one of the most challenging areas for African scholars.

There is mention of a black military commander, Sakanouye Tamuramaro, in the very early stages of Japanese history.[52] Diop mentions a Japanese proverb, "For a Samurai to be brave, he must have a bit of Black blood."[53]

The history of the Black presence in Asian antiquity is one of the most exciting and, yet, least written about aspects of the Black experience. It covers a period of more than 500,000 years and comprises the largest land mass in the world. As the first hominids, simple hunters and gatherers, primitive agriculturists, warriors and civilizers, gods and goddesses, servants and slaves, the Black race has known Asia intimately from the very beginning. Even today, after a series of holocausts and calamities, the Black presence in Asia numbers over a hundred million! Who these blacks were, what they did, and are doing, are questions that beg and demand answers. These answers, which we must diligently seek to supply, are not designed merely to satisfy the intellectual curiosity of an elite group, but to further the vision of Pan-Africanism and reunite a family that has been separated far too long.

Notes

1. Richard E. Leakey, *Origins* (New York: E.P. Dutton, 1977.
2. Gaston Maspero, *History of Egypt*, Vol. 4, trans. M.L. McClure (London: The Grollier Society, 1903) pp. 45-46.
3. Chi Li, *The Formation of The Chinese People* (New York: Russell & Russell, 1928) pp. 259-260.
4. Chen Kang Chai, *Taiwan Aborigines* (Cambridge, Harvard University Press, 1967) p. 76.
5. Albert Churchward, *Signs & Symbols of Primordial Man* (Westport: Greenwood Press, 1913, rpt. 1978) p. 218.
6. Cheikh Anta Diop, *African Origins of Civilization* (New York: Lawrence Hill, 1974) XV.
7. Henry Field, *Ancient and Modern Man in Southwestern Asia* (Coral Gables: University of Miami Press, 1956) p. 89.

8. Ephorus, Quoted by John D. Baldwin, *Pre-Historic Nations* (New York: Harper & Brothers, 1872) p. 219.

9. Homer, *The Iliad.*

10. Strabo, quoted by William Leo Hansberry, *Africa and Africans*, v. 2 (Washington, D.C.: Howard University Press, 1926) p. 193.

11. "The eastern Ethiopians—for there were two sorts of Ethiopians in the army—served with the Indians. These were just like the southern Ethiopians, except for their language and their hair: their hair is straight, while that of the Ethiopians in Libya is the crispest and curliest in the world." Herodotus, *The Histories*, trans. Aubrey de Selincourt (New York: Penguin Books, 1972) p. 468.

12. Uthman 'Amr Ibn Bahr Al-Jahiz, *The Book of The Glory of the Black Race* (Los Angeles: Preston Publishing Company, rpt. 1981) p. 52.

13. Baldwin, pp. 66-67.

14. Genesis 10:6, 15-20.

15. Robert Graves, *The Greek Myths* (Penguin Books, 1955), p. 196.

16. Arthur Keith, *New Discoveries Relating to The Antiquity of Man* (London: Williams & Norgate, 1931) p. 210.

17. Baldwin, p. 74.

18. Major-General Maitland, quoted by Henry Field, *Ancient And Modern Man in Southwestern Asia*, p. 114.

19. Arthur Keith, Appendix, Bertram Thomas, *The Arabs (New York: Doubleday, 1917) p. 333.*

20. George Rawlinson, The History of Herodotus, Vol. 1 (London: John Murray, 1858) p. 442.

21. Al-Jahiz, p. 10.

22. For a summary see Runoko Rashidi, "The Kushite Origins of Sumer and Elam, *UFAHAMU*, Vol. 12, No. 3, 1983, p. 215-233.

23. Genesis 10:8,9.

24. Yekubi, Kings of the Barbar And Ifarik, rpt. in *Sudanese Memoirs*, H.R. Palmer, 2. vols. (Lagos, 1928).

25. Robert Graves, p. 314.

26. Legrand H. Clegg II, "Black Rulers of The Golden Age, *Journal of African Civilizations*, Vol. 4, No. 2, pp. 81-102.

27. "These Syrians were Black, these being the Syrians who live outside the Taurus; and when I say Taurus, I am extending the name as far as the Amanus." Strabo, *Geography*, bk. 16.2.

28. George Rawlinson, *Ancient Monarchies*, vol. 1 (New York: Dodd, Mead, And Company, 1881) p. 50.

29. Rawlinson,

30. Herodotus, pp. 166-167.

31. Patrick English, "Cushites, Colchians, And Khazars," *Journal of Near Eastern Studies*, 18, 1959, p. 53.

32. English.

33. For more information on the black community of the Caucasus, see *Journal of African Civilization*, Vol. 3, No. 1, April 1981, pp. 64-65, See also Allison Blakely, "The Negro in Imperial Russia: A Preliminary Sketch," *The Journal of Negro History*, Vol. LXI, No. 4, October 1976, pp. 351-361.

34. S.R. Rao, "Contacts Between Lothal And Susa," *Proceedings of the Twenty-sixth International Congress of Orientalists*, Vol. 2, 1968, pp. 35-37.

35. Samuel Purchas, *Pilgrimage*, v. 7 (Glascow: James MacLehose and Sons) p. 551.

35a. Ibid.

36. Flavius Philostratus, *Life of Apollonius*, Bk. 3, 271-273.

37. Rawlinson, *Ancient Monarchies*, v. 1, p. 49.

38. *Rig Veda*, 1, 100,18.

39. *Rig Veda*, 1, 182,4.
40. *Rig Veda*, 1, 130,8.
41. *Rig Veda*, 133, 2-4.
42. *Rig Veda*, 10, 91, 12-13.
43. Nripendra Kumar Dutt, *Origin and Growth of Caste in India* (Calcutta: Firma K.L. Mukhopadhyay, 1968).
44. Diop, p. 287.
45. Edward Moore, quoted by Godfrey Higgins, *Anacalypsis*, v. 1 (London: Longman, 1836) p. 161.
46. Higgins, v. 2, p. 364.
47. Nripendra Kumar Dutt, *Aryanisation of India* (Calcutta: Firma K.L. Mukhopadhyay, 1970) pp. 85-86.
48. Romila Thapar, *Asoka And The Decline of The Mauryas* (Oxford University Press, 1961).
49. Christopher Pym, *The Ancient Civilization of Angkor* (New York: N.A.L., 1968).
50. Kwang-chih Chang, *The Archaeology of Ancient China* (New Haven & London: Yale University Press, 1968) pp. 64, 70-71, 74.
51. Graham W. Irwin, *Africans Abroad* (New York: Columbia University Press, 1977) pp. 170-173.
52. Alexander F. Chamberlain, ''The Contribution of The Negro to Human Civilization'' *Journal of Race Development*, April 1911, pp. 484-485.
53. Diop, p. 281.

NILE VALLEY PRESENCE IN AMERICA B.C.

Ivan Van Sertima

> *We can trace the progress of man in Mexico without noting any definite Old World influence during this period (1000-650 B.C.) except a strong Negroid substratum connected with the Magicians (high priests).*
> —Frederick Peterson, *Ancient Mexico*

> *The startling fact is that in all parts of Mexico, from Campeche in the east to the South coast of Guerrero, and from Chiapas, next to the Guatemalan border, to the Panuco River in the Huasteca region (north of Veracruz), archeological pieces representing Negro or Negroid people have been found, especially in Archaic or pre-Classic sites.*
> —Alexander von Wuthenau, *Unexpected Faces in Ancient America*

In my book They Came Before Columbus *(Random House, 1977) I deal with contacts, both planned and accidental, between Africans and Americans in about half a dozen historical periods. In this essay, however, I confine myself to a particular geographical region (the Gulf Coast of Mexico), a particular culture complex or civilization (known as Olmec), and a particular period of history (948-680 B.C.).*

The Olmec are known as the People of the Jaguar or the Jaguar-Mouth People. The jaguar hovered on the fringes of their first major settlements, dominating their consciousness, and so it became a central motif in their art. Yet, contrary to what scholars have claimed, it is often clearly distinguishable from the art of human portraiture. Jaguar mosaics, jaguar masks, even human-jaguar combinations stand side by side and in contrast with some of the most vivid, monumental and realistic human portraits in clay, jade and stone. Therefore, no obsession with the jaguar, no artistic style suggested by this jungle cat with the snarling mouth, can account for the clearly Africoid features of some of the colossal stone heads, clay figurines and masks found in the Olmec world.

Speculations as to a possible African element in the first major American civilization go back more than a century to the year 1858, when the first colossal

This article originally appeared in *Dollars & Sense* magazine, February/March 1983 (vol. 8, no. 6).

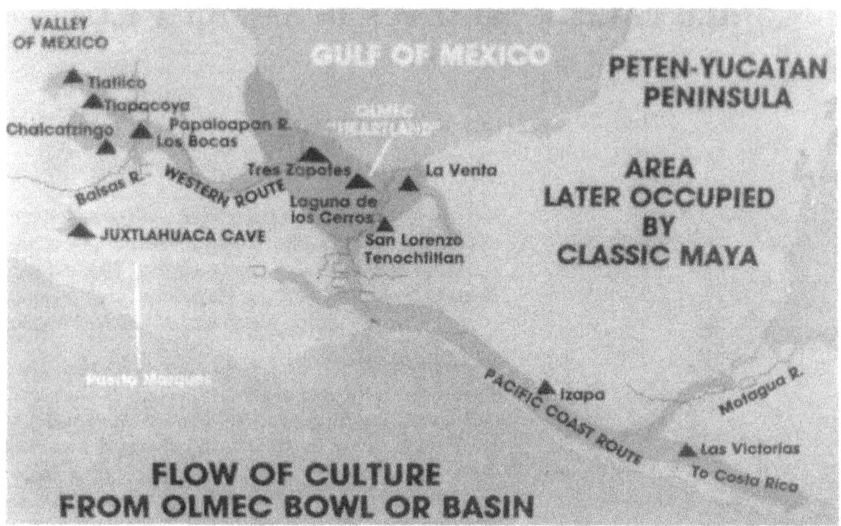

stone head was discovered by Mexican peasants in the village of Tres Zapotes. These very early speculations by scholars like Jose Melgar and Orozco y Berra were easily dismissed because far too little was known at the time. It was not until 1938 that intensive scientific excavations of Olmec sites began. In that year an archeological team directed by Matthew Stirling rediscovered this huge stone head with a helmeted dome. Eight feet in height, 18 feet in circumference, it weighed over 10 tons. Stirling found it, in spite of its great size, to be carved from a single block of basalt and to be a head only. In its realism, its size, its awesome bodilessness, its alien features and headgear, it stood out among American sculptures. Only the colossal bodiless heads of Nubian blacks and other racial types found at Tanis, the harbor for seagoing ships in Egypt, can parallel this head in scale or conception in the ancient world.

"Cleared of the surrounding earth," wrote Stirling, "it presented an awe-inspiring spectacle. Despite its great size, the workmanship is delicate and sure, its proportions perfect. Unique in character among aboriginal American sculptures, it is remarkable for its realistic treatment. The features are bold and *amazingly negroid* in character."

Fourteen years before Sterling's expedition to Tres Zapotes, a team from Tulane University had found a giant stone head pushing out of the ground at La Venta in the Mexican state of Tabasco, about 18 miles inland from the Gulf of Mexico. The Tulane team was only passing through the area and did not have time to dig but they recorded their find in a photograph. After his return from Tres Zapotes Stirling saw this photograph and was struck by something in it: Although only the top of the head could be seen, the domelike helmet on this buried figure seemed to match the one he had excavated at Tres Zapotes. Suspecting a

Among the first stone heads found, with Africoid features. *Front view*. Tres Zapotes. This was found in 1862. It is now located at Tuxtla.

***Side-view* of the Tres Zapotes head.**

Back of the Tres Zapotes head, showing Ethiopian-type braids. This unusual photo is by anthropo-photo journalists Wayne Chandler and Gaynell Catherine.

link, he headed toward La Venta on his next expedition in 1939. La Venta was later to turn out to be the holy center of the Olmec world, the home of the Olmec priest-kings and of the Olmec elite—the very heartland of their civilization.

After a relentless search by Stirling's team, the head recorded in the photograph was located. It was found to be 8 feet high and, like the one at Tres Zapotes, it also looked African. Three more African-looking heads were uncovered at La Venta. Two of them were so realistic in detail that they even had their teeth carved out, a very unusual thing in American art. Massive and military, like tough warrior dynasts they stood, faces of pure basalt stone, dominating the ceremonial plaza in which they were found. The lines of cheek and jaw, the fullness of the lips, the broad fleshy noses, the acutely observed and faithfully reproduced facial contours and particulars, bore witness to an African presence. One

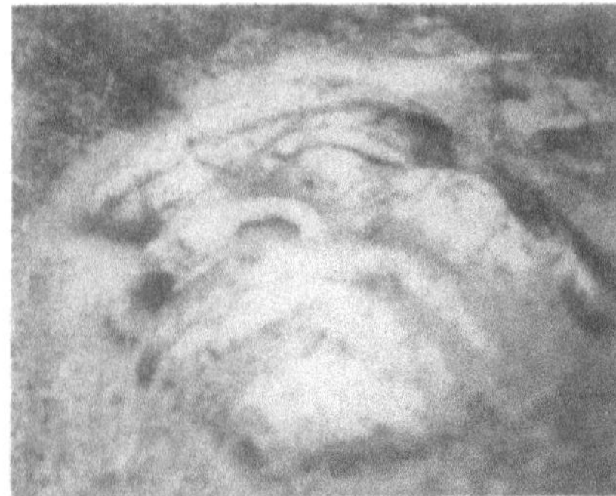

New head found at San Lorenzo, still lying in the swamp.

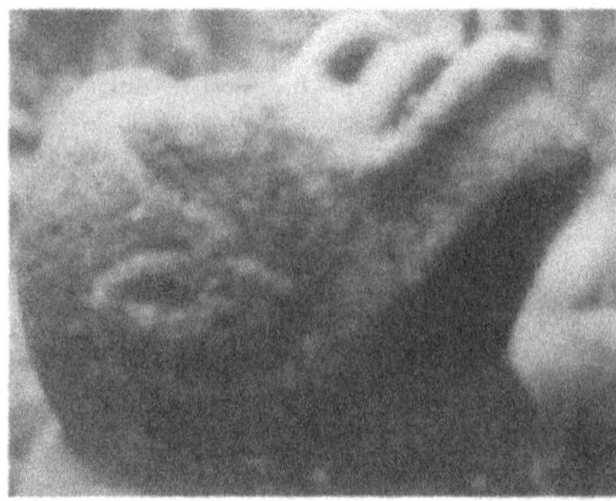

The rain god at La Venta

of the African-looking colossi, 8 feet and 6 inches high and 22 feet in circumference, wore earplugs with a cross carved in each.

The cross, which first appears in ancient America on this site, conveys the same idea of fertility as the Egyptian cross. Like the Egyptian cross it is the symbol of life and generation. The Mexican word for the cross, which was later to appear in the Olmec-influenced city of Teotihauacan is *To-naca-qua-hui-tl* "tree of life." It is possible to argue that the duplication of this motif and its meaning is a coincidence, but how can we explain the duplication of the helmets found on most of the African-type sculptures?

If we examine some of these helmets we find they are uncannily similar to leather helmets worn by the Egyptian-Nubian military in the era of the Ramessids (Egyptian pharaohs) and in the first millenium B.C. They completely cover the head and the back of the neck and they have tie-ons attached to the crest and falling in front of the ears. The details on some of them, although almost 3,000 years old, have become a little obscured, but there is one in particular, now in the Jalapa Museum, which can be examined for comparative purposes. It has the circular earplug and incised decorative parallel lines found on other colossal Nubian heads in the Egyptian seaport of Tanis.

These heads, following the orientation of the ceremonial center on which they were found, were placed on a north-south axis. So was the pyramid at La Venta, the first to be found anywhere in ancient America. This north-south axis corresponds to the axial orientation of the pyramid complex in Egypt and the Sudan. (We shall return to the issue of the pyramid later. Suffice it to say, that although earlier settlements have been found in America—as early as 2,000 B.C. among the Maya—the pyramids are later than the one at La Venta.)

The largest of the African heads at La Venta—9 feet high—had its domed head flattened so that it could function as an altar. A hole may be seen at the left ear, running like a tube through the head itself to form a small opening at the center of the mouth. This head was used as an oracle, a "talking" god. "In grayest antiquity," wrote Constance Irwin in *Fair Gods and Stone Faces,* "a priest of the Olmec whispered into that giant ear, and his sonorous words emerged from the great stone lips." It is strongly reminiscent of the technique used in the talking god of the Egyptians and Nubians in the first millenium B.C.—Amon-Ra. The blacks made Amon-Ra into an animated god. By its oracular pronouncements and the illusion of animation, they could invoke the unchallengeable authority of a god on earth. The statue of Amon-Ra was jointed, a priest being especially appointed to work it, and, in the sanctuaries, hiding places were arranged in the thickness of the wall from which the priest skillfully arranged for the oracular voice of the god to be heard.

The significance of the oracular stone head and of the other objects found on the La Venta site could not be assessed until some very firm dating by scientific methods could be obtained. This was accomplished by means of carbon 14 (a radioactive isotope of carbon) datings during excavations conducted in 1955 and 1956 by members of a joint National Geographic-Smithsonian-University of California expedition. The results were released in 1957 and were astonishing.

At the place where the African-type stone sculptures were found—the La Venta ceremonial court—nine samples of wood charcoal were taken. Five of these samples related to what was believed then to be the original construction of the court. They gave an average reading of 814 B.C., plus or minus 134 years, which is nearly 3,000 years ago.

While most archeologists have accepted the 800 B.C. date as the average of the La Venta ceremonial court, the most recent redatings by archeologists Berger, Graham, and Heizer seem to suggest that the first phase of the ceremonial court is nearer to the 948 or circa 1000 B.C. date. (This redating does not affect my emphasis on the Nubian 25th dynasty, 800-654 B.C., because the earliest dating relates to the first occupation of the La Venta ceremonial site—it was rebuilt twice by the natives—and not necessarily to the later phase of the African colossi and the pyramid. Even if it did, I had made allowance for both extremes of the dating equation.)

Let it be noted that the Nubian military, the most powerful militia in Africa at the time, had become the main force behind power factions in Egypt and had functioned as backroom power brokers in Egyptian politics since 1085 B.C. They held this position of ascendancy for centuries, even though it was not until the beginning of the 9th century B.C. that the establishment of the royal house of Kush in Nubia and the total conquest of Egypt by Nubian kings were finally achieved. Nubia, both as the creator of Egyptian civilization (as the recent archeological discovery of the black kingdom of Ta-Seti has shown) as well as its unifier and conqueror in the 8th century B.C., was the preserve of classical Egyptian culture. It ushered in a renaissance of cultural traits, like mummification and pyramid building that had lapsed in Egypt but had been perpetuated in Nubia all through the period under study (948-680 B.C.). To restore these and other traits to Egypt clearly indicates that the Nubian was in the mainstream of Egyptian culture and quite capable, if thrust by accident or design into an alien environment, of transmitting Egyptian traits.

La Venta was not alone in its sculptural representation of African-type heads in stone. Apart from the four found there, two were excavated at Tres Zapotes and six at San Lorenzo in Veracruz, one of which, the largest known, is 9 feet, 4 inches high. Some of these heads weigh between 30 and 40 tons. The San Lorenzo site was occupied even earlier than La Venta (circa 2000 B.C.) but the Africoid stone heads appear much later.

Even Michael Coe, the leading American historian on Mexico, who has on occasion disputed my findings, agrees that the heads at La Venta are the first in the sequence and that the carbon dating there is the most relevant. Coe, in response to an interview with *Science Digest* in 1981, contended that the reason the stone heads had broad noses and thick lips was because the tools used to cut them were too blunt to make sharper noses and thinner lips. He also contended that the sculptors wanted to avoid "protruding or thin facial features that might break off."

This is the latest explanation by the "establishment." Earlier on, scholars had argued that these were idolized Mongoloid babies or monsters or throwbacks or were influenced by the jaguar motif in Olmec art. These explanations do not take into account that side by side with the stone representations of African types there are also many sculptures in clay with African-type features as well as African-type hair—both head-hair and chin-hair.

When Coe was asked by *Science Digest* whether he knew of these clay sculptures corroborating the stone-head evidence, he confessed that he had never heard of them. Few traditional scholars of Mexico know of these terra cottas (clay pieces). There are only about half a dozen of them among the pieces displayed in the Museum of Anthropology in Mexico City. One must visit the Diego Rivera Museum, the Josue Saenz collection and the Alexander von Wuthenau collection to see these remarkable and unmistakable Africoid men and women—chiefs, dancers, drummers, wrestlers, priests, women of great beauty, men of great authority, Olmec, Mayan, Totonac, Zapotec, Mixtec, Aztec. It is fortunate that in spite of the great official opposition to the idea of Africans in ancient

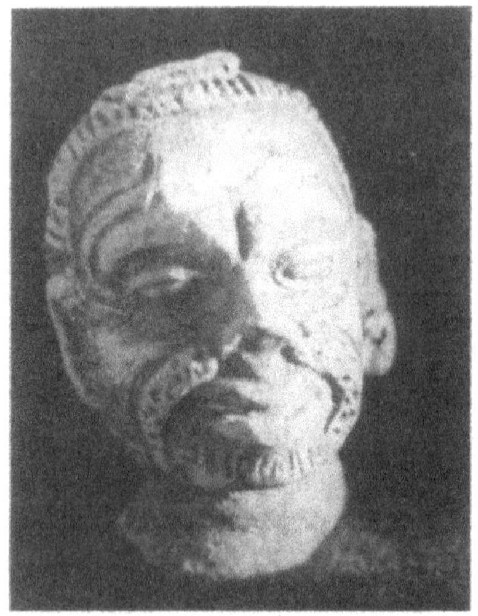

Pre-classic clay sculptures identifiable as African, not only by nose, lips and general facial structure, but also by color of skin and texture of hair. *Top*: Sculpture from the central plateau of Mexico, Olmec period. *Center*: Sculpture from Tlapacoya. (Photos from Homo Americanus Collection: Von Wuthenau) *Bottom*: Sculpture from Chiapas emphasizes moustache and beard. (Photo by Jacqueline Patten)

America, President Portillo of Mexico and the wife of former President Echeverria have given their support to the work of von Wuthenau in establishing this pre-Columbian presence, particularly in the medium of clay.

Clay is the medium *par excellence* for portrait art. It is impossible to list all of the African pieces found thus far in the Olmec world (or in the pre-Classic period when that civilization flowered), but an examination of them reveals the unmistakable combination of kinky hair, broad nose, generous lips, frequency of prognathism (abnormally projecting jaws), occasional goatee beard, and sometimes distinctively African ear pendants, hairstyles, tattoo markings and coloration. With respect to coloration, the clay chosen or the oxide dyes used to evoke the blackness or dark brownness of the skin is particularly striking because they are reserved for the types with the non-native noses, lips, hair textures, etc. These were deliberate choices of artists dealing with living, human models. (I have been to these collections on several occasions and have held many of these pieces in my hands. They are works of incredible skill, some so tiny that only a modern carver of genius could capture the complex delicacy of detail on such a miniature scale. I present with this article some of the terra cottas that were not in my book along with a few that were. I must draw special attention to the drummer from Colima, the three women from Xochipala, Guerrero, and the African acrobat. With the exception of the last named, which is in the Diego Rivera museum, the other four are new acquisitions by von Wuthenau and stand in his San Angel collection, which should become the focus of any pilgrimage to Mexico by African-Americans.)

What clinches evidence of the African presence, however, are skulls and skeletons of Africans found on Olmec sites. The study of crania (skulls) came into disrepute in the early part of this century since it had been used by unscrupulous racists to show that Africans had brains inferior to Europeans. Skull study has matured, however, in spite of early frauds, into a fairly exact science and the Russians can now reconstruct a face with computerlike precision from the skull of the dead. One of the world's leading skull experts, Polish professor Andrzej Wiercinski, announced to the 41st Congress of Americanists in Mexico in September 1974 that African skulls had been found at Olmec sites in Tlatilco, Cerro de las Mesas and Monte Alban.

"These show," said Wiercinski, "a clear prevalence of the total Negroid pattern that has been evidenced by the use of two methods: (a) multivariate distance analysis of average characteristics of individual fractions distinguished cranioscopically and (b) analysis of frequency distributions of mean index of the position between combinations of racial varieties." There is no easy way to break this down into layman's language but, roughly speaking, the three main races of men show differences in skull shape and in the formation of the bones of the face. It is possible to make distinctions in noses, jaws, brow ridges, etc. and in the way these are put together in terms of very minute variations of distance between the parts.

Pre-classic acrobat. (Photo by Jacqueline Patten)

Woman from Xochipala. (Photo by Jacqueline Patten)

Woman from Teotihaucan. (Photo by Jacqueline Patten)

Since in extreme instances, one race may fade into the other, in the sense of unusual types of one race having average characteristics of the other, a further close check has to be made to ensure that this possibility is not distorting the picture. In very mixed populations this would be a very difficult process, open to much error, but in the dry areas of the Olmec civilization Wiercinski found clear evidence of a racial type different from that of the native population appearing as a significant minority. All the indices used to distinguish races through the study of surviving skulls and close comparison with skulls found in continental African and native American graveyards make it quite clear that a foreign racial element (African) entered the Olmec world at this time.

That does not make the Olmecs *African* as some foolish diffusionists have claimed. It means that the African element became a significant group and influence among the native American Olmecs. Africans not only came here (before the Vikings or any other Old World group) but they left an impact upon America's first major civilization. The Olmec civilization was formative and seminal: it was to touch all others on this continent, directly or indirectly. (But I have never claimed that Africans created or founded the Olmec civilization. Such a claim would be absurd. They left a significant influence upon it, as we shall show, and that is more than can be said of any other Old World group visiting the native Americans or emigrating to this continent before Columbus.)

A number of extremely interesting facts emerged from a study of the skeletal evidence. Wiercinski noted that 13.5 percent of the skeletons examined in the pre-Classic Olmec cemetery of Tlatilco were African, yet only 4.5 percent of those found later at Cerro de las Mesas from the Classic period were African. This indicates that the African element intermingled until it almost fused with the native population. Female skeletons found in the graves from the pre-Classic period, and lying side by side with African males, are racially distinct from them (that is, native American Females, foreign African males), but they appear racially similar to their male companions at a *later* "Classic" site, indicating progressive intermixture and the growing absorption of the foreign African element into the largely Mongoloid (Asiatic) American population.

This makes it very clear that the Olmec-African element was a distinctive, outside injection that came and crossbred in the Olmec time period and that it did not represent "proto-Australoid" or "proto-negroid" aborigines who trickled into America from the Pacific in the very ancient glacial epoch when the very first Americans came. According to Wiercinski's skeletal statistics, they would have disappeared millenia ago into the American gene pool if they could fade from 13.5 percent to 4.5 percent in a few brief centuries. The two major Pacific migrations of the first Americans occurred, after all, about 50,000 and 20,000 years ago, respectively, according to the most recent datings. (Some have put it as early as 70,000 years ago, others as late as 13,000. In terms of the point I am making, the fading of an African element that came in at the very beginning of the Bering Strait migrations, the current dispute over those dates does not matter.)

The Ra I built by Africans in 1969 crossed from Safi, North Africa, to Barbados in the Caribbean, using power and the direction of the currents and trade winds.

In the Olmec world (948-680 B.C.) we are not dealing with African elements that survived the Pacific crossing many thousands of years ago. Wiercinski has pointed out that these skulls in Olmec strata are of a continental African type, such as we find in West Africa today, and not those of Pacific negritos, who could have come in much earlier. The continental African migrated in huge waves to Nubia and Egypt in the pre-dynastic era following the drying up of the green, fertile lands of the Sahara. This physical type, in spite of minor Asiatic and Caucasoid infusion into the north of Egypt, remained predominantly unchanged until wave after wave of conquerors and successive invasions of Assy-

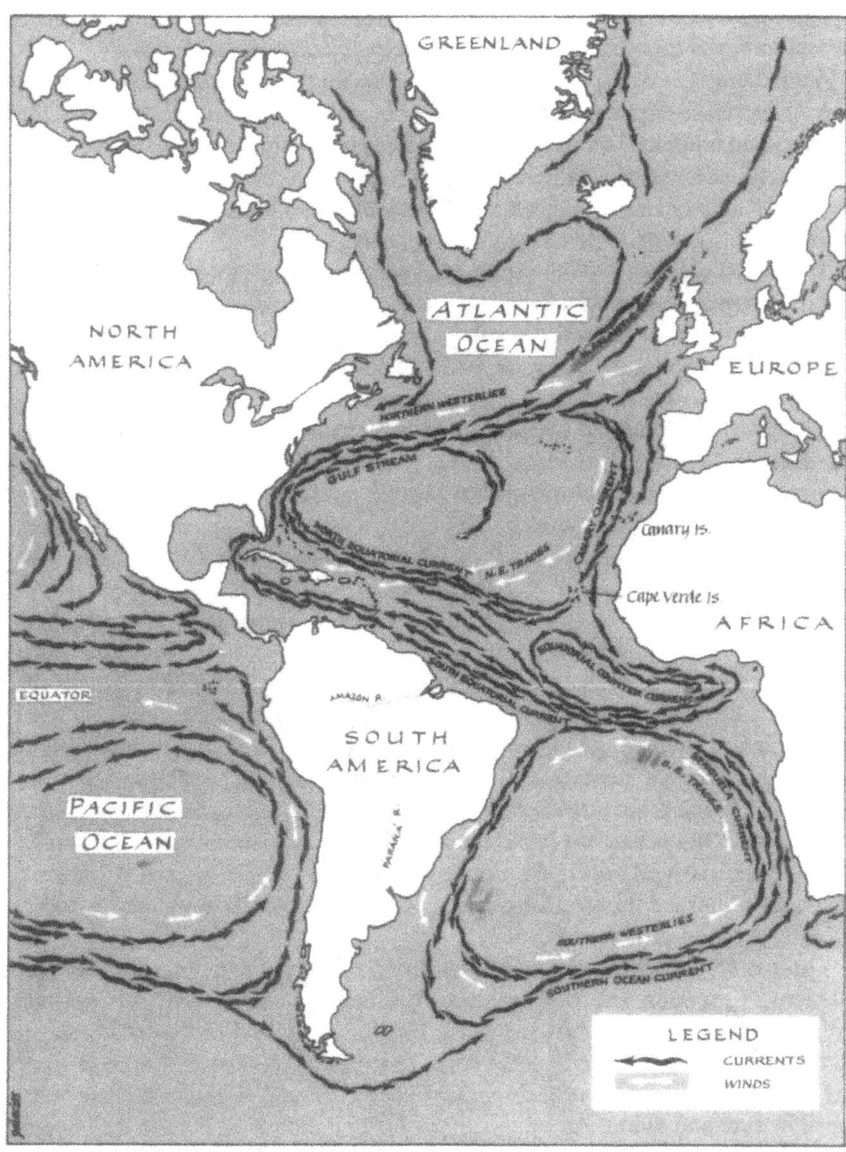

Currents map shows the flow of the ocean from Africa to America.

rians, Persians, Greeks, Romans, Arabs, etc. followed upon the decline of Egypt as a world power at the close of the Bronze Age.

Blacks were particularly dominant in the political and spiritual life in Egypt in the period of contact with the Olmec world and explain the presence of this racial type in colossal African heads in stone, in clay sculptures (terra cottas) and in the skeletal remains found among the Olmec high priests and magicians.

Apart from the African, there is another element that is represented in the native American sculptures of this time. It is not as important as the African in the political and religious hierarchy of the Olmec (no colossal monuments were built to it), but it is associated with the African in the Olmec milieu, with the Egypto-Nubian navies of the first millenium B.C., and even with the indigenous North African on the edge of the Atlantic basin.

That other element is Phoenician. A figure with curved aquiline nose, thin lips, and flowing beard stands on the same plaza as the African figures, although his is a flat representational portrait etched in the slab of stone and does not, therefore, have the same awesome bodiless presence or colossal sculptural proportions of the African figures. The features are clearly outlined, as is the apparel, and it was conceded by even the earliest investigators that this was, to use art historian Miguel Covarrubias' phrase, "a visitor." When it was finally recognized that there was some relationship between this figure and the African-type figures standing beside it on the ceremonial plaza at La Venta, the African types were seen as "mercenary troops" of the Phoenician, or "a cargo of captured blacks."

Let us look closely at this figure. He has been identified as Phoenician by Irwin and others by reference to several details on the stele (engraved stone slab)—his turned-up shoes from a type diffused from the shattered empire of the Hittites in the flight of their upper class to Phoenician capitals; the conversational posture struck by him and his companion on the same stele; the curious figures tilted above him, a floating doll and a man pointing his forefinger down at him—all of which have been shown to correspond to elements in Phoenician culture. Von Wuthenau has presented us with clay representations of figures of this type from several sites in the Olmec world. The Phoenician traveling mascot, Melkart, has turned up at an Olmec site, Rio Balsas. We have no reason, therefore, to question this identification.

There is nothing more natural in this period of history than the association of Nubians, Egyptians and pale-skinned Phoenicians. The Phoenicians became progressively darker and Africoid in the North African civilization of Carthage, so that by the time of Hannibal, the coins and skeletal remains of Carthage show the virtual disappearance of the Semitic Phoenician type as found in their home bases in Tyre and Sidon. An examination of the relationship between the Phoenician and the African is crucial to our understanding, not only of how they could be associated on the same ceremonial plaza at La Venta, but how and why they could find themselves so far away from home.

The relationship between these peoples, their common interests in the face of a threat from the Western Asiatic power—the Assyrian—is an important factor in this period. It helps to explain how this figure with flowing beard, Semitic nose and turned-up shoes appears in association with the African figures in ancient

Mexico and how certain Phoenician elements (including Punic inscriptions, a traveling mascot, and a type of mummy mask) have been unearthed in America in archeological contexts related to the Afro-Egyptian or Egypto-Nubian presence.

Egypt had been trading with the Phoenicians for centuries. These people had once been nomads of the desert but had eventually settled in city-states on the edge of the Mediterranean Sea, colonized islands or built settlements on them. They were, however, a people of nomadic urges and soon made of the sea what they had once made of the desert, a field for their restless wanderings. In the 9th century B.C. (circa 814 B.C.) hundreds of them sailed to North Africa and built a city together with the Africans, which was called Khart Hadast—The New Town—later known by westerners as Carthage.

They trafficked in metals, among other commodities, and their maritime trade in copper, silver, gold and tin took them to Hatus, a Hittite seaport, to an island called Cyprus for its copper, to the Iberian peninsula for silver, to Egypt for silver and for Nubian gold dust, and as far as Cornwall in the British Isles, right out into the North Atlantic, for tin. Although their boats were smaller than those of the Egyptians, 70 feet long was the average, they were extremely maneuverable and were equipped with both sail and oar.

From their settlements they carried linen cloth and wool, fine jewelry, cedar (from which some of the Egyptian ships were made), perfume and spices; and from their major seaports, Tyre, Sidon and Byblos, they exported things that were rare and treasured in the ancient world, particularly a purple dye that came to be known as Tyrian purple, which was reserved for royalty in the Mediterranean basin. It is remarkable that purple, made sacred by the Egyptians and spread by the Phoenicians, was also reserved for royalty and the upper class among the ancient Mexicans as the *Nuttall Codex* (a surviving American book) shows.

The Egyptians, Herodotus tells us, even when they made vassals of the Phoenicians, did not stifle their maritime trade. It was as vital to Egypt as it was to them. The more riches they amassed from trade, the more tribute they could pay to Egypt. A lot of Egyptian trade, particularly the metals so badly needed for the bronze weaponry of their armies, was transported in Phoenician ships. Although merchants in their own right, the Phoenicians were often mercenary seamen for the Egyptians.

During the period under study we have indisputable evidence that Phoenician ships were moving in the waters of the North Atlantic and any examination of the Egyptian or Phoenician navies, from the time of the Ramessids down to the reign of the Nubians, reveals a multi-racial complex and a close relationship between blacks and Phoenicians. Black soldiers, similar to the helmeted ones we find in the Olmec world, were, as indicated above, powers behind the Egyptian throne since 1085 B.C. and they remained so until they established total military and political supremacy over Egypt, circa 720 B.C., under the Nubian king, Piankhy, of the House of Kush.

During this period, corresponding to the middle pre-Classic period in ancient America, the Phoenician was in the position of mercenary, or vassal, in relation to the black power in the Mediterranean. The Phoenician had been cowed by the Assyrian forces of Western Asia, which later threatened Egypt, and, in the cold and hot wars between Egypt and Assyria, which ran right through the 25th dynasty, they were protected allies and mercenaries of the Nubian-Egyptian. This is not to belittle the Phoenician, but to give the lie to speculation that, because the two were found in association on the La Venta site, the Phoenician was the master and the black his mercenary or his slave.

But why should Egyptians, Nubians or Phoenicians cross the Altantic to America? Some have claimed that this voyage was intentional, that the Egyptians had concrete knowledge of a land beyond the western sea. This is not necessarily true. As a result of their astronomy, the Egyptians knew the circumference of the earth. But then there was no way of telling that the missing bulk was not totally covered by water. The evidence points to an accident at sea. But the question arises, could an ancient fleet blown off course, driven toward America by wind and current power, survive the Atlantic crossing?

All the world knows of Thor Heyerdhal's Egyptian papyrus boats, Ra I and Ra II, the former built by Africans, the latter by Americans. Both boats navigated the Altantic successfully, though the first model got into trouble after fully proving itself by drifting on currents off the North African port of Safi to Barbados in the Caribbean. But while Heyerdahl proved that such a journey had been possible from the very earliest of the Egyptian dynasties when papyrus boats were in use, the sophisticated Egyptian and Phoenician galleys of the first millenium B.C. were superior to those earlier models.

We know for certain that the Phoenicians were circling Africa in ships under the orders of the Egyptian king, Necho II, circa 600 B.C. These documented journeys, though occurring later, lend validity to the contention that such journeys were eminently possible in the period under review when similar ships were moving down the Mediterranean into the North Atlantic. Archeology has confirmed that tin was being heavily mined in Cornwall in the British Isles, just 25 miles away from the Scilly Isles, where there are records of Phoenician visits circa 800 B.C. It is only logical to infer that they were in that area in pursuit of their metal trade. Tin was a vital alloy in the manufacture of the bronze weaponry of their allies and sponsors, the Egyptians.

If one looks at the Atlantic currents off Africa and the way they move like conveyor belts to the Caribbean, the northeastern corner of South America and the Gulf of Mexico, one appreciates how easily an expedition into North Atlantic waters could be blown off course into the Gulf of Mexico. According to the later Quiche' Maya people, in whose book the *Popul Vuh* records oral traditions going back to very ancient times, "black and pale-skinned people" appeared from the east in boats. The historian Bernardino Sahagun cites one report, common among the natives, that ancient visitors came by sea from the east: "It is certain that they came in vessels of wood . . . they came out of seven caves and these caves are ships or galleys."

The clear feasibility of the trans-Atlantic crossing to America in this ancient period is of the greatest importance. The winds and currents of the Atlantic have not changed appreciably in this brief span of geological time, less than 3,000 years. Just 28 years ago, Dr. Alain Bombard, a medical doctor in Liberia, crossed the Atlantic in a boat that was far inferior to those used by the Egyptians and Phoenicians in the Bronze Age. In an African dugout, without oar and sail, with little food or water, with only an African fishing kit and an implement to squeeze juice from fish to supplement his supply of liquid in case the rains failed, Bombard completed the journey in 52 days, in less time in fact than the first caravels of Vespucci and Columbus. Current power was his sole source of locomotion. Dr. Bombard not only proved the feasibility of the journey in the most primitive of vessels but also that it could have been an accident (as was Cabral's later "discovery" of Brazil), and that such an accident was not only repeatable but that even a crew, unprepared for such an emergency, feeding on the billion-finned life of the ocean, could still survive the crossing.

It is my contention that a small but significant number of men and a few women, in a fleet protected by a military force, moved west down the Mediterranean toward North Africa in the period 948-680 B.C., probably on the usual metal run, and got caught in the pull of one of the westward currents off the North African coast, either through storm or navigational error. A map showing the flow of these Atlantic currents illustrates how easily such a crew blown off course could land in the Olmec heartland. A study of the same map, however, would show how difficult it would be for them to retrace their course and return to the Old World, unless they were also fully aware of the circular distribution of the currents in the Atlantic. Africans became aware of this circular return route but much later. We are not discussing these later pre-Columbian journeys here. Ignorance of this unknown sea in an ancient time, therefore, not navigational expertise or geographical knowledge, would explain both their unexpected arrival in this area as well as their inability to return home.

But proof of contact is only half of the story. What is the significance of this meeting of African and native American? What cultural impact did the outsiders have upon Olmec civilization.?

A study of the Olmec civilization reveals elements that so closely parallel ritual traits and techniques in the Egypto-Nubian world of the same period that it is difficult to maintain all these are due to mere coincidence. While it is possible to find a cultural trait or a technique in one place which is similar to that in another, *without any contact having taken place*, there is a method by which we can examine a parallel or a series of parallels to determine with relative certainty when something is purely coincidental or whether it is strongly suggestive of contact with, and influence from outsiders.

Let us first look at the monarchic traits, that is, the royal and priestly dress and emblems of power among the Olmecs and the Egyptians. We can point to a cluster of half a dozen royal traits shared by ruling circles in both civilizations that are functionally related and appear in a combination too arbitrary and unique to be independently duplicated.

The double crown. This grew out of special historical circumstances in Egypt, the joining of the "two lands," Lower and Upper Egypt, by the African Pharaoh Menes. The Nubian pharaohs donned the double crown of the two lands in the 8th century B.C. when they regained their power over the north. The double crown appears on an Olmec dignitary at Cerro de la Piedra. He is seen offering a glyph (symbolic object) with the Egyptian cross motif to a seated figure that has African features and African-type hair.

The royal flail. This was part of the ceremonial regalia of the pharaoh. It has one or more pendants hanging from a staff and is usually represented resting on the king's shoulder. In an Olmec painting at Oxtotitlan, the Olmec personage seated on the throne has this type of flail, and it is in the same position behind the head.

The sacred boat or ceremonial bark of kings. This not only appears in both civilizations with the same function and curved shape but it also carries the same name (Mexican *cipac*; Egyptian *sibak*).

The use of purple. The religious value of purple and its use to distinguish priests and people of high rank had its origin among the Egyptians. Sanctity was attached to shell purple because the murex shell, from which it was extracted, revealed, by the sequence of colors through which it moved before acquiring its final fixed purple, a parallel to color changes of the Nile in flood. The Egyptians therefore, considered purple a noble and sacred color, and, through the Phoenicians, who adopted the purple industry, the association of purple with royalty, the priesthood and the high-born spread throughout the Mediterranean.

We find purple having the same value in the Olmec world. Professor Zenil Medellin has noted that a patch of purple dye appears on one of the African monumental heads at San Lorenzo. He claims that these stone heads were originally painted but that the paint faded over time. In the *Nuttall Codex* (one of the few surviving documents of ancient America), Zelia Nuttall, the discoverer of the codex, notes "pictures of no fewer than 13 Mexican women of rank wearing purple skirts and five with capes and jackets of the same color. In addition, 45 chieftains are figured with short, fringed, round, purple waistcloths, and there are also three examples of the use of a close fitting purple cap."

The artificial beard. Another sign of royal or priestly office is the beard. A study of Olmec sculptures, carvings on stelae and paintings sesms to suggest that the beard is alien to the usually hairless American chin. When it does appear on the native American chin, it looks like an appendage, artificially tapered and attached. When found on men with the air and poise of authority, it also functions as a badge of high rank. The use of highly stylized chin stubs as a mark of distinction is a custom of the Egyptian pharaohs.

Feathered fans or sunshades. The Egyptian pharaohs bore feathered fans that are almost identical in shape, style and color to those found in ancient Mexican paintings in the pyramid of Las Higueras. These fans were painted in an Olmec area and in a culture influenced by the Olmec, even though this culture (Totonac) is of a slightly later period. The fans are made of feathers arranged in concentric circles of blue, red and green. In Mexico they are blue, red and light blue. The Mexican light blue is the nearest equivalent on the color spectrum to the Egyptian green.

The parasol or ceremonial umbrella. This is another emblem of royalty in the two cultures. Today, the umbrella is so common and has such a utilitarian function (protection from sunburn or the occasional shower), that its unique ritual use and value as an index of rank has been forgotten. Professor A. Varron has demonstrated the use of the umbrella or parasol as an emblem of dignity and power in ancient times. The parasol is one of the items mentioned as being brought into Mexico by foreigners in an oral tradition recorded in the *Titulo Coyoi.* This is a major document of the Quiche Maya. They were touched by the earlier Olmec and their tradition harks back to ancestral visitors of that time. "These things came from the east," goes the tradition, "from the other side of the water and the sea: they came here, they had their throne, their little benches and stools, they had their *parasols* and bone flutes."

It is important to understand what a great burden of proof is required to establish a cultural influence, even when there is a sound case for a physical presence and contact. Any one of the above traits, standing by itself as a single parallel, can be dismissed as coincidence. When such traits appear as an interconnected cluster, performing a single function and duplicated nowhere else in the world, except where the Egyptians traveled or left their influence, then only a dogmatic conservative or a bigot can deny the possibility of both a physical contact and a cultural influence.

The Indian scholar, Rafique Jairazbhoy, in a book on the ancient Egyptians in America, has pointed to many other ritual parallels. (Although we disagree about the date of the visit of the Egyptians, we complement each other in our study of cultural diffusion. I should point to some of these ritual artifacts, themes and practices he has outlined even though I cannot go into much detail in such a short article.)

There are hand-shaped incense spoons found at the Olmec site of Xochipala in Guerrero and depicted also in one of the Mexican books—the *Codex Selden*—that are almost identical with those of the Egyptians. The name for incense is *kuphi* in Egyptian and *copal* (pronounced *ko-pl*) in Mexican. Again, in Egypt, there are several sculptures in which four figures hold up the sky. These are

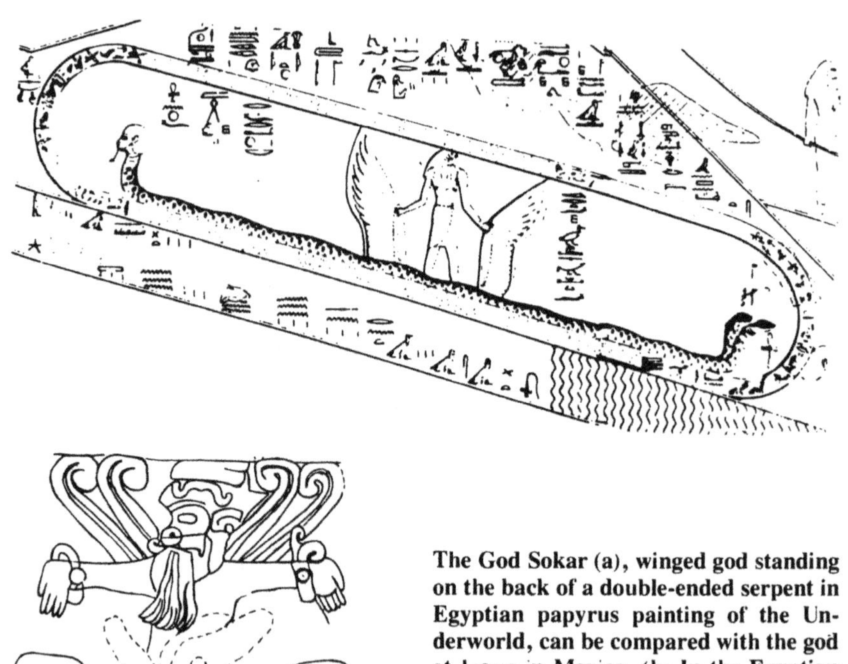

The God Sokar (a), winged god standing on the back of a double-ended serpent in Egyptian papyrus painting of the Underworld, can be compared with the god at Izapa in Mexico. (b) In the Egyptian painting the god stretches out his hands to hold up his wings. The Mexican god does the same. He also stands on the back of the same type of double-ended serpent and wears a foreign beard. (*Ancient Egyptians and Chinese in America*, by R.A. Jairazbhoy)

known as the *Atlantes*. At the Olmec site of Portrero Nuevo two figures appear in the same posture, holding up the sky. While there are only two in the Olmec relief, the four in the Egyptian sculpture are suggested by the use of four hieroglyphs above the two Olmec figures. These are identical with the Egyptian hieroglyphs for sky.

There is the human-headed bird, Ba, which flies out of the tomb in Egyptian mythology. This bird with the human head appears in a relief from Izapa, Mexico, and Mexican sarcophagi leave an opening in the tomb, as do the Egyptians, for the bird's escape from the dead. The Olmec seem also to have practiced mummification. Although the corrosive humidity of the soil in capitals like La Venta destroyed all skeletal remains (Wiercinski's skeletons were found in the drier area of Olmec civilization), Jairazbhoy cites Olmec sculptures at Oaxaca with rib cages outlined as those of a dead man and arms folded in exactly the same way as some Egyptian mummies—arms crossed over chest, fingers open.

The Egyptian papyrus painting (a) from the Book of the Dead depicting the Opening of the Mouth Ceremony can be compared with wall painting (b) in cave at Juxtlahuaca, giant figure wearing leopard skin. He holds two ceremonial objects, similar to the Egyptian before the kneeling man. Both priests wear skins of beasts whose tails hang between their legs, and both proffer a snake-headed instrument to the seated man. (*Ancient Egyptians and Chinese in America*, by R.A. Jairazbhoy)

Another, in the museum of Jalapa, duplicating this ritual posture, wears an Egyptian-type wig.

Jairazbhoy demonstrates the remarkable similarity between several gods in the Egyptian underworld and Olmec Mexico. Two of these are the most visually striking—the winged god Sokar who stands on the back of a double-ended serpent, and the double-rope swallowing god, Aken, "a serpent without eyes, nose or ears, a non-articulated ophidian." There are at least half a dozen that exhibit an identity in complexity that is hard to dismiss as coincidence. Ritual practices, too like "Opening the Mouth Ceremony" (see illustration) and "Heart-plucking," are common to the Olmec and the Egyptians. It is important to note, however, that whereas this was symbolically done in Egypt the later Mexicans (particularly the Aztecs) made it a literal practice.

Similarities between the two civilizations in terms of certain technologies or techniques they used are even more striking. What makes the technological argument easier to prove is that we are certain there are no antecedents for these technologies in America before this period whereas there is a clear series of evolving steps and stages in the Egypto-Nubian world. There is the burial mound or *mastaba* in Nubia which becomes progressively more complicated with interior rooms and underground passages before the black genius Imhotep uses this as a platform for his technological leap into the stepped pyramid. We see the pyramid evolve from "stepped" to "true," taking on a conical form, the steps being filled in but remaining the core of the structure, even when hidden from view. We see the Egyptians stop building the pyramid in 1600 B.C. but the Nubians returning to this in 800 B.C., although on a miniature scale. They were too involved in political and military problems to repeat the architectural monuments of the earlier Africans but they managed to preserve the structural and functional bases of the pyramid in miniature.

Where do the first miniature step pyramid and the first manmade mountain or conical pyramid appear in America? On the very ceremonial court and platform where four of the African-type heads were found in the holy capital of the Olmec world, La Venta. Even among the Maya, where the American anthropologist Dr. Hammond has found 2000 B.C. villages, no pyramid appears until much later. Of course, the Americans introduced innovations, as they continued to build pyramids long after the Egyptians and Nubians had stopped, even down to the time of the Aztecs. But who can categorically deny the possibility of a stimulus from these outsiders at the beginning? Why would the Americans build a pyramid three and a half million cubic feet in volume beside these colossal stone heads when they had never built one before? Why would they place it on a north-south axis, as all Egyptian and Nubian pyramids are placed, when they had never used this axial orientation in erecting buildings in earlier settlements? Why would their pyramids combine the same double function, tomb and temple, and their own great pyramid in the Olmec-influenced city of Teotihuacan have a pyramidal base almost identical in proportion to that of the base of the Great Pyramid in Egypt? Why should the pyramid at Teotihuacan also serve, as does the Egyptian Great Pyramid, as an astronomical observatory and geodetic marker? Why should some of the Mexican pyramids have movable capstones for this purpose as do some of the Egyptian counterparts? And why should the Mexican be found using the same standards of measurements developed by the mathematicians and astronomers of the Nile Valley?

The reconstruction of the ceremonial court at La Venta to accommodate the colossal sculptures, the carving of these and the equally monumental stelae, the erection of th pyramid that took 18,000 men one million man-hours to complete, the planning of all these on the same axis, with the same ritual orientation, called for a new organization, a new technology. It required skills in the quarrying and transportation of massive blocks of stone, a building material rarely used before among the Olmec. It also called for great mathematical precision in the laying, leveling and fitting, all of which had reached a high level of sophistication in

Plan of the La Venta ceremonial platform, showing true pyramid, the first of its kind in America, as well as the miniature step-pyramid.

Egypt but were being attempted for the very first time in Middle American civilization. The slipshod, poorly planned and highly irregular or uneven architecture at San Lorenzo, an earlier Olmec site, is clear proof of the enormous and sudden leap forward in Olmec technology. At the San Lorenzo site none of the structures observes any regular orientation.

The four sides of the pyramidal base at La Venta describe an almost perfect circle. Complex measurements were involved in the erection of a palisade of basalt columns in subsiding sand. Since the sand sank, the builders had to take into account varying degrees of subsidence and so devise a scale of varying heights. Yet they all match evenly at the upper extremities. Apart from this mathematical skill, some of the problems confronting the builders involved the transportation of between 2- to 50-ton blocks of uncut stone from quarries 60 to 80 miles away by way of rafts down the rivers to the island of La Venta. The transportation of massive stones down the Nile by the Egyptians to the sites where they built their pyramids raised problems that would daunt even the best of modern engineers. Vast monuments had to be abandoned recently to the rising waters behind the Aswan dam because of the difficulty even modern technology faces in moving the colossal monuments of the Egyptians who had devised the most ingenious methods for transporting heavy stones. R.F. Heizer has noted startling similarities in the heavy transport techniques used by the ancient Americans and the Egyptians.

This does not mean to suggest that Africans physically built the American pyramids. There were not more than 1,000 Africans in the Olmec world. A substantial number of these, as skeletal studies of the royal graves show, were in the priest caste. What we are speaking of is a stimulus, an influence. The assumption that one can only wield an influence or have a considerable impact on a native population through military conquest or the pressure of great numbers is nonsense. Cabello de Balboa cites a group of 17 Africans shipwrecked in Ecuador in the early 16th century who in short order became governors of an entire province of native Americans. The reason why this African influence is historically significant is because the Olmec civilization was formative. Even Michael Coe has pointed out: "There is not the slightest doubt that all later civilization in Mesoamerica, whether Mexican or Maya, rests ultimately on an Olmec base."

That is why the debate on the African presence among the Olmec is so heated. A whole vision of American history is at stake. When *They Came Before Columbus* was published in 1977, the *New York Times* critic Glyn Daniel launched a savage attack against my thesis. Among the things he said that were downright falsehoods was that I had mixed up step-pyramids with true pyramids and that the American pyramids were temples while the Egyptian pyramids were tombs.

With respect to the first statement, it is clear that this reviewer merely skimmed through the pages of my book since I began my discourse on the pyramids by making this distinction utterly clear. I also pointed out that both step and true pyramids had gone out of vogue until the beginning of the 9th century B.C. when both forms returned in the Nubian renaissance of classical Egyptian architecture. Equally important is the fact that *a true pyramid*, even the Great Pyramid of Khufu at Giza, *has a stepped structure at its core.*

With respect to the second statement, in which Daniel contends there is a clearcut distinction between tomb and temple in the two civilizations, I refer my readers to a letter by Dr. Norman Totten, archeologist-historian, who was site supervisor for the archeological excavation at Deir Alla, Jordan. The following is an excerpt from Dr. Totten's letter, which the *New York Times* would not publish in the heat of a controversy that brought more letters, says *The Washington Post*, than any critique since Robert Frost was attacked:

> Daniel states without qualification, to disprove possible linkage between Egyptian and American pyramids, that "American pyramids are temple platforms; the Egyptian pyramids are tombs." This is news to those of us who have stood inside the tomb chambers of the great pyramids of Cuicuilco and Cholula, Mexico. It disregards the fact that the thousands of earthen mound pyramids across the United States were of two contemporaneous types, temple platforms and tombs. And what of the great stone Maya pyramid with its temple on top and famous tomb with sarcophagus within, the so-called "Temple of the Inscriptions" at Palenque?

> While his understanding of American pyramids is erroneous, his statement about Egyptian pyramids is simplistic and misleading. Certainly the great pyramids at Sakkara, Giza and Dashur were tombs. I have been inside a number of them. There were, however, funerary and valley temples adjoining those pyramids as an integral part of their total plan. The sun temple of Pharaoh Ne-suer-ra (5th Dynasty) at Abusir had a huge kind of obelisk set on a pyramidal platform, and was not a burial chamber but a temple complex. The famous mortuary temple of Mentuhotep I, founder of the 11th Dyansty at Dier el Bahri, Thebes, was topped by a pyramid.

In addition to the evidence in this letter, Rafique Jairazbhoy has cited many pyramids in America which serve the function of both temple and tomb. The superficial face of the pyramid underwent a change as the native Americans introduced their own innovations (they preferred not to fill in the steps and to have a flat top, as in earlier Egyptian and some later Sudanic and West African models), but the structural and functional correspondence remained the same.

Egyptian scripts have also turned up in ancient America. Dr. Barry Fell, formerly professor emeritus of Harvard, has established that some ancient American tribes made use of Egyptian hieroglyphs. Fell demonstrates the Egyptian influence on the writing systems of the Micmac. The Micmac are a tribe of the Algonquian Indians inhabiting the eastern provinces of Canada and closely related to various tribes of Maine, commonly called the Wabanaki or Men-of-the-East.

Fell's examination of the Lord's Prayer in Micmac hieroglyphs revealed that half of the hieroglyphic signs were similar to Egyptian hieroglyphs as rendered in the simple cursive form called "hieratic." He found also that these signs in Egyptian matched the meaning assigned to them in the English transcript of the Micmac text. A limited but recognizable Egyptian vocabulary is present, suggestive of contact with Egyptian (or related peoples speaking Egyptian, such as the Nubian or the Libyan) from whom these words could have been acquired as loans at the same time that the writing system of the natives was affected.

The Davenport stela found in Iowa (now in the Putnam Museum) has inscriptions in three languages, namely Egyptian, Iberian Punic (Phoenician) and Libyan, each in its appropriate alphabet or hieroglyphic character. The stone carries an inscription that gives the secret of regulating the calendar. Fell dates it as circa 800 B.C., which agrees with my dating of the appearance of Egypto-Nubian and Phoenician types in the ancient American world. Fell also notes stone carvings of African animals in Iowa and carvings of African elephants in the fields of Davenport, as well as clay and stone portraits of people with Nubian, Phoenician and Iberian features or clothing. (The party is naturally mixed, as I suggested, and it fits perfectly the historical period I have reconstructed, with all its complex relations between the Egypto-Nubian and the Phoenician and other Mediterranean types.)

The influence spread out from the Olmec center and basin, affecting other peoples on the North American continent. The black figure left an indelible mark. Not only his color but his stature (the continental African is usually a foot and a half taller than the aboriginal American) was remembered in the oral traditions of the Mexicans.

Nicholas Leon, an eminent Mexican authority, reports on the oral traditions of his people, according to some of whom "the oldest inhabitants of Mexico were blacks. . . . The existence of blacks and giants is commonly believed by nearly all the races of our soil and in their various languages they had words to designate them."

Everywhere, from one corner of the ancient American world to the other, blacks were found. Not only were they here long before Columbus, but they were here, not as slaves, but as free men, even as priest-kings among the Olmecs. As Jairazbhoy has pointed out, "The black began his career in America not as slave but as master."

That fact in itself opens a new historical window from which to view the history of America and of the black race.

BIOGRAPHICAL NOTES ON CONTRIBUTORS

AKBAR, Naim

Dr. Na'im Akbar is a Clinical Psychologist in the Department of Psychology and Black Studies at Florida State University. He received the M.A. in Psychology and Ph.D. in Clinical Psychology at the University of Michigan. Dr. Akbar has been appointed to the Editorial Board of the *Journal of Black Psychology*, the National Council for Black Child Development and the Health Brain Trust of the Congressional Black Caucus. Articles by and on him have appeared in *Jet, Black Books Bulletin, Journal of Black Studies*, and the *New York Amsterdam News*. His published writings are *The Community of Self* (1976), *Natural Psychology and Human Transformation* (1977) and *Chains and Images of Psychological Slavery* (1983).

CLEGG, Legrand, II

Legrand H. Clegg II is Chief Deputy City Attorney for the City of Compton, California and vice president of the Compton Community College Board of Trustees.

Mr. Clegg has engaged in research on Black history and culture for 21 years. He has lectured on many college and university campuses on this subject and has made a number of guest appearances on television and radio talk shows.

Mr. Clegg has written many articles for scholarly journals and lay magazines including "Black Rulers of the Golden Age," "The Black Roots of King Tut," "Hawaii: Black Royalty In The Pacific" and "Who Were The First Americans?" He is also co-producer of a film strip, "The Black Roots of Civilization."

Mr. Clegg has been named among the "Outstanding Young Men of America," he has been listed in "Who's Who in Black America" and he was named one of the 1983 recipients of the S.P.I.C.E. Awards (Special People Into Community Endeavors).

COPHER, Charles B.

Dr. Charles B. Copher is former Vice President for Academic Affairs and Professor of Old Testament at The Interdenominational Theological Center in Atlanta, Georgia. He received the B.A. from Clark College, Atlanta, Georgia; the M.Div. from Gammon Theological Seminary, Atlanta, Georgia; the B.D. from Oberlin Graduate School of Theology, Oberlin, Ohio; and the Ph.D. in Old

Testament from Boston University. He has contributed to text books, the *Encyclopedia Britannica* and to numerous scholarly religious publications. He is working on a book, entitled *Black People and Personalities in and of the Bible*.

DIOP, Cheikh Anta

Cheikh Anta Diop was born in Diourbel, Senegal on December 29, 1923. At age 23, he went to Paris to continue advanced studies in physics. Within a very short time, however, he was drawn deeper and deeper into studies of the origin of civilization in Africa. Becoming increasingly active in the African student movements agitating for independence of French colonial possessions, he became convinced that only by re-evaluating and restoring Africa's place in the history of the world could the physical and mental shackles of colonialism be lifted from Africa. His first doctoral dissertation submitted at the University of Paris in 1951—based on the premise that Egypt was a Black African civilization—was rejected. This dissertation was published nevertheless under the title *Nations Negres et Culture* in 1955 and won him wide acclaim. Two additional attempts to have his doctorate granted were turned back until 1960 when he entered his defense session with an array of sociologists, anthropologists, and historians and successfully carried his argument. After nearly a decade, Diop had his 'Docteur es Lettres.' In that same year were published his *L'Unite Culturelle d'Afrique Noire (The Culture Unity of Black Africa)* and *L'Afrique Noire Pre-Coloniale (Precolonial Black Africa)*.

During his student days, Diop was an avid political activist. From 1950 to 1953, he was the Secretary-General of the Rassemblement Democratique Africain (RDA) and helped launch the first Pan-African Student Congress in Paris in 1951. He also participated in the 1st World Congress of Black Writers and Artists held in Paris in 1956 and the 2nd such congress held in Rome in 1959. Upon returning to Senegal in 1960, Dr. Diop continued his research. In 1966, the 1st World Black Festival of Arts and Culture held in Dakar, Senegal honored Dr. Diop and Dr. W.E.B. DuBois as the scholars who exerted the greatest influence on Negro thought in the 20th century. In 1974, a breakthrough occurred in the English-speaking world when *The African Origin of Civilization*, a translation and compilation of the first 10 chapters of *Nations Negres* . . . and three chapters from *Anteriorite des Civilizations Noires*, was published. Since then, Dr. Diop has published two additional books still in French, including his latest, *Civilization ou Barbarie (Civilization or Barbarism)*.

Dr. Diop is currently Director of the Radiocarbon laboratory at the Fundamental Institute of Black Africa (IFAN) at the University of Dakar. He sits on numerous international scientific committees and has belatedly achieved recognition as one of the leading historians, Egyptologists, linguists, and anthropologists in the world. He travels incessantly, lectures widely, and is cited and quoted voluminously. He is the 'pharaoh' of African studies.

FINCH, Charles S.

Charles S. Finch, M.D. is a board-certified family physician who is currently Assistant Professor of Community Medicine and Family Practice at the Morehouse School of Medicine. Dr. Finch completed his undergraduate training at Yale College, his medical training at Jefferson Medical College, and his Family Medicine Residency at the University of California, Irvine Medical Center. He has worked as an epidemiologist for the Centers for Disease Control and was formerly a clinical preceptor at the Duke-Watts Family Medicine Clinic in Durham, North Carolina. He was the founder and chairman of the Raleigh Afro-American Life Focus Project between 1981 and 1982 and is a co-founder and Co-Convener of Bennu, Inc. of Atlanta. He is currently the Associate Editor of the *Journal of African Civilizations* and the author of ''The African Background of Medical Science,'' ''The Works of Gerald Massey: Studies in Kamite Origins,'' and—with Mr. Larry Williams of Bennu, Inc.—the co-author of ''The Great Queens of Ethiopia'' all published in the *Journal of African Civilizations*. In addition Dr. Finch has visited Senegal, West Africa where he has begun studies on the empirical basis of traditional West African medicine. On his most recent visit, he interviewed Dr. Cheikh Anta Diop, an interview which was published in the re-issue of ''Egypt Revisited'' edition of the *Journal of African Civilizations*.

HILLIARD, Asa G., III

Asa G. Hilliard is the Fuller E. Calloway Professor of Urban Education at Georgia State University, Atlanta, Georgia. He holds a joint appointment in the Department of Educational Foundations and the Department of Counseling and Psychological Services. Dr. Hilliard served previously as a Department Chairman and as Dean of the School of Education at San Francisco State University. He is a graduate of the University of Denver with a bachelor's degree in Psychology, a Masters in Counseling and Guidance and a Doctor of Education degree in Educational Psychology. He has had experience as a teacher, administrator, researcher and lecturer throughout the United States and in several foreign countries, including a six-year period of professional service in Liberia, West Africa.

KING, Richard D.

Richard D. King, M.D., is a physician presently engaged in the private practice of psychiatry in San Francisco. He was trained at Whittier College, University of California at San Francisco Medical Center, Los Angeles County; University of Southern California Medical Center; and the Langley Porter Neuropsychiatric Institute of the University of California at San Francisco Medical Center. He continues to seek an education in Ancient African Philosophy through Black Gnostic Studies of Los Angeles, California. Presently, he is a member of the Board of Directors of the Aquarian Spiritual Center of Los Angeles, Assistant Professor of Black Studies, San Francisco State University, and Vice-President of the Black Psychiatrists of America. Formerly, he was a scholar in residence at the Franz Fanon Research and Development Center, Charles Drew Post Graduate Medical School, Martin Luther King Hospital, Los Angeles, M.H.C.D. program-Staff College, National Institute of Mental Health, and a member of the medical school admissions committee of the University of California at San Francisco Medical Center. His primary research interests are Ancient African psychology, Pineal gland, and melanin, with publications in the journal *Uraeus* (From Mental Slavery to Mastership, Black Dot: Archetype of Humanity), *Sepia* and the Fanon Center publications.

LUMPKIN, Beatrice

A retired Associate Professor of Mathematics, Malcolm X. College, Chicago, Professor Lumpkin has written on the Afro-Asian foundations of mathematics and science for *Freedomways*, the *Mathematics Teacher, Science and Society, Historia Mathematica*, and *Journal of African Civilizations*. As a mathematics consultant, she participated in the Multi-Ethnic Curriculum Project of the Portland Public Schools and the Chicago Board of Education Intercultural Project. She is the author of *Young Genius in Old Egypt*, and *Senefer and Hatshepsut*, novels featuring Egyptian mathematicians.

PAPPADEMOS, John

Dr. Pappademos received his Ph.D. in theoretical elementary particle physics in 1964 from the University of Chicago. Since then he has been teaching at the University of Illinois at Chicago, except for the academic year 1980-1981, when he was a visiting professor at the University of Crete, in Greece. He is the author of several articles and a monograph on the history, philosophy, and social aspects of science.

RASHIDI, Runoko

Historian. Born in Stockton, California, August 16, 1954. Special interest in the Kushite nations of antiquity. Founding member of Amenta, 1979. Principal organizer and founding member of the Southern Cradle research organization, 1981. Author of a short series of biographical sketches entitled "Mighty Pharaohs of Ancient Egypt," 1982. Member of the board of directors of the *Journal of African Civilizations*, 1983. His articles and historical essays have appeared in *Return To The Source, Afro-Am*, and the *Journal of African Civiliza-*

tions. 1981 to 1984 African History Research Analyst for Extended Opportunity Programs and Services of Compton Community College.

VAN SERTIMA, Ivan

Ivan Van Sertima was born in Guyana, South America. He was educated at the School of Oriental and African Studies, London University, and the Rutgers Graduate School and holds degrees in African Studies, Linguistics and Anthropology. He is a literary critic, a linguist, and an anthropologist and has made a name in all three fields. He is the author of *They Came Before Columbus: The African Presence in Ancient America*, which was published by Random House in 1977 and is now in its tenth printing.

As a linguist, he has published essays on the dialect of the Sea Islands off the Georgia Coast. He is also the compiler of the Swahili Dictionary of Legal Terms, based on his field-work in Tanzania, East Africa, in 1967. As a literary critic, he is the author of *Caribbean Writers*, a collection of critical essays on the Caribbean Novel. He is also the author of several major literary reviews published in Denmark, India, Britain and the United States. He was honored for his work in this field by being asked by the Nobel Committee of the Swedish Academy to nominate candidates for the Nobel Prize in Literature, from 1976 to 1980.

Professor Van Sertima is an Associate Professor of African Studies at Rutgers University in New Jersey and Editor of the *Journal of African Civilizations*.

PATTEN-VAN SERTIMA, Jacqueline

Jacqueline Patten-Van Sertima is photographic consultant, art director and cover designer for the *Journal of African Civilizations*. Mrs. Van Sertima has also recently established the Journal's new audio arm, Legacies, Inc. As director, she produces companion audio cassettes to each volume of the *Journal of African Civilizations* as well as of various presentations made by Dr. Van Sertima and colleagues.

As a photographer, Mrs. Van Sertima has won international distinction for her hand-painted photography and its significant contribution to social awareness. Listed in the Cambridge *World Who's Who of Women* for "distinguished achievement," their *International Register of Profiles* and their *International Who's Who of Intellectuals*, she is given equal acclaim in the United States in *Who's Who in America* and *Personalities of America* for "outstanding artistic achievement and contributions to society." Mrs. Van Sertima received her B.S. degree in Psychology/Sociology and M.S. in Education from Hunter College, New York.

WILLIAMS, Bruce

Bruce Williams received his Ph.D. in Near East Archaeology from the University of Chicago. Since 1976 he has been responsible for publishing the excavations of the Oriental Institute Nubian Expedition between Abu Simbel and the Sudan frontier, and is presently engaged in preparing the volume on New Kingdom remains. His interests include the archaeological and historical relations of the Second Intermediate Period, the origins of pharaonic culture, and the development of Kushite civilizations.